inside the

magic

rectangle

Victor Lewis-Smith

inside the
magic
rectangle

VICTOR GOLLANCZ
LONDON

First published in Great Britain 1995
by Victor Gollancz
An imprint of the Cassell Group
Wellington House, 125 Strand, London WC2R 0BB

The reviews in this book first appeared, some in slightly
differing form, in the *Evening Standard*

A catalogue record for this book is
available from the British Library

ISBN 0 575 06119 7

Designed and typeset
by Fishtail Design

Printed in Great Britain by
St Edmundsbury Press Ltd
Bury St Edmunds, Suffolk

Acknowledgements

Thanks are due to: Stuart Steven, Adam Edwards and Alex Renton at the *Evening Standard*, and also to Sarah White and Emma Messenger for fearlessly obtaining VHS review copies from recalcitrant or cowardly programme makers; to Gollancz's libel lawyer, John Rubinstein, without whom this book would have been considerably longer; to Dr Peter Lee for his trenchant views about many programmes, the strength of his opinions being not one whit diminished by his having never owned a television set; to Robert Robinson for his inspiration over the years and for coining the phrase 'the magic rectangle'; to John McVicar and Laurie Taylor for the matutinal chats; to my co-writer Paul Sparks, who shall remain nameless; and to my mother and father, who, during my childhood, were smart enough never to utter the knee-jerk parental reproach 'You're watching too much television.'

A Year in Provence

It's a funny thing, onomatopoeia. In France, I am told, the cats in children's stories don't go *meeow meeow*, they go *wrillou wrillou*. Our geese honk, but over there it's *oie! oie!* But, on last night's *A Year in Provence*, the French and English dogs were in complete agreement: rough, rough, rough.

I knew that this channel crossing was going to be bloody rough as soon as I clapped eyes on the opening titles, a montage of images so stereotyped that even *Wish You Were Here . . . ?* would consider them trite: a game of boules, a bunch of grapes, a bottle of wine and a fat rustic Provençal, all accompanied by crass accordion music and a foil-embossed typeface reminiscent of the front cover of a cheap novel. The only thing that prevented me developing travel sickness was the realization that what I was watching was not Provence at all; it was British Sunday-evening television, scheduled by someone who still believes that we all ought to be in church, and should undergo penance if we're not.

The template for this series is *The Good Life* with sunshine – characters from 50s Oxo ads, whacky idealistic husband Peter and sensible down-to-earth wife Annie, chucking in the rat race and rediscovering the simple joys of life in the south of France. TV has produced many sit-coms full of funny foreigners over the years, but this time they have come up with a whole new genre: a sit-trag, full of unfunny foreigners. Last night's episode, a feeble storyline about tracking down truffles, aimed at low farce but badly undershot the mark. Stereotype I sported a silly hat and inane grin and arranged a visit to a truffle den, where Peter and Annie bought a kilo from Stereotype II, a local wide-boy. While trying to locate their errant builders, Peter got splashed by lawn sprinklers and met Stereotype III, a wealthy Parisienne who 'zinks all ze Eeenglish are très chic' (she'd only just met the Mayles) and offered Peter (you'll never guess) *chocolate* truffles! Together with Stereotypes IV and V, Peter searched for more truffles with a large pig, whose performance was far and away the least hammy of the evening. Then Annie suddenly said she hated Provence and, rather like *The Prisoner*, they suddenly escaped back to London; unlike *The Prisoner*, nobody forced them to return, but sadly they did anyway, so we shall have to endure another nine episodes of this pointless bilge. Then Alfred Molina appeared for the final thirty seconds and I'm almost sure he was acting. Yes . . . believable character, convincing gestures, three-dimensional performance . . . I'm sure that was acting.

This expensive nonsense is no more than *Allo Allo* for the middle classes, presenting a xenophobe's view of France under the guise of an affectionate portrait. Mayle's original diaries were never intended to be dramatized, and there is an emptiness at the heart of each TV episode that no amount of Gallic shrugging and absurd haw-hee-hawing can disguise. Worst of all is the terminal miscasting of the two central characters. John Thaw's performance is so wooden you constantly fear he may ignite in one of those nasty forest fires you hear so much about down there. As for Lindsay Duncan, she is totally unbelievable as his wife, and seems more like his daughter. When she claimed to have been a tax inspector for two decades, I found myself wondering about her early years in the job; I for one would have strenuously objected to being quizzed about my expenses by a twelve-year-old.

Following hard on the heels of *Eldorado*'s abortive Year in Spain, *A Year in Provence* fuels the suspicion that the primary motivation of some BBC producers is not excellence of programming, but where they'd like to go for an extended foreign visit while getting paid for it. I had already heard that filming in Provence began too late in the year, and that they had to bring in thousands of bunches of plastic grapes; but plastic actors, that's a new one on me.

It takes more than a few clichés strung together to make a believable programme. So far, the series is looking like a load of boules.

Metroland: Card Game

These days, there's a vast array of specialist services on offer via the telephone. Every interest is catered for, although, if the pre-recorded medical helplines I phoned yesterday were a representative sample, then most are a load of rubbish. The Tinnitus line just rang and rang, the Circumcision line cut me off, the Diarrhoea line was engaged all day, the Premature Ejaculation line was all over in a couple of seconds and, as for the Amnesia line . . . well, I couldn't remember the number.

Last night's *Metroland* (Carlton), which looked at the specialist sexual services advertised exclusively on the walls of London's public phone kiosks, began by panning across a multicoloured selection of paper promises, everything from the prosaic *Tall leggy blonde gives massage* to the more perverse *Whipping and canning* (no canning for me, thank you, I might cut myself on the sharp edges of the tin). 'My name's Derek,' said a Glaswegian (clearly not called Derek) who earns a grubby living by wandering along Oxford Street, placing prostitutes' cards in every BT booth he passes. He was a nasty piece of work, but smart enough to treat the cameras as a PR opportunity, helpfully holding open doors for old ladies, and emphasizing the positive aspects of his trade: 'At the end of the day, we're doing a service . . . otherwise, members of the public would be harassed by kerb crawlers.' His central thesis was simple but compelling: the only way to get prostitutes off the street was to allow his cards on to the street.

Whether it's cottaging in public lavatories or phoning whores from BT kiosks, the smell of stale urine (like cats' spray) must possess aphrodisiacal properties for certain men, because dozens phoned in each day in response to the cards. Their calls were fielded by a 'maid' (so fat she could have fallen down and not noticed it), who promised them the services of 'an eighteen-year-old masseuse' – although, from the glimpses we got of her, I reckon she'd been eighteen for several decades. 'Bubble service, sir?' the maid enquired, 'that's a specialized . . . half an hour, and it entitles you to the assisted bath and hand relief at the end' (strange – I thought only the NHS did assisted baths, helping geriatrics to get off their Zimmer frames). She certainly felt no shame about working in the oldest profession, declaring defiantly that 'We don't sell our bodies,' although they clearly weren't averse to renting them out on an hourly basis. When she wasn't answering the phone, she spent her days designing new cards, and laminating by hand. Which sounded rather like a perversion in itself.

Strike me, all of a sudden a load of feminists started taking them down. I refer to a somewhat stagy sequence during which they indignantly ripped cards from kiosk walls, vehemently complaining about a public nuisance although, as Derek pointed out, throwing litter on to the pavement is an offence, and 'Look at all the work you're causing the poor street cleaners.' A priest thoughtfully stuffed the cards into a carrier bag and carried them away, probably to add to his private collection, but a woman who looked like Barbara Woodhouse (the late dog trainer who spent her life advising us to give our pets a stroke, yet tragically succumbed to one herself) angrily trampled *Korean model will suck* underfoot – a hasty decision since Electrolux have a factory in Korea and it might have been a perfectly innocent vacuum-cleaner ad. A confrontation between Derek and a deranged Italian woman was conducted in a language tantalizingly close to English, which I now quote verbatim: 'Wha err doin' ken?' 'Bosh on the gantry. Regresshin, soona seenis God, yo bloddy lie-ya.' The card game is illegal, but Derek was philosophical about the fines he'd suffered, admitting that 'At the end of the day, the police are only doing their job.' And meanwhile, the prostitutes were doing their hand job.

This was a perfectly structured programme, frank without being salacious and, in its non-judgemental approach to its subject, it recalled the 1950s Associated Rediffusion series, *Out of Step*. It's rare that I find myself able unreservedly to praise a Carlton-commissioned programme, and I'm delighted to do so now, although that company will doubtless be quaking in its corporate boots when CH4's *Vintage Thames* season starts this Saturday, and reminds us yet again of the quality of the station we lost. Curiously, when Carlton's head of publicity phoned me last year to complain about a run of negative reviews, he made a most bizarre comment: 'You clearly have a problem with Carlton, is there anything we can do . . . ?' I wondered what on earth he was suggesting, but I soon came up with a solution. 'Yes, make better programmes,' I replied. Perhaps, belatedly, my remark is sinking in.

Arena: The Peter Sellers Story

Analysing humour is like dissecting a frog – few people are interested, and the frog dies – but there is, nevertheless, no shortage of glib theories on the subject. One hypothesis claims that there are only seven jokes (in which case Hale and Pace have not yet heard six of them). Another asserts that all comedians were fat shy children, who were bullied at school and developed their humorous abilities in self-defence (in which case Hale and Pace weren't bullied nearly enough).

My own theory, for what it's worth, is that you don't have a sense of humour, a sense of humour has you. Comedy, like opera and sex, is a gloriously irrational experience, where sudden inspiration and subtleties of timing can make all the difference between delight and disappointment. Presumably it was a desire to capture his own sense of humour in action that led Peter Sellers to record every aspect of his own life so obsessively, and his resulting home-movie archive was certainly not just a load of old Bolex. As Saturday night's *Arena: The Peter Sellers Story* (BBC2) made clear, he was a proficient cameraman who always used the latest pro equipment, unlike his less pecunious friend and colleague Spike Milligan: 'I could only afford eight-millimetre, Peter had sixteen-millimetre. He was eight millimetres richer than me.'

Juxtaposing fragments of his home movies with clips from his feature films and comments from friends and family, this second part (of three) presented us with a life so tangled that it made R. D. Laing's *Knots* look like *Janet and John*. The influence of his dominant mother undoubtedly coloured all his subsequent relationships with women, as his first wife found out when he expected her to sympathize with him over his unrequited lust for Sophia Loren. And, when his public career took off in the early 1960s (with *The Millionairess* bringing international celebrity status), he became increasingly estranged from his own private life. He turned his house into a permanent film set, cynically used his children as unpaid extras and, as the love affairs multiplied, so did the family arguments.

We heard from his former coterie of hangers-on, all now well into their anecdotage. His chauffeur ('the Great Bert') recalled Sellers' clinical depression after the break-up of his marriage (regular applications of Britt Ekland soon cured that), while fellow-actor David Lodge claimed to have performed the role of 'court jester' to the King of Comedy. His directors seemed to understand him better, with Blake Edwards divulging, 'I think he lived a great part of his life in hell,' and Stanley Kubrick declaring, 'He was the only actor I know who could really improvise . . . most actors stray into a repetitive hotchpotch . . . Sellers got the spirit of a character and just took off. It was miraculous.'

The programme featured a wonderful illustration of Sellers' aural (and oral) skills when, in a US TV interview, he mentioned that the voice of Dr Strangelove was modelled on a New York photographer named Weegee. Other documentaries might have left it at that, but a tape of Sellers talking to Weegee had somehow been unearthed and, yes, the similarity was striking. In fact, Sellers was clearly a human weegee board himself, allowing hundreds of souls to express themselves through him, yet having no personality of his own. Comedy at this level is akin to a neurological disorder, and Jonathan Miller put his finger on it (it's OK, he's a doctor, he's allowed to put his finger on it) when he said: 'The chameleon that so enabled him as a performer had a double function . . . it was a talent that was marketable and it delighted an audience, but it was also a sanctuary, enabling him to fight off some sort of demons about which we know nothing, or the hideous knowledge that he might have been, personally, a nonentity.'

During my brief stint at TV-reviewing, few programmes have provoked a sharp intake of breath, but this documentary left me pretty well hyperventilating. Dazzlingly directed by Peter Lydon, it worked superbly on many levels – biographical, historical, psychological. Rehearsal footage of Ealing comedies could have sustained ten programmes by themselves, and every movie clip was woven seamlessly into the whole, rather than being merely illustrative. The brilliant score (by Andy Sheppard and Steve Lodder) relaxed the programme, yet had its own complex structure (with subtle allusions to the *Pink Panther* theme), and the series is a fitting tribute to the late Nigel Finch, the co-producer (with Anthony Wall) who died last week. Amongst the many BAFTAs it will undoubtedly win, it deserves a special one for finally letting us hear the B-side to 'Goodness Gracious Me'. No more sleepless nights for me.

Praise Be!

I can't quite put my finger on Thora Hird. When Alan Bennett provides the script she can give a genuinely moving performance yet, when playing herself, her demeanour is that of a mawkish WRVS lady hovering over a bedside, the sort who offers a cup of hot sweet tea and says, 'You've had an accident, dear.' From the way she hosted the first in the new series of *Praise Be!*, she clearly assumed that her typical viewer was either a dim five-year-old or a confused inmate of a geriatric ward. And, having watched the programme, I think she's probably right.

For verily, a miracle hath occurred, and the moribund format of *Stars on Sunday* has been raised from the dead. True, *Praise Be!* does not have the late Jess Yates, but Thora, with her fruity Sister George hat and cape, is a worthy successor. She smiled her sweet-tea smile, read, 'I mean this sincerely, I'm enjoying myself so much' in dispassionate tones straight from the autocue, and told us that 'Tonight's hymns will all be sung to praise the Lord for the wonderful world he has created.' And the requests flooded in from the handicapped, the arthritic, the lonely, the deaf, the blind and the very, very old: all recipients of blessings of the Lord God's wonderful world.

On with the hymns, selections from *Ancient and Modern* sung by congregations consisting entirely of cute gappy-toothed children and gumming OAPs, with a few social misfits for leavening. Various denominations were represented but one thing was certain: there were no charismatics. On *Praise Be!* the hopeless sang of their hope in an orgy of dour melody, inept scansion and archaic vocabulary, making a joyless noise unto the Lord. Hymns were accompanied by soft-focus Athena-poster shots of the wonderful things for which the Lord can take credit – raindrops on roses, bright-coloured posies and nesting mallards, rather than, say, muscular dystrophy or dandruff – while Thora linked the twee shots with philosophical observations so crass they made the average Christmas card read like Wittgenstein's *Tractatus*. 'I'm sure there is something we can all learn from the faithfulness of our animal friends,' she said, as Roger her vicar blessed the local pets on the village green. Faithfulness? My own cats made their loyalties perfectly clear to me long ago; if I ever mislay the tin opener, they're off.

Then another miracle occurred; it seemed impossible but the programme actually got worse. Thora visited Paul Heiney's farm where, although he ploughs a few fields of root crops, the really profitable vegetables are the witless TV presenters continually turning up to film it. 'I'll only farm organically,' he proclaimed, meaning that he grows those shrivelled, emaciated mud-covered things you see in supermarkets, costing four times as much as the healthy, succulent, chemically grown produce on the next shelf. As for his animals, the lambs had 'a splendid life' on Jollity Farm (at least until he sold them to the abattoir for immediate slaughter). By now the programme had degenerated into that ritualistic Sunday myth of rural England that begins with the omnibus edition of *The Archers* and unfailingly delights a certain type of city dweller. If God's countryside is so idyllic then why have figures for unemployment, alcoholism, violent crime and suicide rocketed amongst country folk, with most of them desperately trying to move to the city?

And why do such dreadful religious programmes survive in prime-time slots? Are they a part of the 'Keep Sunday special' ethos (a euphemism for 'Keep Sunday miserable')? Genuine worshippers are at church, not glued to TV sets, but of course these programmes are not intended for Christians, just the rest of us. They can't force us to believe, but they can ruin early-evening television so, out of sheer Christian compassion, that's exactly what they do. ITV has erased the early-evening God-slot and it's high time the BBC did too.

Religious programmes are often treated as sacred cows, beyond all criticism, but frankly there is only one sacred cow on *Praise Be!*. However, she must go unnamed, in case the programme's libel lawyer is tempted to perform a miracle of his own: the courtroom miracle of turning a TV review into a huge amount of bread.

Libby Purves, wife of Paul Heiney, later wrote to me, suggesting that perhaps I was losing my mind, and denying that her husband was interested in his farm being featured on TV or radio. In fact, she claimed that he had refused a great many offers from the media, and only accepted this one because he was an admirer of Thora Hird. The animals on the farm were reared in a traditional way, she insisted, and were killed under the most humane conditions in low-stress slaughterhouses.

I replied . . .

5. v. 93

Dear Libby,
God bless you for your letter.
I was touched to hear that your husband – sole instigator and executor of the twelve-part radio series *A Year in Harness* – is so media-shy about his farm, and that, when it comes to TV, 'a great many offers are refused'. Perhaps you could let me know the names of some of the TV programmes that have been banned from filming in Heiney areas? I'd like to contact the producers and console them.
    Referring to my remarks about the killing of livestock as 'verging on the libellous' in infantile and silly, and you must have known that perfectly well when you wrote it. You object to the nasty brutal word 'abattoir', and prefer nice fluffy words like 'low-stress slaughterhouse', but the only way to make a slaughterhouse happy is to remove its first letter. I'm not a vegetarian, and I see nothing wrong in defenceless animals being killed in order to satisfy my jaded palette; slit their little throats, I must have more meat. You're presumably not vegetarians either, but you *do* think it's wrong, so you take refuge behind euphemisms. The distinction may make you feel better, but I doubt if the animals would appreciate it; they're going to end up just as dead in either case.
    I'm all in favour of traditional farming, just as I thoroughly approve of charity work and helping old ladies across the street. What sets my alarm bells ringing is when someone is continually appearing in the papers, or on TV and radio, talking about their good work instead of just quietly getting on with it. Chez Heiney-Purves, you are certainly ecologically sound in one respect: every last scrap of your lives seems to be recycled endlessly in the media.
    Yours in Christ,

    Victor Lewis-Smith

Two years later, when Ms Purves was asked if she would agree to allow her letter to be included in this book, she declined, brusquely refused my offer of a donation to charity and called me a smartass. I understand that she has taken a course of Prozac, which would account for her unusually benign response.

Concerto!

The British are notoriously suspicious of humorists who dare to display competence in the serious arts. Jonathan Miller as opera director? Clive James as serious poet? Barry Humphries as art historian? The multi-talented are greeted with scepticism, as though diversity inevitably equates with superficiality. Of course the irony, on British television, is that a large proportion of performers can't even do the one thing they've been booked for.

Dudley Moore is undoubtedly a Renaissance man, despite being born 450 years too late to qualify; but, although his abilities as a comic actor and screen writer are universally acclaimed, his remarkable skills as an orchestrator and all-round musicologist are seldom acknowledged. Sitting beneath what looked like a McDonald's arch, his introduction to the first programme in the *Concerto!* series was concise and authoritative, yet engagingly conversational and informal, proving that (in moderation) to 'er' is humanizing. With the help of soloists and conductor, he reflected on Mozart's Flute and Harp Concerto, combining Radio 3 standards of scholarship with a Classic FM desire to enthuse and entertain. Cutting between rehearsals and interviews, the discussion neatly appraised this serene eighteenth-century work from historical, structural, instrumental and emotional viewpoints, presenting its analysis in bite-sized pieces suitable for those of us with twentieth-century attention spans.

The concert harp is a bewildering instrument, with more pedals than the starting line of the *tour de France*, and Marisa Robles' heavy Spanish accent allowed us only a limited insight into the workings of its mysterious double action: 'Let's put it this way, if you start on the harp when you're a few days old, and practise until you die, you'll basically get there.' Partnering her was James Galway, whose darting eyes give the impression of a man permanently watching tennis at Wimbledon; his haunted expression may well be divine retribution for the appalling recording of 'Annie's Song' he made in the 1970s, a rendition that inspired a million tone-deaf kids to take up the flute. Michael Tilson Thomas tried to impose his own interpretation on to the soloists, but had to roll with the punches from Galway: 'We've been playing it this way for thirty years. If we changed now, we'd need a month in psychiatry.' Throughout, Moore was disarmingly irreverent, but without sabotaging the discussion. The late 1770s, when people were reluctant to employ Mozart, was dubbed his 'acne period', and Moore's musings on the eighteenth-century flute moved rapidly from technical to farcical: 'Everything was different in those days, there was no refrigeration – a flute going off must have been a tremendous pong.'

The red-tinted lighting and hazy visuals used for the concerto's performance took us into a shadowy world reminiscent of Disney's *Fantasia*. Lavishly staged and shot (with imaginative use of crane shots), the direction resisted the temptation to wander beyond the studio, allowing us instead to see the soloists' hands in macro close-up; how can a man with Walls tomato sausages instead of fingers play the flute like an angel? Having been recorded for future broadcast on a high-definition format, the image was rectangular (although I'm convinced that cameramen often simply stick strips of cardboard on the top and bottom of their lens so they can *pretend* it's high-definition), and the only flaw in the presentation was that the performance appeared to be mimed. If it was, it's a pity that the sound and vision boys couldn't have reached a happier compromise.

On the evidence of this first programme, *Concerto!* is a perfect vehicle for popularizing the classical repertoire, making great works accessible to a wide audience without demeaning either the music or the audience. This is a world away from *Harry Enfield's Guide to Opera*, which succeeded only in alienating aficionados and insulting the intelligence of the non-expert viewer. Po-faced musicologists may be horrified by Moore's flippancy, but he evinces more enthusiasm and understanding than the average academic, and his scatological tendencies precisely mirror Mozart's own penchant for obscenity (so graphically displayed in his letters). Like a sufferer from Tourette's syndrome, Moore frequently seems on the verge of subverting our expectations of fine art by shouting out the occasional 'bollocks'. Indeed, when one of the performers remarked that 'Mozart had a very wide gamut,' Dud drew in a breath. I suspect his reply lies for ever on the cutting-room floor.

Celebrity Squares

So there is hope for the future of television. Just when it seemed that the medium had nothing more to offer than endless reheated productions of burned-out formats, Central Television has come up with an entirely new genre and produced a masterpiece of parody. You've heard of period drama: now there's period game show.

Older viewers might remember the original *Celebrity Squares*, an absurd 70s game show where square celebrities gave heavily scripted ad-lib responses to trivial yes/no questions, laboriously fed to them by an old-time music-hall comedian called Bob Monkhouse. No doubt he retired long ago (probably to a bed-sit somewhere on the south coast, where all past-tense people end up) but, for Friday night's spoof re-creation, Central had located an actor uncannily similar to the original, though of course much older. The greasy charm, the slimy wink, the fake tan and the fake personality, all had been captured perfectly. Even the opening material had the flavour of that bygone era about it: 'My first wife left me because I didn't have a big endowment . . . at ninety-two my grandfather stains floors . . . he doesn't mean to' – exactly the kind of crass jokes that comedians used to tell in the 70s, before their audiences became too sophisticated.

Within the squares of the enormous noughts-and-crosses board sat a nonet of spoof 'celebrities', ingenious imitations of the various second-division media types who used to appear on the original show; the sort whose brains and talent would fit inside a matchbox, but whose egos wouldn't fit inside the Albert Hall. Some (with instantly forgettable names like Glenda McKay and Benjamin Mitchell) pretended to be minor actors from minor soaps, only giving themselves away by occasionally using two- or even three-syllable words. Others (Jakki Brambles, Derrick Evans) cleverly mocked those sad people who deliberately misspell their Christian names in a pathetic bid to draw attention to themselves. One was a black woman (with the surreal name of Floella Benjamin) and was obviously a cruel parody of Rusty Lee, since she did nothing entertaining, except laughing uproariously every time she appeared on camera. There were a couple of concocted comics too (creations worthy of Steve Coogan), including the hilariously named Bradley Walsh ('Star of the Royal Variety

Performance,' fake-Bob jested), who insisted on wandering out of his square and into someone else's, just like every 'zany' comedian used to do back in the 70s. The other was Paul Shane, a burlesque of the worst kind of outdated club compère, with his 'Is there anyone here from Yorkshire? They're worse than the Paddies, they're all over the world.' The knowing audience rocked with laughter at his subtle combination of anachronistic racism and mindless inanity.

But the crowning touch of genius was the inclusion of a couple of genuinely forgotten celebs amongst the soon-to-be-forgotten hoaxes, giving a verisimilitude to the show that it would otherwise have lacked. Gareth Hunt (a man whose career peaked with a coffee ad involving a hand gesture that could get you hanged in Puerto Rico) was precisely the sort of pointless human Polyfilla that made the original series so unutterably dreadful, and it was good to see that he could take a joke against himself by agreeing to play himself in this merciless send-up. And, of course, while no one would book Henry Cooper for a game show nowadays, back in his 'Splash it all over' days people were prepared to overlook his uncompromising inability to deliver a joke. Everything about the parody was perfect, from fake-Bob's banal catchphrases ('We'll be back in a flash with double the cash') to the phoney prizes at the end, where they trailed an oxymoronic 'fun-filled holiday in Brussels' just so that the host could say, 'It's the centre of the EC and, after sampling sixty-five types of beer, Eur-o-peeing.'

Sick joke? Some may think so. Others will realize that *Celebrity Squares* is a near-impeccable spoof, and it's to Central TV's credit that they have made an entire series, rather than limiting themselves to a one-off. Three cheers to ITV who, rather than merely revamping one of their old, clapped-out game shows, featuring clapped-out guests and a clapped-out host, have been brave enough to schedule such a devastating parody in prime time. It's easy to pull off a once-a-year April Fool's spoof, but to make an entire series of outright fiascos: frankly, that takes a type of bravery that's very close to imbecility.

The Invisible Wall

It's not often that the fair-minded general public spontaneously applaud a man for punching the occupant of a wheelchair, but I know someone who once received that remarkable accolade. A pacifist by nature, he was acting as doorman for a private party (only accessible via a narrow and precipitous staircase) when a severely disabled person arrived and demanded admittance. For over an hour, my friend patiently and logically explained the reasons why he and his wheelchair couldn't come in (fire regulations, no access, no invitation, no manners), but received such an irrational stream of abuse and belligerence in return that he eventually snapped and lashed out, much to the approval of admiring bystanders, who'd wanted to hit the man themselves. After all, the assault was proof of my friend's lack of prejudice ('See the person, not the disability'), and the occupant of the wheelchair was a thoroughly bigoted individual. Hitler on four wheels would still be Hitler.

That incident flitted through my mind last night as I watched *The Invisible Wall* (BBC1), a series which claims to highlight the discrimination faced by Britain's disabled population, but has mostly given unreasonable people the opportunity to make unreasonable demands of a well-intentioned but imperfect society. 'There are six and a half million disabled people in this country, and each of us has faced the invisible wall,' began the eminently reasonable Richard Jobson. 'Each of us'? Richard Jobson *disabled*? Then it struck me that he was once married to the celebrated Scandinavian thinker Mariella Frostrup and, let's face it, a man can't get much more disabled than that. Six and a half million others there may be, but this programme ignored the vast majority of them, those who strive uncomplainingly against adversity and don't expect favours, only tolerance. Instead, it gave airtime to a vociferous, aggrieved few, who wanted equal rights *and* special treatment, and whose chief disabilities proved to be not their physical impediments but their cripplingly obnoxious personalities.

Whenever you hear the phrase 'using our secret hidden camera' on a television programme, you can be sure that the producer never quite got *The Man From U.N.C.L.E.* out of his system in the 60s, and the clandestine footage we saw confirmed that its use was nothing but a gimmick, capturing no evidence whatsoever of prejudice by the able-bodied against the disabled. Andy McLay (wheelchair-bound and obviously still bitter about it) wanted to qualify as a sports instructor, and arrogantly demanded that the University of East London should, therefore, change its syllabus, rudely brushing aside objections that 'The course requires demonstration of leg movements which you can't do' with a brusque 'I can demonstrate leg movement with my arm.' Ambition is a laudable quality, but it needs to be tempered with realism, and his sheer lack of dignity recalled the old Peter Cook and Dudley Moore sketch about the one-legged man auditioning for the role of Tarzan. Clearly, Mr McLay's real problem wasn't below the waist but above the neck, though he was correct when he blamed his rejection on 'an attitude problem'. *His* attitude.

Joanne Eaton 'was fitted with the secret camera' next, a rather pointless exercise because a film crew was following her as she wheeled herself round her college, unable to open doors or use ramps. A helpful administrator agreed with her that the old building ought to be modernized, although the programme was curiously unopinionated about where the college might find £100,000 to install a lift. As for a third 'hidden camera' investigation, into access problems at a Job Centre, it was certainly top secret; so secret, in fact, that they'd senselessly filmed it in a completely different building to the one under discussion.

The secret camera failed to capture any discrimination, but, worse, the entire production lacked discrimination. The opening titles, showing a nimble mime artist prancing about, were woefully insensitive (like starting a programme for asthmatics with shots of healthy people enjoying mountain air), while the use of the secret camera was an unjustifiable invasion of privacy, permitted only because BBC executives wouldn't dare turn down a request from its Disabled Unit. None of the disgraceful instances of genuine discrimination we heard about (being sacked for having an epileptic fit at work, enrolling into a college and finding no suitable lavatories) had been captured on camera, but they still made a far more persuasive case for change than all the surreptitious nonsense (which was doubtless as enjoyable to film as it wasn't to watch). Ostracizing the disabled is contemptible, but it's equally true that being disabled doesn't automatically make you socially more acceptable than anyone else. The programme makers failed to recognize that, which is why this has been a series without legs.

Men Behaving Badly

If we are to believe scientists, according to the ineluctable laws of time and space, somewhere in a parallel universe there must be a planet (let's call it Tharg) which is an almost exact replica of Earth but full of strange and subtle differences. On Tharg's BBC1, their star presenter Roland Rivron is hailed as a comic genius (while our one, tragically, only stars on schools programmes at 10.25 a.m.). Tharg's *Songs of Praise* is presented by Arthur Mullard, their Thora Hird is a professional wrestler, while their Angus Deayton never resorts to the clichéd phrase 'So no change *there* then' when he can't think of a punchline. And, on that distant planet, the ratings for Anne and Nick are even lower than those for the Test Card (so no change *there* then).

Last night on Tharg, the new series of *Men Behaving Badly* (BBC1) very probably bombed, but in this solar system it went off with a big bang, shooting meteorically across the night sky (rather like an over-extended metaphor). Itself the very antithesis of the dire *Game On* (which briefly dis-graced our screens earlier in the year), this superb chronicle of the sordid joys of bachelor existence never lost its momentum for a second, hitting the screen running, and ducking and diving right up to the closing credits. As in past series, Simon Nye's scripts are adept at putting bitter coatings on sugar pills, using a compellingly irreverent mixture of comedy and profanity to discuss archetypal human concerns, and occasionally creating moments of surprising dramatic intensity. Last night's episode, for example, brought Gary (Martin Clunes) face to face with his own destiny, and forced him to make a choice between yet more parallel worlds, both of which looked like heaven from a distance, but like hell in close-up: the worlds of the single and the married.

When you see a church marriage service in which the organist is wearing a tutu, and the congregation are whipping each other while the heavily pregnant bride is engaging her tongue in mid-air refuelling with the vicar, you know you're either watching Oliver Reed's wedding video or, as was the case here, witnessing Gary's worst nightmare. Dorothy (Caroline Quentin) was desperate to have children ('I don't know why, I just want them . . . it's like you and lager'), yet Gary was equally desperate not to talk about it, his fear of marriage and babies seeming curiously appropriate for such a foetal-looking actor (Clunes is blessed with the sort of lips that, if you pushed him against a plate-glass window, I suspect he'd remain stuck there all day). But permanent solitude was no more attractive an option, once he'd asked a spinsterish work colleague to remind him of the benefits of being single: 'Well, you can drop off while listening to Melody Radio, or you can have a bit of a cry, that cheers you up . . . then sometimes you can go really mad and have sardines on toast.'

Meanwhile, Deborah (Lesley Ash) unwisely entrusted her front-door key to her besotted ex-boyfriend Tony (Neil Morrissey). He took the responsibility seriously; so seriously that, within seconds, he and Gary were in her flat, rummaging through her pants drawer, gawping at her photo album ('You can't beat the old red-string micro-bikini can you?'), with Tony pulling her knickers over his head (who hasn't?) while Gary searched hopefully for vibrators, and found them, not realizing they were hair-curling tongs. The farcical plot hurtled on with a speed and logic worthy of *Fawlty Towers*, with stupidity, dishonesty, prurience and sheer bad luck each playing their part, yet the script never lost sight of its central premise, brim-full of quotable lines about the perils of marriage and reproduction. When Martin boasted that 'A single yoghurt pot of my sperm would be enough to repopulate the whole of Ireland,' Dorothy replied, 'Haven't they had a tragic enough history without you turning up at the border with your yoghurt pot?'

The central quartet of actors in this near-perfect comedy series have now achieved a mutual sense of timing worthy of a first-class rep company, while the relaxed, free-wheeling style of Nye's scripts is reminiscent of *Sorry* at its best. Together with producer Beryl Vertue (who, in true Hitchcockian style, makes a brief silent appearance in each series) and Hartswood Films (under the aegis of Thames Television), they're proving that the US doesn't have a complete monopoly on wonderful sit-com in the 90s. Thames? You remember Thames, from the days when London had a TV station it could be proud of? Apparently, on the planet Tharg, it replaced Carlton at the last franchise renewal, and is now producing some fantastic shows.

Noel's House Party

Throughout history, Little Man Syndrome has had a lot to answer for. Napoleon was a runt, Genghis Khan was a dwarf, Emperor Hirohito only came up to Churchill's waist, while Goebbels wore lifts in his shoes yet still qualified as a midget. As for Herr Hitler, what else could you have expected from a man who stood five foot nothing in his stockinged feet and suspected (correctly) that everyone was laughing at him behind his back?

Television, being today's power centre, is equally full of little men, busily building themselves little media empires. Which brings us to Emperor Noel Edmonds, the host of *Noel's House Party* (BBC1), back on Saturday night for a fourth series with his ratings still buoyant, thereby constituting official proof of the theory that no one ever went broke underestimating the intelligence of the general public. 'The nation's number-one party is back,' boasted the man with the modesty by-pass as he ran squealing on to the set, wearing a shirt that appeared to have been designed by the blind seamstress of Jermyn St. He's never quite outgrown the 70s Radio 1 culture that spawned him, still believing that mental vacuity can be disguised with mere physical speed, that the presence of 'stars' automatically improves a show even if they don't do anything, and that shouting, 'We're live' from time to time can compensate for a moribund programme. But worse, the man clearly still believes that his incessant affability somehow gives him the moral authority to humiliate 'the punters'.

'The show is new and improved,' he claimed, as the same old ritual began again. We were invited to guess, at 39p a minute, how many beards there were in the audience, and someone was forced to sit in a giant pastry crust, only to be told moments later, 'You have failed to beat the big pork pie.' Terry, a bovine hairdresser from Up North, was roundly insulted, with Mr Edmonds laughing at unfashionable pictures taken on the gentleman's wedding day (our host had presumably forgotten that old *Top of the Pops* from the 70s are currently being screened, or he wouldn't have laughed quite so loudly). Viewers in the Birmingham area were encouraged to drive, as quickly as possible, across town to a telephone box in the city centre; the lucky winner promptly found himself locked inside for twenty minutes, then was told he'd won nothing and had gunge poured over him. Eamonn Holmes had gunge poured over him too, after which it was time for a star – Roger Moore. He and Noel performed what was not so much a comedy routine, more like two men standing in a room talking, and it was exquisite to watch the pair corpsing at their own material, while simultaneously dying on live television.

There was more, I'm afraid. 'When the Naughty Boys arrive, you never know what's going to happen,' said Mr Edmonds, but it wasn't true. You knew they weren't going to be remotely entertaining and, sure enough, within seconds they'd stripped Terry to his underpants, sat him in a tin bath and filled it with frozen peas, all pretty much as you'd have expected. Allan Lamb was spoofed by Noel (who had cleverly disguised himself by pretending to be a crass, insensitive broadcaster), and somebody entered the Grab-a-Grand box, and tried to grab handfuls of dosh in one minute. That's what Mr Edmonds does too, only he has fifty minutes each week to grab it. This is business for him, not showbusiness, and his apparent contempt for his audience shines like rotten wood in every matey aside he utters. How ironic that this fake TV stately home should pay for the real mansion he lives in the rest of the week, a secluded country seat from which his doting public is thoughtfully excluded.

Saturday-night schedules have long been a case of the bland leading the bland, but *Noel's House Party* is currently the bland leader, with big money being thrown at a clapped-out formula. Isn't Mr Edmonds now a little bit too old for local-radio pranks and larks? And anyway, have we all forgotten what happened last time he was given too much licence? When I hear him telling viewers to get into their cars and rush across a busy city very quickly if they want to win a prize, alarm bells start ringing. Someone will soon be crashing red lights and, sooner or later, television will have another Michael Lush incident on its conscience.

Wildlife on One

One of the most powerful animals in the bush is the Whispering Attenborough (*Attenbore susurrus*). Rarely straying from its natural habitat in Shepherd's Bush, it makes regular half-hour forays during the early evenings, but observers report that they have only ever seen its top and its tail. For the rest of the time, it is invisible to the naked eye, and can be identified only from its low, hushed, distinctive but apparently meaningless whine.

Keen-eyed viewers will have briefly glimpsed the Attenbore topping and tailing *Wildlife on One* (BBC1), which looked at 'the real world of the African leopard'. Nature programmes have a special dispensation to show scenes of frenzied carnage that would otherwise be deemed unacceptable for broadcast (much as schoolboys used to be allowed to see pictures of bare titties only if they belonged to African tribeswomen and appeared in the sober pages of *National Geographic*) and, with one of the world's fiercest predators cast in the starring role, last night's gore score was bound to be as high as ever. 'It has been almost impossible *until now* to film wildlife at night,' he claimed (a mantra programme makers have repeated for years, from *Twentieth Century Fox* to *Flamingowatch*, to justify their enormous budgets), while introducing nocturnal footage from South Luangwa National Park in Zambia, shot on the world's most sensitive video camera. As he did, you could almost hear him panting with anticipation at the thought of all those cute fluffy Bambis, about to be transformed into the sort of small bits the butcher can hose down his plughole.

Once the film began, the Attenbore communicated with us in his usual peculiar, hushed, staccato phrases. Typically, he rejected imaginative adjectives in favour of obvious ones – so that food was 'abundant', groves were 'thick', land was 'fertile', while the moon 'waxed and waned' – and whenever he talked of 'she', he really did mean the cat's mother, a leopard on the prowl in search of food for her cubs. Laughing hyenas mocked her when she narrowly missed a zebra (the only food that comes with its own natural bar code) and, when she spectacularly failed to catch any of a family of baboons, her expression reminded me of the way my (now deceased) cat Pickles used to look at me when I couldn't get the lid off the Kit-e-Kat quickly enough. 'She has a hidden family dependent on her for food . . . with hungry cubs waiting, she must persevere, despite the moon,' the Attenbore intoned, anthropomorphizing in his desire to forge an artificial relationship between ourselves and the leopard. But his attempts to endow a simple animal with complex human motivations were both unconvincing and bland: Johnny Morris without the jokes.

While human qualities were being ascribed to the leopard, the viewers were treated as though they were dumb animals, being asked to believe that what they were watching was reality, the genuine record of a single night in a leopard's life. Yet the advance billing proudly proclaimed that cameraman Owen Newman spent sixty nights in South Luangwa, armed with the world's only production model of the Sony 7000 and, since many of the sequences intercut five or more different camera positions, the programme was clearly the usual wildlife fiction, constructed in an edit suite around an imaginary tale in which the cutest animals escape being eaten, moonlight temporarily makes hunting difficult, but then clouds come to the rescue and Mummy eventually catches a meal for her cubs, so that viewers can enjoy the mandatory crunching of cartilage.

I'm rarely happy with nature films. The genre has been indulged for years, because these programmes apparently combine respectable ratings with educational worthiness, but I'm increasingly convinced that they're simply how people who live in Pinner and don't have access to snuff movies get their regular fix of sex and violence. Worse, they're now being held hostage by technological gimmickry. Before night-time photography was possible, we used to see documentaries about leopards hunting in daylight but, now that cameramen have ultra-sensitive equipment, we're told that they spend all day up a tree, fast asleep, which is simply not true. But my biggest problem is with Attenbore, a latter-day version of those humourless men who used to turn up at school with a slide projector to present 'improving' natural history lectures. For all that, I'd rather not get any closer to these creatures than when I'm flying overhead. Talking of which, I wonder if leopards think of airplanes as canned food?

Budgie the Little Helicopter

It's no secret that the Queen – a regular reader of this column – often gives me a ring, requesting my advice about what to watch on 'the idiot's lantern' (as Her Majesty so amusingly puts it). She is a woman of the world, and naturally, at such times, we exchange off-colour tittle-tattle. Only yesterday, she told me that Prince Edward likes nothing better than waking up with a soft-boiled egg and some lovely thick soldiers. She also hinted that she wasn't surprised by the Duchess of York's preoccupation with choppers, claiming that the fixation runs in the family.

Budgie the Little Helicopter (ITV) has taken to the air, in an animated children's series 'adapted from the original stories by HRH Duchess of York' (a quaint use of the word 'original', since the first Budgie book bore uncanny similarities to a story published decades earlier). The tales are also indebted to Thomas the Tank Engine, dealing as they do with a group of anthropomorphized public transport vehicles, all of them far too busy getting into scrapes ever to carry any passengers. There is, however, one striking difference. Unlike staid trains, helicopters exist in a continual state of angst, living their entire lives on the edge. Why? Because they're completely reliant on the essential Jesus bolt, the piece of metal connecting the rotors to the engine. Should you happen to be in one when the bolt fails, you'll only have time to say, 'Jesus' before you plummet to certain death.

Yesterday's episode began with Budgie and Pippa (a chubby little Fokker) on the prowl for extra-terrestrial beings; but, while they scoured Harefield airport for alien craft, I was puzzling over a greater sci-fi mystery: time travel, which had caused the participants to slip back a generation. I thought expressions like 'Gosh,' 'Crumbs,' 'Good show' and 'Crikey' died out with Enid Blyton, but apparently not, because this royal author liberally sprinkled her dialogue with such obsolete expressions. By 1969, every British schoolchild knew what Concorde looked like, yet here it was, supposedly being mistaken for a spacecraft. Crass stereotypes from that generation were perpetuated too, so the French wore moustaches and berets, working-class people said, 'Cor!' 'Give 'em what for!' and 'Bomb the perishers!' while Budgie's commander, Lionel, was a Battle of Britain type with a handlebar moustache and metal landing bumpers for legs (the spit and image of Douglas Bader, in fact).

The feeble storyline proved to be a shameless lift from Orson Welles' *War of the Worlds* incident. Budgie's radio was malfunctioning and, when it retuned itself to a sci-fi play, he heard a few words about little green men and naturally thought that aliens had landed. In the caring, sharing 90s, some might consider the arrival of extraterrestrials a well-timed potential boon for this sad planet, but not Budgie and his chums, who immediately decided to kill them (rather than find out, say, whether they'd come in peace with a cure for cancer). Getting hold of sandbags, they attacked some local roadworks, demolishing several dozen workmen's flashing lights which, in their high spirits, they foolishly mistook for invaders. Everyone laughed when they realized their error, council-tax payers presumably footed the bill, and I'm sure that this part of the plot, at least, came entirely from the duchess's own experience. After all, smashing up traffic cones has long been a traditional speciality amongst drunken Hooray Henrys and Henriettas.

Opinion is divided on the merits of the duchess's latest *oeuvre*. Some say that we are dealing here not simply with characters but with Jungian archetypes, and that the obsession with flying objects reflects the emotionally charged conflicts currently taking place within the collective unconscious of a technologically driven species. Others, however, say that it's simply a hastily written pile of derivative, one-dimensional cack, execrably drawn, badly voiced and cynically sold not on merit but on the strength of tarnished royal connections (mentioned four times on the credits), all so that some idle, red-haired lardbucket can go skiing down the slopes at St Moritz (bet you could break your neck if you fell into her tracks). Who is right? Ladies and gentlemen, it's a mystery.

10-2-95

Dear Sir,
                I am writing to you
re- your article in the "Evening
Standard" Wed 1st February,
regarding "Budgie the little Helicopter"
I was interested in the paragraph
referring to the originality of the
book, which bore uncanny
similarity to a story published
decades ago, this is something
I noted — I have enclosed
a photo-copy from T.V Comic
Annual, dated 1954 : Drawn
by George Moreno + written by
Dorothy Dee — who were my

This review inspired a letter from J. Moreno, who wrote to me
enclosing a copy of a children's story written by her parents and
published in the *TV Comic Annual* of 1954. I should like to make it

father and mother (now both deceased)
and I think you will also note
similarity in the character,.
only Budgie has been modenised
I was wandering if you were
referring to these stories, as
it would be nice to know
that people still remember,
one of many characters
and stories my father created
and also my mother wrote,
and am suprised that
nobody has noticed this
before.

Yours Sincerly

J. Moreno

clear that there is absolutely no question of plagiarism on the part of
the duchess. After all, her creation is called *Budgie the Helicopter*,
while the Morenos' was called *Polly Copter*. Completely different.

Polly Copter's Adventures

with ROY ROGERS

by Dorothy Dee

ILLUSTRATED BY GEORGE MORENO

ONE BRIGHT MORNING Polly suggested to Copty that it might be fun to go to one of the big airports to watch the giant air-liners leaving for their various destinations.

"What a splendid idea!" agreed Copty. "We might pick up a few useful hints on how to fly the Atlantic!"

"Come along then," said Polly, who was anxious to be off. "I hear Roy Rogers is leaving on a plane this morning, and we might be lucky enough to get his autograph."

Copty needed no further urging when he heard this; and the thought of seeing him in person filled him with excitement.

They arrived at the airport just as a huge liner was taking off.

"Look out!" yelled Polly, as the bird-like plane swept towards them.

Without a moment's hesitation, Copty went into a dive and so missed it by a split second.

"Phew," gasped Polly. "That was a close thing, although I'm positive that liner winked as he passed us. I'm not sure he didn't do it on purpose!"

They had no time for further speculation on this point, however, for as they landed in

Extract from 'Polly Copter's Adventures'
reproduced by kind permission of the *News of the World*
and Jane Moreno.

To Play the King

'They don't like it up 'em,' 'Points mean prizes,' 'It's the way I tell 'em.' No matter how popular a catchphrase becomes, they've hitherto always been a little too vulgar to appeal to refined sensibilities. But recently we have witnessed the arrival of the first ever middle-class catchphrase, which I've heard being quoted everywhere from Hampstead wine bars to gentlemen's clubs in St James's. Ladies and gentlemen, I give you 'You might think that – I couldn't possibly comment.'

In the final episode of *To Play the King*, revenge tragedy came face to face with that longest-running farce in the West End, the House of Commons. Michael Dobbs' *roman à clef*, superbly dramatized by Andrew Davies, has presented the viewer with more keys than you'd find on a Chinese typewriter: crapulent, ten-chinned newspaper proprietors, ex-BBC director generals, divorced princesses saying 'Yah' a lot, an ineffectual leader of the opposition, and Michael Kitchen getting only the ears wrong in his otherwise uncannily accurate portrayal of a certain maverick monarch keen on talking to moolies and reincarnating as a tampon. Only one Major figure remained unidentifiable – the scheming, murderous PM himself, Francis Urquhart. Number 10 may have housed some pretty disreputable characters over the decades, but so far we still haven't seen a resident whose initials reveal quite so blatantly his intentions towards the entire country: F.U.

This was a government poisoned at the head, and anyone who believes that all conspiracy theories are simply made up by a couple of people in a room somewhere would have been foaming at the mouth with delight. The PM (addressing us directly in the true Websterian manner) found himself outmanoeuvred, and trailing in the polls to an opposition unexpectedly united behind the King. Haunted by Banquoesque images of his murder of Mattie Storrin – 'I am in blood steeped in so far' – his resolve temporarily faltered until his Lady Macbeth of a wife persuaded him that, if he screwed his courage to the sticking place, he wouldn't fail. Acting on her advice, he also screwed Sarah, his special adviser, making the beast with two backs while the King's press secretary was making the beast with one back, a homosexual tryst that forced his resignation when Urquhart's buggers leaked news of royal shirt-lifting to the press.

With the PM determined to conquer in the end-game, the King sat in his chessboard-tiled room planning his offensive, forgetting that, in chess, an attacking king soon becomes outflanked and vulnerable. While naïvely touring a deprived inner-city area, he found himself the victim of an ever-so-convenient kidnap attempt, even-more-conveniently foiled by the Army, and his credibility was shot for good. Back in Downing Street, reference was made to a bomb going off as 'not one of ours', the implication being that HM Government could 'fake an IRA bombing in ninety minutes'. Possible? *You* might think that – I couldn't possibly comment. Ultimately, Urquhart's instinct for survival triumphed over the King's intellect and cold compassion. The government was returned on a platform of 'Bring back National Service', the PM was saved, the King was forced to abdicate, and some young pliable rubber stamp of a brat from Sloane Castle was installed on the throne. And, just like a revenge tragedy, the final scenes were littered with dead bodies, with Sarah and disaffected Party Chairman Tim Stamper both making spirited attempts to break Admiral Carrero Blanco's world record for the high jump in a limousine.

Just occasionally, television disproves Marshall Macluhan's definition and reveals itself as a hot medium. *To Play the King* and *House of Cards* are two such rare examples, albeit that a knowledge of British Constitution and Grub Street rumour are a definite advantage in following the intricate weaving of the tangled webs. This has been the BBC at its best, from the breathtaking opening steadycam helicopter shots of Parliament to the closing credits. Andrew Davies' screenplay has been a model of economy, the acting – especially from Ian Richardson, Michael Kitchen and Colin Jeavons – was quite brilliant, and the eye of the casting director (who can often make or break a series) has been faultless. With Jim Parker's exceptional score – quintessentially British yet subversively sardonic – and the matchless direction and production from Paul Seed and Ken Riddington, there hardly seems any point in the BAFTA jury bothering to turn up to decide on next year's drama award.

A follow-up to the series? *You* might think that – I couldn't possibly comment.

Men's Rooms: Pointing Percy

It may sound like a mishmash of ads from the *Sunday Express circa* 1961, but my motto has always been 'An overactive prostate can increase your word power.' There's nothing like the peculiarly evocative brand names of public urinals for stimulating the subconscious and, at the end of an afternoon's mild incontinence, an author, staring vacantly at various latrines, can find that his latest thriller has mapped itself out for him. There's the CIA hero ('The name's Sheldon . . . Sankey Sheldon'), who teams up with MI5's dapper Armitage Shanks to investigate why scientists on the Bolding Vedas project mysteriously keep going round the bend. In Twyford they attempt to flush out Vitrok, the Russian spy, and discover his secret mission: to smash the capitalist cistern.

Last night's *Men's Rooms: Pointing Percy* (CH4) also found inspiration in the smallest room, as an all-woman crew ventured into the innermost sanctum of the male: the gentlemen's lavatory. Dressed in Groucho Club black, Nigel Floyd covered the spectrum of euphemisms for urination – from the infantile 'pee' to the robust 'shaking hands with the wife's best friend' (though my preference, 'straining the potatoes', was sadly absent from his list) – his words accompanied by a sampled sound collage of splishes, sploshes, parps and poops, much the same technique as the opening sig of *Food and Drink*, only recorded all points south rather than north of the navel. Putting down his slang thesaurus, he then started reciting from the Ladybird Book of Sociology, offering truisms of the 'When a boy stops going to the lavatory with his mother, it's a rite of passage' variety, as he tested the superior plumbing at the Grosvenor House Hotel. When radio's *Stop the Week* used to address this topic, it provided us with a glorious golden stream of observation but, regrettably, all Mr Floyd could produce was an attack of verbal diarrhoea.

In a cubicle at the Manor House municipal lavatory, someone had relieved a massive internal blockage by causing a massive external one. Forgive my coarseness, but a delinquent driver of the porcelain bus had just deposited a glorious high-fibre bog blocker – the sort of unflushable horror that one usually only produces when staying with friends – which the hapless attendant was vainly trying to persuade downstream with a mop. Never mind about knighthoods for luvvies who hang around the Ivy, Olu Oyesana deserves the OM at the very least for his fearless work as the Red Adair of the public carzey. 'Does it ever make you feel sick?' said a queasy voice (so off-mike that I suspect she was not merely outside the loo, but outside the city too), and received the reply 'Yes, that's why I have to eat a lot of mints.' Now there's an advertising angle that the After Eight Mints company haven't yet pursued. Things looked up. They have to, because, apparently, if your gaze drifts sideways, you might be accused of breaking the ultimate taboo: 'willy-watching'. Being as ocularly challenged as Mr Magoo, I've hitherto been blissfully unaware of potential pitfalls, but a gentleman named Madge soon filled me in (so to speak) on the etiquette of cottaging. Absolute silence at the urinal indicates interest, followed by eye contact and a quick dash to the nearest cubicle, where holes in the door are plugged with lavatory paper ('putting up the curtains') to evade prying eyes. One man sits, while the other stands erect with his feet in a shopping bag, to confuse the vice squad, who might peer beneath the door in search of excessive legs (a great idea except that, in the throes of congress, the bag doubtless moves about like a sack of ferrets). Sadly, the programme then anti-climaxed with several limp minutes at the Oxford Union, in the company of a tubby gentleman who sat on a lavatory bowl and displayed an ability all too common on TV nowadays: he could produce exactly the same substance from both ends.

Well, I'm sorry if you're eating your sandwiches, but that's what I watched last night. *Pointing Percy* was a fascinating yet revolting look by women into the least exclusive of all men's clubs, and I look forward to a male team laying bare the secrets of the women's lavatory in the near future. Following on from a somewhat humourless look at strip clubs, this was an inspired piece of scheduling although, at only fifteen minutes, it couldn't plumb the deeper mysteries, such as the identity of the lone maniac who follows me around, separating the two plys on lavatory rolls, then folding them so that the perforations are constantly out of sync. But, despite that deficiency, this was wild and hilarious stuff. Like lavatory paper itself, in fact. Off the wall.

This, and other references to the problems of incontinence, provoked letters of protest from the Continence Foundation and the Association for Continence Advice.

I was interested to note that both organizations are based at 2 Doughty Street, London WC1. Presumably, there was originally only one society, so had there been a schism? Factions? And, with two organizations now crammed into one building, do they both have adequate bathroom facilities?

Association for Continence Advice
The Basement, 2 Doughty Street,
London WC1N 2PH
Tel: 071 404 6821
Fax. 071 404 6876

14 June 1993
The Editor
The Evening Standard
Northcliffe House
2 Derry Street
London W8 5EE

Dear Sir

I write on behalf of our membership to complain most strongly about the introductory paragraph in Victor Lewis-Smith's article on Wednesday 28 April 1993 on your TV Review page (copy of item enclosed).

These remarks perpetuate the INCORRECT stereotype of the incontinence sufferer being elderly and in residential accommodation.

The ACA is a membership organisation. Our members include Consultants, Doctors, specialists in Nursing, Physiotherapy and Occupational Therapy. We have Company members and Groups (such as Nursing Homes) as part of our membership.

We are all working to the same goal – that of raising awareness that this secret, stigmatising problem affects all age groups. Most importantly, this is a symptom which can often be cured following an assessment and diagnosis of the underlying disorder.

Mr Lewis-Smith is indeed fortunate if the indignity of incontinence has not affected him directly or indirectly, as over 3 million adults in the UK experience regular urinary incontinence.

His remarks have offended the sufferers and the professionals alike.

I hope that you feel able to restore some dignity to those you have degraded by retracting this paragraph.

Yours sincerely
Wendy Colley (Mrs)
CHAIRMAN
cc Major Vivien Harmsworth, Readers' Representative, Evening Standard, E Margaret Moore PhD

The Continence Foundation
2 Doughty Street
London WC1N 2PH
Tel 071 404 6875
Fax 071 404 6876

23 May 1993
The Editor
Evening Standard
Northcliffe House
2 Derry Street
London W8 5EE

Dear Sir

I write to protest about the introductory paragraph in Victor Lewis-Smith's article on Wednesday 28 April 1993 on your TV Review page.

Incontinence is a problem which effects over 3 million adults in the UK today and most of them feel embarrassed and ashamed about the symptom and are unwilling to seek professional help. Comments such as those by Mr Lewis-Smith do nothing to help break down the image of incontinence as a condition associated with elderly people in residential care. In practice, the majority of people with problems are young, otherwise fit, healthy adults and I find the remarks unnecessarily degrading to elderly people.

We hope that the 'Evening Standard' will feel moved to publish a retraction of this paragraph and an apology for any offence that is caused.

If at some time in the future you would like to cover the subject of bladder and bowel problems, we would, of course, be delighted to participate in this.

Yours faithfully

Christine Norton

Development Officer

cc Major Vivien Harmsworth, Readers' Representative, Evening Standard, E Margaret Moore PhD

29 June 1994

Dear Victor,

Your review of Men's Rooms: Pointing Percy (28 June), rather than plumbing the depths, scaled new heights. Whilst reading the review on the tube home I startled a number of fellow travellers by laughing out aloud so amusing was its content.

My main purpose in writing to you is not to compliment you on your review, funny though it was, but to put you out of your misery once and for all regarding the dreaded misalignment in perforations in ones two-ply. I cannot throw any light on the identity of, or motivation behind, the 'lone maniac' to whom you referred. However I can offer a solution to the problem.

I am no artist but I trust you can follow the drawings below which show that the solution to this most dastardly of problems is startling in its simplicity.

BEFORE   SOLUTION   AFTER

OUT OF SYNCH

Take the outer ply and pass it over the top of the roll so that it becomes the inner ply

PERFECTLY IN SYNCH

In a flash you can forever more put the misery of out of synch perforations behind you and startle friends at parties at your ability to unravel (literally) one of life's great mysteries.

Yours sincerely,

Frank Johnson

Honey for Tea

It's hard to believe nowadays, but there was a time when putting an American character in Oxbridge was a sure-fire comedic winner. In numerous films of the *A Yank at Oxford* type, unsuspecting Americans were thrust into a world of stuck-up toffs, jolly boating on the Isis, cockney porters and dotty professors, overcoming cultural differences to earn a degree and grudging respect from the university. Of course, such portrayals were already anachronistic in the 1930s, depending on mutual misunderstanding to a ludicrous extent, and no modern writer in their right mind, you might think, would even consider reviving such a moribund genre. Which brings me to Michael Aitkens and his latest comedy series, *Honey for Tea* (BBC1).

Accompanied by probably the most appalling rendition of 'Gaudeamus Igitur' I've ever heard, the opening titles depicted Mr Belasco, a Californian, in the throes of a fatal heart attack: the only character in the show (it soon transpired) not to outstay his welcome. His West Coast widow Nancy (in Cambridge to see her son Jake through college) was played by Ms Kendal, but Felicity had precious little to do with her LA accent, surely belated revenge for Dick Van Dyke's notorious 'Maori Parpens'. In a single phrase, she veered uncontrollably from the Bronx to South Africa via Surrey, like some linguistic Spruce Goose, awkwardly taking off only to crash-land again within moments. Her opening soliloquy – full of absurd pronunciations like 'podahdoes' – was a clumsy attempt to recap last week's plot, but only made one thing clear: one pair of swallowed Ts doesn't make a summary.

What followed was thirty minutes of superannuated stereotypes, crassly contrasting Americans (brash, ostentatious, money-obsessed, all breast implants and analysts) with the English (stuck-up, class-ridden, ill-dressed, eccentric fogeys) in a series of confrontations from which all traces of humour had been surgically removed. Jake (Patrick McCollough) was a muscle-bound fool, only there on a sports scholarship, and asking crusty old professors to 'Gimme five.' Leslie Phillips, as Master of the College Sir Dickie Hobhouse, was hamming it up so much he could have opened a chain of pork butchers. As for Professor Simon Latimer (Nigel Le Vaillant), his one facial expression was of fixed disbelief, although he didn't do it as convincingly as I did, while watching the burgeoning of an ultra-predictable love-hate romance between his snobbish character and the self-made Nancy; a sort of *To the Manor Stillborn*.

The dialogue plumbed depths of imbecility seldom encountered since euthanasia was justly administered to ITV's *Doctor in the House*. I call exhibit A – 'Now where was I?' 'Here in the room, sir.' 'I was not speaking geographically' – and rest my case. When Jake, preparing for a disputation, was asked to knock on the door and enter, he misunderstood the instructions for a full three minutes, a display of dimwittedness that even Norman Wisdom might consider a little unsophisticated. When it wasn't puerile it was portentous – 'We can't let the untutored through our exclusive portals' – or else so glaringly plotladen as to be embarrassing. In short, the whole programme was reminiscent of a dismal matinée by a dreadful local rep, with an audience of OAPs only there because it's raining outside.

This is, without the slightest doubt, the worst sit-com the BBC has produced in a decade, stunning even the studio audience (who are let in free, and are therefore always grateful) into occasional silence. When a show's denouement is a shot of a punt shipping water, you suspect it's holed below the waterline itself, but, when exactly the same joke appeared ten minutes earlier, you know you're watching a disaster of *Titanic* proportions. As for the casting director, lynching comes to mind. While no one can doubt Ms Kendal's naturalness in *The Good Life*, her presence here is about as believable as Arthur Mullard playing the eponymous role in *The Marie Curie Story*. The only positive aspect of this shambles is that Cambridge will at least be spared the ignominy of becoming 'Honey for Tea Country'. If this drivel makes a second series, I'll eat my mortarboard* because, frankly, it doesn't merit a two-two or a third, and even a fail would be too dressy. A series like this deserves the ultimate disgrace: an aegrotat, awarded due to chronic infirmity.

* Two years later, and I still haven't had to place an order with Messrs Ede & Ravenscroft, suppliers of academic caps and gowns by appointment to Her Majesty the Queen.

Copacabana

If ever there was a profession awash with fatuous expressions, surely it's
that wonderful business we like to call the show. 'Always refer to it as
the Scottish play in the theatre, luvvy,' actors tell each other, even
though they're continually declaiming Macbeth's name while on
stage. 'What's my motivation, darling?' they ingenuously ask directors, when everyone knows it's a combination of money and egotism.
But most absurd of all is undoubtedly 'The show must go on,' which
is clearly a misspelling. This weekend, while watching excerpts from
Barry Manilow's dismal stage musical *Copacabana* (BBC1) in between
the two halves of Claude Lanzmann's epic film, it became obvious that
the phrase really ought to be 'The Shoah must go on.'

Here was yet another example of a genre that's grown rapidly on
the BBC in recent years, the extended free plug masquerading as
documentary. Under the guise of chronicling the shambolic opening
of the West End dead-end show, it actually consisted of fifty minutes
of uncritical adulation, interspersed with an interview-cum-hagio-
graphy of its homely creator. In fact, I am surprised that Zoë Heller
(who'd lost her umlaut on the credits – probably mislaid it in the dress
circle) didn't require an emergency proctologist to remove herself
from Mr Manilow's nether regions, after she bowled a succession of
gentle full tosses (all variants on 'Tell us, why are you so wonderful?')
to this man, who has the sort of face you usually only see when you peer
through security spyholes in hotel doors.

Sporting a pair of Gustav Mahler glasses (in a futile Paul Scofield-
esque quest for intellectual cred), and leaping as sure-footedly as a
chamois from one cliché to the next ('I live in Jet Lag City ... We want
this baby to fly . . .'), the great composer insisted that '*Copa* is not a
camp show.' And to prove it, on to the stage came twenty definitely-
not-camp-dear-me-no male Carmen Mirandas in a feathery explosion
resembling a mortar attack on Bernard Matthews' abattoir, accompanied by sailors in sequins nervously hoisting aloft a dozen girls dressed
in eight-foot New York skylines and mermaid tails. If that's not camp,
then Larry Grayson is fronting tonight's *Newsnight*. 'For me, Gary
Wilmot is the find of the past ten years,' Manilow gushed, apropos of
the show's star, 'I was just hoping that he could sing.' Well, after

listening to a few bars, I could see what he meant (I'd like to know what Mr Wilmot did with the money. What money? The money his mother gave him for singing lessons). Let's put it this way: either Mr Wilmot was permanently sharp, or the entire orchestra was permanently flat. Take your pick.

As the cast finished their Edinburgh try-out and headed for London ('We've tied up the Prince of Wales,' the executive producer told us, without a hint of irony), it emerged that, like all great musicals, *Copacabana* possessed a genuine show-stopper. Unfortunately, it wasn't any of the many unmemorable tunes, but the choreography, which ground to a complete halt so many times during final rehearsals that the opening matinée had to be cancelled. A disaster, you might think, but not according to this documentary, which showed punters smiling through tears and saying, 'It's because they're such perfectionists' (although newspapers at the time reported scenes of fury and mayhem, with irate ticket holders threatening violence and legal action). But finally, with the show in a state of advanced unreadiness, the first night went ahead, before an audience that included such luminaries as Gaby Roslin, Gloria Hunniford and Anita Dobson, a veritable walking definition of the celebrity B-list. 'The show opened to mixed reviews,' we were told (in the sense that 'dreadful' and 'atrocious' have subtly different meanings) but, to be fair, it did get a standing ovation. And, to be even fairer, the first out of his seat was Gustav Manilow, the fish-eye-lens king.

'*Copa* is a love letter,' the composer swore at the outset to Zoë Heller.* But this documentary was a love letter too, a narcissistic exercise in self-promotion, trying to attract sympathy for the manifest inadequacies of a commercial venture, and for the hubris of Mr Manilow and his acolytes (I can never remember, are acolytes the ones that hang down or up?). Any documentary with even a glimmer of integrity would have torn to shreds this feeble show, with its fatuous plot and banal music (carbon copies of 'Mañana'), performed by the

---

* I received a love letter from the *Copacabana* producers' lawyers, alleging defamation and demanding damages. I rebutted each and every one of their complaints, and they were told to go away and never bother me again. They did and didn't respectively. If only all things in life were that simple.

sort of luvvies who claim to have been born in a trunk in a theatre. What a pity they didn't all stay locked in.

Just before the curtain went up, we saw technicians making last-minute alterations to the audience's chairs. Just as well, because there was obviously something wrong with them. They were facing the stage.

Top Gear

Formaldehyde must be arriving by the lorryload at the BBC Pebble Mill studios. How else could *Top Gear* (BBC2) have been preserved all these years? A living fossil in the schedules, everything about it screams 'Trapped in the 70s', from the Allman Brothers' sig and the low-tech opening graphics to its very title, a homage to the young John Peel's progressive rock show. As for the presenters, they're 70s guys through and through, from their taste in music right down to their IQs. I bet, even as I write, they're standing in front of bedroom mirrors with their tennis racquets, miming to Dire Straits guitar solos.

The new series began last night with Jeremy Clarkson, a man with the self-awareness of Alan Partridge and the physique of an endo-morphic Stephen Fry. Addressing us with all the vacuous, locker-room matiness of a local-radio DJ, he showed us a trio of coupés called something like the Vauxhall Farrago, the Volkswagen Excreta V12 and the Honda Caliper 1.2, delighting that one would 'knock on the door of a hundred and fifty mph' while lamenting that another was 'flat out at a hundred and forty mph', although I'm sure he'd be the last person to encourage motorists to flout the law. There were plenty of toys for this boy, but his favoured plaything was the Ford Probe, which he claimed 'looked good enough to snap knicker elastic at fifty paces'. It was a jelly mould on wheels, as far as I could see. Still, the engine made a 'sexy, very loud noise', and that was all Mr Clarkson cared about. I bet he was the sort of boy who placed lolly sticks in his bicycle spokes so it sounded almost like a moped.

As with *Food and Drink*, *Holiday* and *The Clothes Show*, *Top Gear* is cursed with presenters of restricted vocabulary trying to find new ways of expressing the same few observations week after week.

Unequal to the challenge, Mr Clarkson fell back on analogies so fatuous ('This car may have film-star looks, but it's no harder to run than the girl next door') that they could have made the wind fairly whistle through Alan Whicker's dentistry. As for grammar, our Jeremy clearly thinks subjunctivitis is some sort of eye infection, because he misconstrued one conditional clause after another: 'If this car *was* a city, it would be San Francisco . . . If this car *was* a dog, it would be a big lazy labrador.' This hiding behind analogies, hoping we wouldn't notice he had nothing to say, reached its ludicrous conclusion when he embarked on an extended coffee metaphor – 'This one's a cappuccino, beautifully presented but not fulfilling, this is filter coffee, does the job, hits the spot, this is espresso, one shot blows your head off . . .' – and I had a vision of a bleary-eyed presenter on the final day of his freebie in Cannes, hung over, staggering down to breakfast, no end to his report and in desperate need of inspiration, looking down at his table, and . . . Eureka! I rest my case.

There was more. Quentin Willson talked contemptuously about second-hand car salesmen, little realizing that with his pompous put-it-on-for-TV accent (which should be called Royal Dalston) he sounded like one himself. Quentin had an allergy to analogies, seeking refuge instead in alliteration ('levitating limos . . . cufflink carriages . . . hot-shot hatches . . . speedy slingshots suffering') to dress up research that apparently consisted of merely reading second-hand car prices out of the *Sunday Times*. And Steve Berry – a prototype Andy Kershaw unlikely ever to be put into mass-production – patronized and ridiculed the 'appalling' Indian Enfield motorcycle range (utterly reliable machines and the backbone of that country's personal transport system for decades).

Paraphrasing Mr Clarkson, I wrote not so long ago that, if *Top Gear* were a car and you took it to a garage, the diagnosis would be 'Battery's flat, timing's all wrong, no spark, it's scrap, guvn'r.' I'd go further now. If I were a controller, I'd crush this programme into a six-inch cube, and replace it with a motoring show that didn't only address itself to overgrown schoolboys obsessed with speed, posing and reliving their adolescence. And, as punishment for the current team, I'd present them with a fleet of Thundersley one-seater battery-powered invalid cars with GT go-faster stripes down the sides, make them drive out through the main entrance of BBC Pebble Mill, and tell them not to come back until they hear that the late Douglas Bader has been appointed captain of the All-England Synchronized Swimming Team.

We Have Ways of Making You Think

The one fact everyone knows about Joseph Goebbels is that, according to the popular song, he had no balls at all. In an effort to present a more rounded picture of the man and his work, the first programme of *We Have Ways of Making You Think* dealt with his years as minister in charge of propaganda films in Nazi Germany, a chilling account that left the hairs on the back of my teeth standing on end.

All propaganda is deeply suspect, but the dissonance between the superficially innocent films he produced, and the sinister subliminal messages they contained, made these the most improperganda movies ever shot. He understood that people were either bored or repulsed by overt proselytizing – 'All political films turn out dreadfully' – and instead made entertaining musicals and historical romances that packed the audiences in. His favourite film was *Snow White*, his role model was Walt Disney, and ninety per cent of his output was not overtly propagandist at all; in a Goebbels film, the sun was shining, the dancing girls were kicking high and there was not a canister of Zyklon B in sight.

He was smart, and understood mass-manipulation far better than the monorchid Führer. When Hitler supervised an anti-Semitic film and juxtaposed footage of Warsaw Jews and rats, people were repelled by such crude and obvious manipulation and refused to watch it. At the same time Goebbels made *Jud Suss*, a wicked but compelling film about an evil eighteenth-century Jew who torments an upright Aryan family; audiences flocked to see such a great storyline, and swallowed their mind poison along with the plot. Through such films he softened up a nation's psyche to tolerate, and even welcome, the Holocaust.

Not that Goebbels himself ever believed in practising any of the ideals that his films preached. Good Germans, he said, should only have one house, should be happily married, and should despise decadence and the sub-human Slavic races. Meanwhile our Joseph was hanging around nightclubs, and conducting countless extra-marital affairs in his various houses, including a long-standing one with Lida Baarova, a Slavic actress. Hitler found out about Ms Baarova but, we were told, refused to accept Goebbels' resignation. Now where have I heard that one before?

Out of such dismal stuff, writer-producer Laurence Rees managed to capture some amusing moments. Aged film stars and producers recounted their memories of the period – 'It vas so alive, it vas so important, darlink' – proving that luvvies, even ex-Nazi ones, are the same the whole world over. A clip from a film about the British upper class depicted them all as decadent and effeminate, and who can argue with that? The most unfortunately named Wilfred Von Oven played with the electric windows of a house built for Goebbels by a grateful film industry, and told us that, despite Joseph's phocine looks, women found him extremely attractive and he could get his disabled leg over almost any actress he cared to pursue although, surprise surprise, the legion of actresses who were interviewed all said that they had rejected his advances.

This was a promising start to the series, with some astounding and obscure footage, and imaginative use of talking heads. However, the tone of the narration was rather lifeless, and someone should have had the sense to edit out several predictable minutes of ex-Nazis saying, 'Of course, we didn't know what was really going on.' The programme's only major failing was the lack of time for a thorough analysis of the content of the films themselves; the material touched on in this first programme was enough to last an entire series.

As for the denouement, the man who had fed a nation sugar-coated pills for a decade now fed cyanide-coated pills to his wife and six Shirley Temple lookalike children. But, as they used to say in the 40s, it turned out nice again, because he then put a bullet through his bonce. I wonder, if he had lived, whether he'd have gone into advertising?

Away the Lads

In London Zoo, there is a placard that invites you to stick your head through a hole, while you remain oblivious to the fact that a sign on the other side reads MAN – THE MOST DANGEROUS ANIMAL OF ALL. In last night's *Away the Lads*, John Alexander and his *40 Minutes* team managed a neat trick: they transferred the idea to television.

The documentary could well have been shot in a zoo, since the group of bovine, foul-mouthed Geordies we followed on holiday in Benidorm boasted (correctly) that they had turned their apartment into a pigsty. A lumpen mass of British brutish bone, bristle, tattoos and earrings, these delegates from the north-east branch of DENSA had left chilly Tyneside behind in the hope of a fortnight of sun, swill, sex, sex, sex and sex. Nine obstreperous, bellowing louts, they were crammed into room 100 of a shoddy cardboard hotel with paper-thin walls; whoever was staying in room 101 last August really did come face to face with their worst nightmare.

The programme was a random scraping of life at the very very bottom of the barrel. The lads swilled lager for breakfast in the shower, wore items from Top Man that sparked in the dark, ate with wide-open tumble-drier mouths, exposed their genitalia to each other, headbutted a 'Test Your Strength' punchball to the point of near-unconsciousness, simulated a sense of humour by reciting old Tango TV commercials, intimidated the elderly on the streets, ogled titties on the topless beach and spoiled for a fight in the nightspots. For them, evenings would end either in getting laid or getting laid out.

But it wasn't all refinement. A philosophical discussion about what constituted a lager lout was held, while one of their number ripped the cap off a Carlsberg bottle with his teeth. 'We never go out looking for trouble,' they swore, but the sounds of their knuckles scraping on the ground as they walked made me doubt their claim. The Benidorm phenomenon became clearer when we were introduced to its arbiters of taste, a pair of British pimps from the local night club who simulated troilism with a succession of real live Fat Slags fresh from the pages of *Viz*, and wore T-shirts emblazoned with the uplifting slogan NEVER MIND THE LOVE AND PASSION, WHACK IT UP HER DOGGY FASHION.

In an attempt to turn this grim litany into a piece of worthwhile television, some sneaky tricks were used. The lads were given a camcorder to record their holiday, allowing the programme to include plenty of ratings-boosting tit and bum, while exonerating the BBC film crew from accusations of prurience. Most irritatingly, an extended apologia was cut into the programme, showing the lads at work as welders and carpet fitters in their home village. Presumably, we were supposed to swallow the message that their terrible circumstances justified their terrible behaviour. But they had good jobs, money in their pockets, and neither deserved nor wanted our pity; the truth was that they were simply seeking escapism through sensual degradation. As Dr Johnson once said, 'He who makes a beast of himself loses the pain of being a man.' These were their fleeting moments of painlessness, before the inevitable marriage to some no-messing fat slag.

This was supposed to be a them-and-us film, although the division did not concern class, rather the unbridgeable gulf between the sublimely stupid and the rest of us. At the end, I was left wondering about its motivation; lift a stone and film what crawls out into the sunlight? No rhyme nor reason to the movement, so why bother to take off the lens caps? Overall, the film's tone was equivocal – reverential when filming within punching distance, sneering in the cutting room – and I somehow doubt whether the lads were invited for finger sandwiches at the press screening. If so, knuckle sandwiches would have been the order of the day.

40 Minutes claims that its purpose is 'to take the temperature of Britain'. It is a pity that this week John Alexander chose to use a rectal thermometer.

Minders

Am I the only person in Britain who was not sexually abused as a child? Every day, I hear adults blaming their dysfunctional personalities on unwanted advances during childhood, yet the bitter truth is that I was a plain boy, and nobody really fancied me. Scout masters, vicars, little old ladies in tea shops – not one of them offered me so much as a sweetie or muttered, 'It's our little secret,' and I've been traumatized ever since by the rejection. And worse, because of their callousness, I'm unable to appear on television, dimly lit and in silhouette, smoking nervously and dumping all my inadequacies on to a long-forgotten grope in Akela's hut.

Fortunately, as last night's *Minders* (BBC2) revealed, professional help is at hand for those who feel in need of psychiatric assistance. Simply phone the North Battersea Community Mental Health Team, and they'll send a female social worker with a severe haircut and dangly earrings round to listen to you, nod sympathetically and then go away again. Over the past five weeks, the psychiatric team featured in this fly-on-the-wall medical series has visited the distressed, depressed and possessed (even one eloquent black man who insisted he was white with blue hair, and the Queen's nephew to boot), but it's shied away from the conspicuously, barkingly, anti-socially mad. *Really* mad people are far too unsavoury and unphotogenic to be allowed on to the small screen, although there are plenty of them in society at large nowadays. Mrs Thatcher, you may recall, took the precaution of decanting most of them on to the streets several years ago, so that her Cabinet ministers would seem more rational.

'Depression is the single most common mental illness,' the voice-over intoned, and last night's programme focused on two young mothers who'd diagnosed themselves as sufferers, and wanted therapy. Jeni, who was fronting a rock band, told us, 'I've always wanted to be a singer,' so, having heard the caterwauling sounds she produced on stage, there was no great mystery about why she felt depressed. She'd been abused as a child, and hoped that a therapist would compensate for the rapist, but her real wish was something we'd all like: 'All I want is someone to listen to me.' Pauline, with several screaming kids, a recent cot death and a husband in jail, also wanted some 'me' time, and indeed the two women seemed to have a lot in common. Both wanted attention, both were intensely stupid and both (mercifully) were tattooed. Tattoos: stupid people's way of announcing to everyone that they're stupid before they open their mouths.

The Mental Health Team, led by psychiatrist Frances Raphael, duly conducted 'home assessments' on the two mothers, but made a fundamental error, assessing the state of the women when they should have been assessing the state of the housing. Dr Raphael may have been born on the right side of the tracks, but Jeni and Pauline clearly hailed from the wrong side, dwelling in places so rough they should have been pulled down to build a slum. The well-meaning social workers, sitting awkwardly in these squalid council flats, were quite unable to provide any long-term assistance, listening helplessly to the incessant complaints, and offering only trite observations of the 'If you kill yourself I personally think this would be a disaster' variety. And I couldn't help thinking that, if the entire North Battersea Community Mental Health Team were disbanded and their wages spent on improving housing, family support and nursery facilities in the area, that might be a far better use of limited resources. Better certainly than the hopeless confrontations we witnessed: on the one side, attitude, on the other, platitude.

To be fair, there were some interesting moments. I'd like to have heard more details about a third woman, Pamela, who was given to 'lashing out at people in a self-destructive way', and, had Pauline's observation that 'I don't think there's such a thing as cot death, I think I laid on the baby' also been followed up more assiduously, this might have been a fascinating series on its own. But as it was the coverage was so superficial as to be meaningless, cataloguing some everyday human misery with neither the desire nor the ability to alleviate it. Every aspect of infirmity seems to be captured on camera nowadays, be it chronic ill-health (*Jimmy's*), accident (*Blues and Twos*), mental distress (*Minders*), even your dog's distemper (*Animal Hospital*). In fact, there are currently so many fly-on-the-wall documentary series on television that someone really ought to call the health authorities in.

Antiques Roadshow

Today I am launching the start of National Honesty on Television Week, during which the titles of selected programmes will be subtly modified to reveal their true intentions. And so, the *Antiques Roadshow* now becomes the *For God's Sake Stop Telling me How Rare and Delightful This Heirloom is I Just Want to Hear How Much it's Worth and Even Though I'll Tell You That I'll Never Sell it Because it Has Sentimental*

Value as Soon as the Show Finishes I'll Shoot Off to Sotheby's and Flog it and Blow the Lot on a Fortnight in Majorca show.

Now in its fifteenth year, *Antiques Roadshow* is ushered in by a synthesized Vivaldi-style sig (a modern reproduction of little value), and continues to delight those who find conversation pieces in glass cases fascinating. But, for the rest of us to extract anything from the programme, it must be watched like the specialist rounds on *Mastermind*. The information may be incomprehensible, but what makes it enjoyable is witnessing the success and failure of the participants. It would be a cold and heartless viewer who did not roar with laughter at the look of crushed misery on the face of an elderly spinster, as she discovers that her great-grandmother's cherished Delft dish is, in fact, a load of old toot.

Yesterday's edition came from Berwick-on-Tweed. It is a little-known fact (and not mentioned on the programme) but the town is technically still at war with Nazi Germany. Sadly, most of the residents looked as though they were still preoccupied with defeating the Kaiser. A long queue of Monty Python clapping grannies formed outside the hall with their white knuckles clutching possessions wrapped in newspaper. Before them stood Hugh Scully (who I am convinced is Chris Kelly without the bouffant wig). In his heyday, Scully was the hip, thrusting young star of the regional opt-out *Spotlight South West*, but his years with the roadshow have taken their toll, and his foppish speech is now as antiquated as his subject matter, littered with 'It was not forever thus' and other archaic phrases that Fowler contemptuously defines as Battered Ornaments.

The battered ornaments on display were examined by a team of experts, whose demeanour lay midway between eminent Harley Street consultants and dodgy second-hand car salesmen. They pretended never to have seen the objects until that moment, when really they had been researching for hours and had their prompt-notes just out of shot. A pin-stripe suit with the Elgin marbles in his mouth elaborately pointed out the Buddhist emblems surmounting a pair of jars from Jingdezhen, but the owner only emerged from his coma when the magic words 'four to six thousand pounds' were spoken. A beautiful Restoration-period chair would have been worth a small fortune, if it were not for the restoration. The two gumming OAPs who owned it also had an *Awakenings* moment when the expert said 'sixteen-seventy-five', thinking he meant price not year. Saddest of all was a once-valuable teddy bear with missing growl and alopecia that someone had recently stuffed with kapok; they'd stuffed the owner too, because his teddy was now worthless.

I am no cynic. Two paintings – by Fuseli and Melville – were astonishingly beautiful, and there were many other splendid antiques on display. But there is an uneasy dissonance on the show, between the gentility of the experts and the vulgarity of money, and the greed of the punters comes across more strongly than any genuine interest in history. Worse, some are perfectly well aware how much their antiques are worth, and are simply parading them to make their neighbours envious. They are the real cynics, whom Oscar Wilde defined as people 'who know the price of everything, and the value of nothing'.

For all that, Henry Sandon remains a thoroughly likeable presenter. Henry, I'd like your opinion on this item here. 'Now, let me see . . . it's rather worn . . . oh dear, it's fallen apart and been stuck back together again . . . it's had its day. Look, someone's ruined it by trying to disguise it with a new sig tune, but scratch away the paint and you can see the inscription . . . it was originally *Going For a Song*.'

Vanessa

Many's the programme I've seen, since embarking on this reviewing lark, that's made me want to go to the lavatory afterwards. But, until yesterday afternoon, I'd never felt an urge to suggest to a television company that they ought to design their studio like a lavatory. The idea struck me while watching *Vanessa* (ITV), a programme whose content was so unremittingly vile that, for health reasons, the doors should have been sealed after recording finished, while the whole studio, like a giant Superloo, was inverted and flushed with disinfectant. And, hey presto, the place would be completely sterile, ready to be soiled by the next repulsive audience.

I never thought anyone could make Chrystal Rose shine like Jacob Bronowski, but I'd reckoned without her successor, talk-show host Vanessa Feltz. Yet another swollen ego who starts each show by standing in front of her own giant-sized signature, she's encouraged comparisons between her inane Anglia chat show (now being networked) and American ratings successes like Oprah (who recently lost seventy-two pounds) and Ricki Lake (who lost 115 pounds), but the only apparent connection is that Vanessa seems to have been the recipient of the missing 187 pounds of fat. One cannot help feeling cruelly cheated: we get the body of Libby Purves *without* the mind.

Yesterday's theme (if half an hour of verbal diarrhoea can be dignified with such a term) was 'people who take their clothes off in public', allowing Vanessa to talk coyly about nudism and exhibitionism, a TV discussion topic born dead on early-60s chat shows. Advance billing for the programme promised us 'real people' (as though other talk shows were plagued with visitors from Westworld), but what we got were the usual sad bunch of dysfunctional daytime TV groupies, wanting the cameras but, actually, *needing* social workers. Tony and Wendy were the couple who'd recently been filmed *in flagrante* for Desmond Morris's *The Human Animal*, and were keen to explain that 'We didn't do this because we're exhibitionists' (I couldn't see the man holding a gun to their heads and forcing them on, but I suppose he was just out of shot). Vanessa, displaying an immaturity that belied her age, launched into a stream of single *entendres* of the 'Did you rise to the occasion?' variety, and asked whether it wasn't just porn, but Tony explained it was really educational because 'There's an eight-page booklet that goes with the video.' As for Vanessa's proud pre-series boast that 'We won't fall into the trap of giving free publicity to boring people peddling their latest film,' I can only assume that either a) she couldn't hear Tony when he said, 'Wendy and I have set up a company and produced a series of videos,' followed by the inevitable prolonged clip; or b) the man with the gun was at work again.

'Please join us after the break,' she implored, with desperation in her voice as though her first set of ratings had just come in. In part two, on came someone who spent his evenings asking his wife to drop her knickers while he took snapshots and sent them off to 'Readers' Wives' (as usual with amateur porn, acres of anaemic flesh confirmed that the film was more over-exposed than the wife). The couple both said they loved exhibiting themselves, but Vanessa called it 'pure tack', shook her head and said, 'I don't understand the thrill.' Which was odd, because getting a cheap thrill by publicly displaying smut was exactly what she'd been doing all afternoon. Never mind the nudists, the strippers and the tattooed lady, Vanessa was the biggest exhibitionist of all.

'It's been a hell of a programme,' said Vanessa at the close, and I could scarcely disagree. Technically, this is one of the most ineptly edited shows I've ever seen on British television, with questions being asked long after answers have been given, and continual cutting that prevents any possibility of a train of thought developing. In fact, the cutting amounts to butchery, but there's only scrag end and offal with which to work, since the hostess appears intellectually incapable of sustaining rational discourse. From the producers (Colin Eldred, Lisa Woodward and Malcolm Allsop) down to the researchers (Marissa Weinstein and Clare Ely), and down lower still to Vanessa Feltz herself, it's impossible to detect any sign of an intelligence at work on this show, and Anglia should note – pay peanuts, you get monkeys. And if you'd given typewriters to this simian lot, and revisited the studios a thousand years hence, I bet you none of them would have managed so much as the first letter of *Othello*.

Ms Feltz BA (Hons) Cantab subsequently described me in a national newspaper as the living person she most despised, and suggested that I was obnoxious, repellent and impotent. I sent her a Polaroid of myself in a state of full tumescence, and have heard nothing since.

QED: The Bike

I've only ever had two decent brainwaves. In 1988, I planned to publish a book called *My Lips*, to cash in on the free endorsement from President George Bush, who was continually on TV urging people to 'Read *My Lips*.' The other was an invention to combat bicycle theft by incorporating a spring-loaded six-inch knife beneath the saddle. Any unauthorized rider would immediately trigger the mechanism and, hey presto, instant retribution would follow, of a savagery to delight the heart of any Old Testament prophet.

Sadly, neither of my ideas ever got past the planning stage but, on last night's *QED: The Bike*, tribute was paid to an admirable chap with the determination to pursue his dream in the face of public indifference, until eventually it became reality. Mike Burrows' lifelong ambition had been to make man the fastest animal on earth and, with his carbon-fibre Windcheetah bicycle, he succeeded. As usual, television chose to cast him as a lone English eccentric – something documentary makers often do in the hope of zapping a technical subject with some human interest – but he was really just a small-scale inventor with the sort of creative vision that is seldom tolerated within large corporations. His brainchild proved to be the most remarkable innovation in bicycle design for a century, and it soon became clear that reasonable car drivers like myself, who had always regarded cyclists merely as annoyances to be sworn at and crushed against walls, would have to re-evaluate this mode of transport.

In an age when significant developments in engineering only ever seem to be made by anonymous research teams working for multinational conglomerates, it was heartening to see that the Burrows prototype was largely knocked up in a shed in Norwich, with a jig-saw and a bit of sandpaper, by his Mr Kiplingesque father. It was British through and through and a world beater, winning the first race it entered in 1982. But no sooner had I put my Union Jack hat on and started humming 'There'll Always be an England' than the documentary took a downward turn; pedalling the bike was easy, but when Burrows tried to peddle it to industrialists, no one was remotely interested.

The bike was ahead of its time and Burrows was obliged to freewheel until the rest of the world caught up. Then, in 1991, fate intervened in the shape of Rudi Thomann, a driver for Lotus. He took the design to his bosses and suddenly Lotus took over the show. Roger Becker, a designer who declared, 'I am Mr Lotus,' told us that the firm had 'a highly developed company philosophy'. You bet; in films it's called 'Keep the writer off the set.' After computer analysis in wind tunnels by the company's aerodynamicist, Richard Hill, the Windcheetah reappeared as the Lotus Sport, and the rest is history:

Chris Boardman in his wilting Pixie crash helmet, crushing the world record and winning a gold for Britain in Barcelona; Lotus making two thousand bikes a year; and Mike Burrows still working from his shed. Hill diplomatically told us that Burrows 'was always around to give us valuable advice', which I suspect roughly translates as 'He was a bloody nuisance.' Burrows himself was sanguine about the offhand treatment he had received, saying that the group produced something marvellous but 'Like the Beatles, we've all fallen apart and now we're slagging each other off.' Although Burrows is clearly the John Lennon of the outfit, I fear that Lotus would like him to be the Pete Best.

Television does many things badly, but it excels at science documentaries, especially those emanating from the BBC. The end of the programme, when *QED* commissioned a new bike from Burrows, seemed tacked on, little more than a trailer for the forthcoming *Radio Times* competition. But overall Linda McDougall has produced a cleverly directed, fascinating programme, and John Peel's narration was, as ever, perfectly understated and quietly droll, making science accessible even to me. And I speak as someone who, twenty years on, is still trying to work out what you were supposed to do with the tiny little tube and the metal grater in the puncture-repair kit.

Goodbye to Cloughie

There are two continuity announcements guaranteed to make this viewer's blood run cold: '. . . and the programme is introduced by Ross King' along with 'This programme was originally transmitted on BBC East Midlands.' Luckily, East Midlands is seldom asked by BBC1 to contribute to the network but, on those rare occasions when it happens, I imagine it to be the televisual equivalent of the Royal Train stopping briefly at a minor station. Bumbling, red-faced men with flags try to wave and bow simultaneously. The stationmaster desperately searches for some red carpet. Feverish cries of 'It's Mr Yentob' echo around the station. Everyone rushes around, but the result is hopelessly chaotic.

Goodbye to Cloughie chronicled Brian Clough's traumatic last days as a football manager, and BBC East Midlands Region had pulled out all the stops. One camera, a PP3 battery and a local TV reporter turned up at the Nottingham Forest ground to record the vital relegation game with Sheffield United, and we were soon knee-deep in bathos. The usual trite shots of eerie empty stands and echoey, distant chanting were intercut with mawkish tributes from colleagues, grown men hugging and sobbing while 'My Way' blared over the tannoy. All that, and we were only just two minutes in. Suddenly, the great man himself appeared, shot initially through a mysterious crimson filter, but then a curious thing happened. The filter was removed but most of Mr Clough's face stayed exactly the same colour, spotty purple, and resembling a cross between Worzel Gummidge and Gustave von Aschenbach after his make-up has run during the closing scene of *Death in Venice*.

What followed was Ron Knee territory. We saw tight-lipped (tearful) Brian brushing past dejected fans, emotional (tearful) Brian hugging Barry Davies on *Match of the Day*, and defiant (tearful) Brian giving interviews to journalists from those thunderers of the printed word, the *Nottingham Advertiser* and the *Derby Free Press*. Local hacks they may be, but they found exciting new ways to describe the day's events when they phoned in their copy: 'The age of miracles is finally over . . . the living legend has paraded before his adoring fans.' Clough was also interviewed at length (though certainly not in depth) by Paul McCrea. Here, indeed, was a meeting of minds. Brian Clough has too many years of heading the ball as his excuse, but what can Mr McCrea blame? Here was a man so cerebrally challenged that he made Paul Gascoigne look like Bamber. 'I don't want a yes/no answer, if you don't mind me being preposterous,' he insisted, attempting to pin Clough down on his future plans. Even his attempts at sycophancy nose-dived: 'The nice thing is you're still alive, if you don't mind me saying so.'

Clough's four turbulent decades in the sport were traced: his 251 goals as a centre forward, his OBE and honorary degree, his alleged fondness for the falling-down water, his innumerable arguments with chairmen and press, and his famous partnership with Peter Taylor which ended in acrimony when Taylor once dared to cross him. With Clough, it seems that once is all it takes, so even those who have never crossed him at all are permanently on probation. Then came a succession of testimonies of the *This is Your Life* sort from a series of

Wilfred Pickles clones, all with 1950s names like Tommy Bilton and Billy Thompson, and with tongues endlessly flicking from left to right under the upper set to keep it in place. A former Derby captain revealed that the only advice Clough ever gave players during the pre-match pep talk was 'Get hold of the ball'; sensible enough, though maybe a trifle limited. The entire programme was marinated in gallons of Clough's tears, which he alternated with intimidation to keep awkward questions at bay. So irrational and agitated was his behaviour that, by the end, this man who has for so long been a national institution was starting to look as though he should perhaps be in one.

This was a ridiculous programme and, frankly, a gold watch or a carriage clock would have been a more imaginative retirement gift from the BBC than such a shoddily made tribute. A tyrant in decline, Clough cut a pathetic figure on screen, still using menace as a substitute for wit, and relying on snatches of old Frank Sinatra records to proclaim his innermost feelings. There was a feel of Saturday night in a dodgy pub about the programme – the man who has been threatening violence all evening suddenly starts singing sentimental songs and weeping openly. None of the contributors seemed able to express themselves and, if they had, there wouldn't have been much to say.

True, no one actually said 'sick as a parrot'. But I bet you they were thinking it.

French Cooking in Ten Minutes

It's par for the course for TV critics to be called a rat by disgruntled programme makers, but I'm beginning to think they're right. I'm half human and half rodent, with a squirrelish urge to store away my most cherished discoveries, and keep them to myself. I rarely tell anyone about my favourite restaurants, music or books because I like them to remain obscure; I'm glad that *archy and mehitabel* and the tales of Alphonse Allais are little-known in this country and a few years ago, when *Augustus Carp Esq. By Himself* was republished by Penguin, I remember feeling horrified, as though its widespread availability would somehow devalue its worth.

So I confess to having been full of resentment when I saw that another of my treasured books, *French Cooking in Ten Minutes*, had been turned into a six-part series on BBC2. Although this quirky, 1930s masterpiece by Edouard de Pomiane has been well-loved in France for over half a century, comparatively few people know of it here, and I wanted it to stay that way, but the adaptation has been so perfectly conceived and executed that (in spite of my selfish instincts) I'm delighted to see it reach a wider audience. Christopher Rozycki is perfect in the role of the Franco-Polish author (part Robert Hardy, part Fawlty Towers' Kurt), offering to teach us the secrets of great cooking, and modestly confiding that 'You are fortunate to have the guidance of a man of great skill, elegance, culture and wit, just like I had when I began, for I of course was self-taught.' Food is very important to him, but life is more important (which is why he maintains that an excellent four-course dinner should be prepared in ten minutes, leaving time for more pressing pursuits), and he's the living embodiment of the fable of the tortoise and the hare as he moves around his pre-war kitchen at a funereal pace, yet simultaneously out-gallops the Galloping Gourmet; the secret being, there's no room for hysteria in his kitchen.

His unlikely catchphrase 'Good, our water is boiling' underlines his philosophy of cooking. The instant you arrive home for lunch, always put a saucepan of water on to boil, because it's bound to be useful for something. Yesterday's menu was guaranteed to frighten off the 'Never eat anything you can't pronounce' brigade, with *escargots de Bourgogne* (which should be cooked facing upwards, so that the butter can't run out), *filet de flétan* (poached fillets of halibut with basil and vinegar), *salade de tomate* (simply slice and add vinaigrette) and a *plateau de fromage*. There was something Taoist about the way he did almost nothing with the food, yet left nothing undone, jokingly saying that 'You do not often associate snails with speed' as the sumptuous dinner quickly came together. Not to mention a pudding that involved double cream, cream cheese, lots of sugar, more double cream, a defibrillator, the phrase 'We've lost him' and no flowers please, just donations to your favourite charity.

Despite its title, the programme was not really about preparing meals in ten minutes at all, but about an attitude to existence. Even though Rozycki found time to dramatize the preparation of a basic roux ('The sauce thickens . . . starch in the flour binds together with milk and gives a velvety quality to the sauce'), the basic ruse of the series is that cooking is merely an offshoot of philosophy, which itself is merely an offshoot of living. Like Ruth Mott's excellent *Victorian Kitchen Garden*, it reminds supermarket shoppers that food is traditionally seasonal and that, in bygone days, occasional recourse to a tin of peas need not undermine the quality of a dish.

Too short, yet absolutely perfect, this series is proof (as was Danny Baker's *TV Heroes*) that less can be more. It's a Fabergé egg of a programme, with painstaking attention to detail (witness the subtle changing of the seasons outside, with the sounds of playing children gradually increasing as summer approaches) and the seduction of Madame X concluding each episode (she's the real dish of the day, although no love is sincerer than the love of good food). From its opening titles (Grappelli sig and Gitanes graphics by Exess) to its closing remarks ('I wonder if the snails are an aphrodisiac') this was a gem, and Large Door's Nicholas Cooper, who adapted and (with Candida Julian-Jones) produced the series for BBC Education should both take a bow. Most cookery programmes glumly devote their full thirty minutes to the mechanics of preparing a dish. So how is it that this programme, only ten minutes long, can teach us how to cook superb food, yet spend half of the time talking about the glories of being alive?

Chef!

It's not every day you tune in to BBC1 and see somebody doing a hand job for Lenny Henry. Don't misunderstand me; as media types will know, plenty of actors and actresses get a foot on the showbiz ladder by performing hand jobs, hiring out their perfectly manicured digits and palms to do washing-up in the Fairy ads, model diamond rings or, in this case, wield razor-sharp kitchen knives at lightning speed (curiously enough, this particular handman was called Mr Headman).

It's a pity that the director didn't hire a couple more extras while he was at it – one to do a writing job, another to do an acting job –

because *Chef!* (BBC1), which limped to the end of its second series last night, is quite astonishingly weak in both departments. Not funny enough to be classed as a sit-com, nor believable enough to be classed as drama, forensic science has been unable to detect any trace of humour or subtlety in this dismal hybrid, whose title proves yet again that exclamation marks are TV's equivalent of signs on Old Testament doors, indicating those we should pass over. Peter Tilbury's laugh-free scripts are (paradoxically) a complete joke, supplying no shred of subtext or shading; but that scarcely matters when the series is based around a performer who acts in such a don't-know-how-to-change-gear, didn't-bother-with-acting-school sort of a way.

This week, in *England Expects*, chef was angry. But then chef is always angry, shouting like Basil Fawlty, only without the jokes. This was dialogue with the emphasis on dire, the sort of middle-class-speak reminiscent of so-called toffs in vintage episodes of *Crossroads*, with 'of whom's dropping like bombs, and a succession of conversations so stilted that someone should have passed the port. '"Chef" is a small monosyllabic word, brief in duration and yet, in its tiny utterance, you manage to effortlessly convey an infinity of foreboding,' shouted Henry (torturing the English language so cruelly that I almost phoned Amnesty International), and what sounded like canned laughter dutifully roared its approval. Strange, you'd think a top chef wouldn't have canned anything in his kitchen.

There was a plot, though it was so thin that a ton of cornflour couldn't have given it substance. Chef was competing in a *concours gastronomique*, so he and his sidekick Everton selected some bottles of 'Chiltern Valley' English white wine, and caught a flight to Lyon (the most unconvincing scene of all, since the British Airways hostess wasn't patronizing or churlish). Once there, all attempts at humour were blatantly racist: the French were frogs, English were *rosbifs*, Belgians were 'bloody detectives', Norwegians didn't deserve to win anything, Mauritius and Madagascar had no culture. Did the politically correct Mr Henry *really* think that such naked xenophobia could be neutralized by the occasional interpolated cry of 'Don't be racist, chef'? I rather fear that he did.

Then came an unexpected change of gear, a whole scene in which chef wasn't angry because he was too busy tasting 'Chiltern Valley'

wine: 'This is very nice, very nice.' But, never fear, soon he was shouting again, this time in the sort of Franglais – 'I will frappez votre teeth so far down votre gorge, you'll be able to manger avec your derrière' – that third-form schoolboys often mistake for wit until fourth-form schoolboys set them straight. There was a moment of panic when the 'Chiltern Valley' wine went missing, but luckily his wife turned up with some more 'Chiltern Valley' wine and, would you believe it, Gareth's cooking won first prize thanks, not least, to the 'Chiltern Valley'. When the show finished with a close-up of a bottle of (yes) 'Chiltern Valley' wine, I became so intrigued that I tele-phoned a wine expert and, sure enough, Chiltern Valley is a real company, and this was real product placement. I knew that Mr Henry did voice-overs, but on his own TV shows? I'm surprised we didn't see NOW AT LOW LOW PRICES flashing on the screen.

Chef! is not a bad show. It's an *embarrassing* show. Lenny Henry is a talented stand-up comedian, but he can't act for toffee (nor even for Chiltern Valley wine), so how on earth did he ever get this job in the first place? Well, Crucial Films (the production company) must have looked far and wide before casting the lead role in such a high-profile series and, after much deliberation, clearly decided that Lenny Henry was the best possible candidate for the job. And I'm sure the boss of Crucial Films – a certain Mr L. Henry – would confirm my every word.

Charles: The Private Man, the Public Role

Well yes, he's not normal, but then how could he be? After all, the subject of *Charles: The Private Man, the Public Role* (ITV) has spent a lifetime surrounded by the nodding men – who, like nodding dogs in the back windows of cars, are enough to drive anyone insane – and last night was no exception. Narrating in the portentous royal media language invented by his father – Dimbleballs – Jonathan Dimbleby began by intoning, 'The house of Windsor, scorched by adversity blah . . . thousand years of history blah . . . foibles, mystique . . .' making it clear from the outset that this was to be an almost-all-holds-barred account of a year in the life of the Prince of Wales. Watching two and a half hours of thinly veiled public relations, interspersed with questions so innocuous that the interviewer might as well have had BY ROYAL APPOINTMENT stamped across his forehead, one nagging thought kept recurring: isn't there another man of the same name who makes those sharp, penetrating comments each week on *Any Questions?*

In an area of Birmingham so rough that the butcher probably sells *broken* leg of lamb, we saw the prince on a *Meet the People* awayday, shaking hands with life's flotsam and indulging in the old royal trick of thinking of the next superficial question while not listening to the last answer. 'How old are you?' he asked one man (a dead ringer for Michael Jackson, only he was black). 'Twenty-five.' 'Jolly good,' said the prince, and moved on. Back in his St James's apartment, we heard the first of a dozen laments about the horror of having one's life planned out for months ahead, although (as with opera singers and convicted murderers) that surely goes with the territory. A sickly *Hello!*-style skiing photoshoot was followed by a discourse on religious faith, with embarrassingly simplistic pantheistic beliefs (which even Blue Mink would have thought unsophisticated) presented (and, worse, received) as though they were arcane profundities. As for his interminable observations on the meaning of *Fid Def* – 'I think of it as Defender of Faith, not *the* Faith' – the prince did the seemingly impossible: he reduced the complexities of theology to the banality of the -ology.

Soon, the end of each commercial break was coming like the next wave of peristalsis during a night of vomiting, that Oh-God-it's-starting-again feeling. Was this 150-minute ordeal simply the prince's revenge for all the tedious formal events he's had to sit through over the years? Today's newspapers have plucked the few juicy titbits on offer – the marriage breakdown, the infidelity, the call for national service, the disestablishment tendencies – but they were so few and far between that (as with trying to find the dirty bits in *Ulysses*) the game simply wasn't worth the candle. We saw him boosting Britain's arms sales to the Middle East, justifying the trade with the supremely moral argument that 'If we don't sell them, someone else will.' I only hope the weaponry provides a better defence than the prince did, or it'll be shot down in flames. We heard him talking about divorce over footage of the Bach double violin concerto, the tears he shed for the music left unedited (by the editor, a certain P. Charles) to drum up sympathy for the intolerable pressures of royal marriages. True, his nonchalant response to the gunfire in Australia was impressive, but was it traditional British sang-froid or just slow reflexes? However, more contentious issues, such as the Tampax call and the cold-shouldering of Princess Diana, were utterly glossed over by an interviewer who plainly knew which side his bread was buttered. The future isn't hard to see: Dimbleby gets knighted, Diana can get knotted.

Ah well, from one near-disaster in a plane, to one plain disaster on television, and all in a day's work for a prince. Not only did the programme lack teeth, it wasn't even capable of inflicting a mild gumming on its subject, although doubtless Dimbleby Martin Productions will do very nicely out of world-wide sales. Not so much money for old rope, as old espadrille. This was nothing more than an evening's improperganda, made with the full co-operation and approval of the prince's press office, and full of unchallenged self-justification, so much so that I'm surprised he didn't end with a song. Something, perhaps, like 'One Did it One's Way'.

Brighton Belles

An acquaintance of mine, who once spent several months in a psychiatric hospital, remembers a curious fact about the television set there. It was permanently tuned to ITV, with tape stuck over the selection buttons, and he had to apply for a special chit to watch any other channel. BBC1, 2 and CH4 were deemed too upsetting and challenging for patients, but the safe, anodyne output of ITV – epitomized by its cosy, womb-like sit-coms – was considered a suitable environment in which the mentally disturbed could gently recuperate.

Carlton has clearly produced its latest sit-com, *Brighton Belles*, with the needs of mental hospitals uppermost in its mind. The show may have been modelled on the sharply acerbic US series *The Golden Girls*, but the format has suffered a time-warp while crossing the Atlantic, and has arrived (or rather washed up) in the Brighton of the 50s. Every aspect of it – plot, dialogue, cast and acting – belonged on the stage of a grotty provincial rep in a period light comedy, not on a 90s TV screen.

The characterization of the four ageing *provocateurs* was so thin as to be positively anorexic. Annie was dizzy, Frances was simple and trusting, Bridget was top-heavy and post-menopausal and Josephine had an accent that seemed to veer alarmingly between Irish, Welsh and Devonshire. It was only when she uttered the phrase 'dinna' that I realized she was supposed to be a wise-cracking Scot, but, as it transpired, she could only manage a sort of dumb-cracking John Laurie in curlers. The four shared a middle-class Shangri-la on the seafront where, just like *Peter Pan*, everybody was called Darling, and they talked to each other in a strangely ossified language – 'What kind of a friend would I be to hurt her so? . . . I'm glad, nay, happy that this has happened' – as though Enid Blyton were the show's script editor.

Last night's feeble, inconsequential plot certainly wouldn't have caused unrest in the TV room of a psychiatric ward. John Stride entered stage right, as a philandering doctor whose histrionic gestures and incessant marching about (he's not called Stride for nothing) suggested he'd really be far happier appearing in provincial rep. He started dating Frances but also flirted with Bridget, and jealousy and mistrust reigned in the house. At one point, Frances even said she was leaving for good and I began to cheer up; one down, only three to go. But no. Annie tricked the doctor into making a secret confession in a boomingly theatrical voice, which must have been heard by most of Hove, let alone Frances who was standing three feet away. Unmasked as a cad and a bounder, he was booted out of the house, and the girls made it up. 'There's no fool like an old fool,' they chorused; love the fancy philosophy, girls.

The show established the same comedic rhythm as *The Golden Girls*, with space for three jokes a minute, but unfortunately didn't possess a single gag worthy of the name. Still, thanks to the miracle of artificial laughter enhancement, dismal lines like 'Frankly Annie, I'd rather wash Bob Geldof's socks' were greeted with mass hysteria, while the word 'bonking' brought the house down. If this was really the best the writer could come up with, then what was the point of adapting the original at all? British audiences had no difficulty in understanding the references and humour in the American series and, in spite of the change of location, this anglicized version seemed to emanate from a far more remote and irrelevant world.

Carlton obviously thought that, by casting four undeniably suc-cessful actresses in a tried and tested format, they would come up with a sure-fire winner. But comedy only succeeds when script, perform-ance and direction are all simultaneously superb, and what they have ended up with instead is a sure-fire turkey. From the awful musical links reminiscent of BBC Radio LE in the 50s, to the pasteurized inanity and mundanity of the dialogue, the show reeks of embalming fluid.

While the programme is simply too lightweight to despise, it turned out to be rather like Brighton itself, relying on an elegance and charm that has long since faded. By the end, I fully expected to see Kenneth More drive past in *Genevieve*, hoot and shout out, in his own waggish way, 'Hey, you old girls with the flat, that old crock of yours is no vehicle for comedy.'

Frost in the Air

One of my strongest TV memories from the 60s was hearing someone on the David Frost show referring to the Prime Minister as 'Kipper Wilson – two-faced and no guts'. Even as a child, I could detect from the excitement of the studio audience and the outspokenness of the participants that something extraordinary was going on.

By a cruel twist of fate, the young nowadays believe Frost to be little more than Loyd Grossman's aging sidekick, peering through the keyholes of the famous. But BBC2's *Frost in the Air* trilogy has been recalling his glory days back in the 60s and early 70s when, despite resembling one of those photographs of groomed men that still adorn the walls of provincial barbers, he pioneered TV satire and the audience-participation show, becoming indisputably the most famous personality that television had yet produced. Indeed, by spending virtually his entire waking life in TV studios or on transatlantic jets, he managed to achieve a seemingly impossible feat: he regularly hosted live television shows eight evenings a week, three in Britain and five in the States.

Last night's second programme focused on his remarkable encoun-ters with the eminent, the powerful and the corrupt, in an age when such people were still televisually naïve enough to be tricked into occasional bouts of honesty. Frost's intellect proved ideal for the medium – not particularly deep but almost infinitely broad – and (with the notable exception of his dismantling of insurance crook Emil Savundra) his interviewing technique relied more on persuasion than confrontation, the living embodiment of the fable of the wind and the sun. Frost gently repeated the awkward but pertinent question that everyone wanted answered, and suddenly Cardinal Heenan found himself telling Catholics to ignore the papal bull and carry on taking the Pill, Robert Kennedy found himself admitting that yes, he was a reckless, ruthless man, and Richard Nixon found himself confessing, 'I let down my friends and my country.' Most remarkable were Frost's unwavering powers of concentration. It's a perennial mystery that he could continually travel between New York and London without any apparent tiredness whatsoever, whereas Wogan always managed to appear severely jet-lagged after a ten-minute taxi ride to Shepherd's Bush.

A curious thing about those who spend their time with powerful magnates is that they eventually become powerful magnets themselves, attracting or repelling those around them. Frost's international celebrity made him a desirable TV property, but it also engendered a great deal of professional jealousy, still apparent in many of the present-day contributions. Richard Ingrams savoured some vintage *Private Eye* parodies of Frost's mannered speech patterns, and even though John Cleese tried hard to be generous, the effort showed: 'His feelings about his own work depend on how it's received by others, he doesn't have an internal taste meter.' But what Cleese identified as a weakness was probably Frost's greatest strength in those days: his ability to focus on what an audience wanted and to deliver it, unfailingly, night after night.

But this programme was far more than a barbed tribute to a man who rose without trace. It also gave us some exquisite moments as a series of enfeebled not-so-clever-now-eh? has-beens watched younger, smarter versions of themselves jousting with Frost twenty-five years ago. Wafts of formaldehyde filled the room as a decrepit Enoch Powell watched a crepit Enoch Powell being taken apart by Frost after his 1968 'rivers of blood' speech ('I won the contest,' he croaked, apparently still proud of his arrant, spiteful nonsense). Savundra and Oswald Mosley are, thankfully, no longer with us, but we still had The Death (well-known anagram of Ted Heath). 'See, he got nowhere, I didn't answer him,' gloated the Grocer, shoulders heaving, little realizing that his repeated refusal to reply to the simple enquiry 'Do you like Wilson?' was the most eloquent answer he could possibly have given.

John Bush has produced a dense, brilliantly constructed programme that managed to be both chronological and logical. The caustic narration, the painstaking, inventive playing-in of archive material on period monitors, and the smart use of rostrum work on a well-researched collection of obscure documents have made this a stylish documentary that added weight to BBC2's Sixties Day. Anyone can broadcast archive programmes. UK Gold plays old tapes all the time. Any silly sod can. But, throughout the day, BBC2 avoided merely wallowing in a bygone era and marbled the schedule with creative, thoughtful and crafted material such as this.

Nineties programmes being made with the same substance, care and energy that once went into 60s programmes? It almost makes you optimistic for the future of television.

The Chrystal Rose Show

Every Daz has its Omo, every Bob Dylan his Donovan, and every Coke its Pepsi. Hard on the heels of any genuine innovator there is always a *doppelgänger* on the make, so it's no surprise to see that Oprah Winfrey now has her imitators. Chrystal Rose looks like Oprah, and walks like her too, but the moment she opens her mouth it becomes clear that the boffins at Carlton have not yet been able to duplicate the Winfrey brain. If Oprah is Pepsi, then Chrystal is not so much Coke as fizzless, insipid Panda-brand cola, served lukewarm from a transport café.

From the opening titles onwards, an air of disaster surrounded yesterday's edition of *The Chrystal Rose Show*. Whereas the audiences on American people shows always hit the ground running – alert, informed and eager to perform – on Chrystal's show the London studio audience resembled a coach party from Remploy after an accident on the M1: bemused, bewildered and trying unsuccessfully to regain a fragile grip on just what was going on. They clearly had no idea why they were there and, although Chrystal tried to bring them out of shock by getting them to talk, what they really needed was not inane discussion but some blankets and a few cups of hot, sweet tea.

It took eight members of the production staff and God knows how many months to come up with the theme for this week's programme: 'Is marriage outdated?' Chrystal introduced Marje Proops, who, as we all now know, follows in the long line of Miss Lonelyhearts whose own private lives invariably turn out to be far more screwed up than any of the readers they so glibly advise. For decades, while she has been publicly insisting that her readers should remain devoted to their spouses and forsake all others come what may, our Marje was privately refusing to sleep with her husband and conducting a twenty-year-long extra-marital affair, while telling everybody that she had an ideal marriage. 'I destroyed his life,' said Marje nonchalantly, to a ripple of applause from the studio audience. Some might call all this the most grotesque hypocrisy, but Chrystal simply hugged her and said that 'I'm sure you'd all like to join me in saying a special thank-you to dear Marje.'

Insubstantial themes deserve incoherent questions, and Chrystal is unrivalled when it comes to the ill-formed interrogative. I quote her first question to the audience verbatim: 'Do you think that erm . . . especially if with marriage, Marje's experiences do you think now that we should marriage is outdated as we know it do you think that affairs are acceptable who thinks it should last for ever?' The audience were temporarily wrong-footed by this intellectual googly, although a woman with one tooth in her head eventually stood up and said that 'nobody should be condemned'. The unsuccessful poetess Fiona Pitt-Kethley was introduced with the caption *Faithful for short periods*; I wish that they could have put *Interesting for short periods*, but I suppose there would have been trouble with the Trades Descriptions people. A man in baggy trousers said that he regularly cheated on his wife – 'As long as you're clean and, like, be nice then I think it's nice' – and his wife said, as though uttering a Zen koan, 'Would you bake a cake without an egg?' She reappeared later on and asked, 'The main thing is, how do you bake a cake?' I suppose that, if your husband is constantly out sleeping with other women, then cooking is a great consolation.

This programme is desperately poorly presented, researched, shot, lit, directed and produced. Apart from that, though, it's dreadful. Worst of all is the crude editing. Most television now uses digital techniques, but this looked as though it had been cut by a man wearing boxing gloves using scissors and a tube of Uhu glue. One was left with the impression that the show was originally intended to be an hour long, and that Carlton are now deserately attempting to salvage twenty-five minutes from the wreckage.

Overall, *The Chrystal Rose Show* has all the intellectual muscle of a Tupperware party. Actually, that's unfair. At least at a Tupperware party they know how to keep the contents fresh.

The Mousehole Cat

Last January, my New Year's resolution was instantaneously to ex-ecute anybody who asked me, 'Isn't Christmas is getting too commer-cial these days?' Since the purge, nobody's said it this December so, like the nuclear deterrent, the mere threat of retribution must have been enough. This year, I propose summarily to hang anyone who tells me, 'I'm a cat person: dogs are so reliant on their owners, but cats are so independent.' OK, show me a cat who has a private income and can use a tin opener, then we'll talk.

Even so, I have to admit that animals don't get much more independent than the star of yesterday's animated tale, *The Mousehole Cat* (CH4). Mowzer, an irresistible rug wrapped around a purr, lived her fictional existence in the real Cornish fishing village of Mousehole, 'at the far end of England, a land of rocks and moorland stretching itself out into a blue-green sea'. Time and again, successful children's literature is situated in the comforting safety of a symbolic womb (islands, caves, tunnels, secret passages), but this one went further, even including the cervix and the waters breaking: 'a harbour so small, and the entrance so narrow, that fishermen called it "The Mousehole".' Mowzer shared a cottage with Old Tom the fisherman, whom she'd house-trained so well that he willingly spent his days gently rocking her chair, scratching her behind her ear and cooking her so many regional fish dishes that he might have been sponsored by the Cornish Tourist Board. With every week an endless feast of fish stew, baked hake, kedgeree and stargazer pie, it was small wonder that Mowzer grinned as she settled down for yet another post-prandial cat-nap. She may have been drawn, but you could hardly describe this lazy moggy as animated.

Then . . . (as in all great stories, some grit has to enter their life's Vaseline) winter brought cat-astrophic weather, preventing the hungry villagers from reaching their fishing grounds. In a strikingly powerful image (beautifully understated by the illustrator), the storm 'clawed with its giant cat's paw through the gap in the harbour wall', while the fishing boats sheltered 'safe as mice in their mousehole'. But, did I mention earlier that cats were independent? On Christmas Eve, just when every scrap of food had been eaten (and the famished villagers had probably started looking at the local cats in a new light), Mowzer and Old Tom decided to brave the storm, because 'I'll not see the children go hungry at Christmas, and the young men can't go, they have families.' Could this humanity-loving cat, walking purposefully towards the harbour and vowing to catch fish for the people or perish in the attempt, *really* belong to the same species as my neighbour's flea-ridden feline sprinkler, which regularly and spitefully urinates against my front door? Believe me, Dettol will not do. It's a case of knocking the house down and building again.

By the time the intrepid duo were reaching the open seas, I was reaching for the Kleenex. The tom-cat storm cruelly toyed with the little boat as though it were a helpless mouse, but Mowzer had an Orphic belief in the power of music to calm the natural world. I'd heard of sopranos being catty, but never of cats being soprano, yet there she was, sitting in the prow, a feline Queen of the Night bobbing on the high Cs, serenading the gale and lulling it to sleep. The nets were hauled in to reveal a bounteous catch (this wasn't a pilchard-friendly tale), and the little craft headed back to land, where the entire village were waiting by the quayside, anxious for Tom and Mowzer's safety. Somehow, you never get that same sense of community when somebody goes missing in Clapham.

Antonia Barber's story (splendidly told by Siân Phillips) was so strongly and simply constructed that it would have seemed complete on radio, but the captivating animation (adapted from Nicola Bayley's original book illustrations) added another layer to the production, as did Ian Hughes's score, which started out simply and expanded into Hollywood lushness. I remember John Hallas (of Hallas & Bachelor fame) telling me many years ago that computer graphics were the future of animation, and *The Mousehole Cat* demonstrates what can be achieved by the restrained, artistic use of digital techniques: computer animation doesn't have to equate with the hyperactive, characterless efforts that form the backbone of morning children's television nowadays. Joy and Max Whitby have produced a little modern masterpiece, which will be repeated for many years to come, and everyone at Grasshopper Productions deserves a BAFTA. Indeed, if they don't get one, I'll eat my cat.

Shortly after this review appeared, I received a letter from Mowzer himself, written (I suspect) with the assistance of author Antonia Barber. The famous moggy told me that he spat not only in the face of tinned cat food, but in the face of fame itself, turning down all photo opportunities and refusing to give interviews. Strange indeed that a celebrity cat should display such a mature attitude towards fame, while celebrity humans continue to indulge in cattiness.

Jan 23 /1995.

Dear Victor Lewis-Smith,

Living as I do, and as any intelligent cat
would, in the depths of the country, your review of 'The Mousehole
Cat' has only just reached me. My woman, Antonia, is quite made up
with it, subjecting her long-suffering friends to large portions of
it read out over the telephone, but I take strong exception to your
opening remarks about cats. 'Show me,' you say, 'a cat with a
private income, who can use a tin-opener, then we'll talk.'

My personal bank takes the form of of a large shed full of
grain on the edge of my property, which supplies me with a steady
income of thieving rats and mice. As for tin-openers, I laugh at
them and spit in the face of tinned cat-food. Nature has equipped
me with deadly mouse-openers which make me quite self-sufficient,
unlike the foolish Labrador bitch which vies with me for Antonia's
attention, and lives in grovelling dependence upon the tin-opener
and the biscuit box.

Not only do I provide for myself, I also do my best to support
Antonia, a pathetic creature with claws worn down by constant
typing. I pile her front doorstep with the choicest morsels each
night, in spite of her continuing ingratitude and irritated cries
of 'Bloody cat! look at this mess again!'

I need hardly tell you who was the inspiration for her story,
but I spit in the face of Fame. (Actually, I spit in the face of
most things, being, as you will have guessed by now, a Real Cat.)
Stand-ins have to be used for photo-calls, except on one rare
occasion when I was conned into an appearance.

I therefore send you a photograph of an Independent Cat just to
prove that they do exist. Sorry it's rather spoilt by Antonia in
her silly hat: she always tries to get into my act.

Mowzer: her mark

Blind Date

This has been a weekend of gross obscenity. Not CH4's *Love Weekend*, with its naked chat show, its lesbians doing a spot of all-night mid-air refuelling, its close-ups of secreting glands being thrust hither and yon. All that *and* Nina Myskow. That was a harmless and well-constructed affair compared with the wanton prurience of LWT's weekly meat rack of a game show, where the guys find the gals and the gals find the guys – *Blind Date*.

Blind Seamstress might have been a more appropriate title in view of Cilla Black's hastily made pearly queen outfit, with its three huge buttons standing in for the customary ten thousand little ones. She introduced three 'hunks', dressed in cheap nylon suits packed so full of static that they had become walking Van de Graaff generators: Andy, Neil and Mark, six hundredweight of steak (brains already removed), marinading in Brut aftershave and laughing at anything their lederene said, in a desperate bid for approval; they could have been the team from *That's Life!*.

On walked Lisa, who seemed to possess a Barbie doll's looks and personality, and Klaus Barbie's sense of humour. Her smutty questions received nudge-nudge answers that would have seemed sub-normal if they had been ad-libbed, but they were not; they were written weeks in advance by brilliant LWT script writers.

Q: 'What were you champion of at school?'

A: 'You should have seen the size of my conkers.'

Q: 'If you were trying to impress me, what uniform would you wear?'

A: 'Nothing suits me better than a uniform so I'd wear nothing.'

These toe-curlingly feeble interchanges had the studio rocking with laughter, and Valentine's Day mascara ran freely down the faces of the predominantly female audience. The questioning over, Barbie picked guy number two (trying her damnedest to pretend she hadn't chosen the ugly one) while he made a rudimentary courting display by revealing his chest hair, and suddenly Darwin's theories began to make a lot of sense.

Next, last week's winners. We saw Steve and Michela on their filmed 'holiday', an Esther Rantzen-inspired montage of faked hilarious moments which reduced them to the level of performing seals in the cause of Light Entertainment. They pretended to get along but clearly the only thing they had in common was that they'd both won a holiday on a rather sad game show. Back in the studio, the pair departed from the text and discovered that they really hated each other, and the show briefly came alive as the audience got its teeth into a good old-fashioned slanging match.

The only thing the next trio wanted to get their teeth into was a foaming mug of Steradent. Club 30 became Club 70+ as Nellie, Vangie and Betty, three post-menopausal blue rinses, went through the same puerile, scripted questioning. Nellie said, 'I like me drink' and really wanted to win Michael Barrymore, but had to make do with cravat-wearing Bob. The muted audience response suggested that they love to fantasize about what the twenty-year-olds get up to on holiday, but are not yet ready for images of heavy petting with zimmer frames.

Blind Date is an undeniably ingenious format: moronic television with universal appeal. The show tempts our voyeuristic appetites, although what everybody *really* wants to see would require infra-red cameras and a team from the BBC Badger Watch Unit. They can't show that, but they can broadcast the heated arguments in the studio, nasty bickering that often crackles with sex. Only Cilla could make it all work. She has the niceness that Dame Edna sings about and, like a human Haze Pomander, can cover up the slightest whiff of unpleasantness, leaving only pleasantly scented air. But the show is a pretence: pretend dubbed laughter, a pretend presenter who isn't really the scally from our alley she'd like to think she is, and pretend couples reading pretend chat-up lines. No genuine relationship could flourish under these circumstances and the biggest pretence is ours, watching this patently fake romance and wanting to believe it might be genuine.

But that is the way LWT works. I once phoned the company with a game-show idea of my own: film condemned men on death row in Kentucky State Penitentiary playing the buzzle game (move the ring over the wiggly wire – freedom if they didn't make contact, instant electrocution if they did). The LWT game-show chap listened intently: 'The problem with that is I'm afraid we haven't really got the budget to get over to Kentucky State. I mean I'd *love* to be able to go abroad and do it.' Lorra morals.

The Michael Jackson Interview

Roll up, roll up, for all the fun of the fair. It's a thriller. Gasp at the sight of a twenty-stone woman crawling right up the fundament of the world's only ninety-eight-pound white black man.

It's official. Michael Jackson is 'very normal'. If you didn't believe the assurances of Oprah Winfrey, a self-confessed bulimic and abused child, then how about Liz Taylor, who popped in to tell us that 'Michael is the least weird man I've ever known.' Coming from a woman who gets through husbands the way most of us get through Kleenex, has a history of chronic alcoholism and is yet another bulimic, this endorsement of Mr Jackson's normality seemed about as convincing as a diploma in public relations from the Pol Pot School of Charm.

Speaking from his Santa Barbara ranch, Jackson gave us his interpretation of normal: clown-white face; mascara-pencilled, emotionless, lizard-like eyes; armband, lipstick; and Pinocchio voice and nose. It's surprising that the nose wasn't fifty feet long by the end, the way he squeaked out one implausible statement after another: 'I haven't read LaToya's book . . . I've had *very little* plastic surgery apart from my nose . . . I'm proud to be a black American . . . I date Brooke Shields, but I'm married to my music . . . I do not know what questions you're going to ask me.' As one reverential enquiry followed another, he needn't have worried; for sure, Oprah wasn't going to ask him anything that would make him pale.

Schmaltzy, soft-focus archive clips chronicled Jackson's early career – practically born in a trunk at the Idaho Theater, on stage from the moment he could walk, swapping his childhood for world stardom. Then we had that famous Oprah moment. True to form, twenty-six minutes in, the CS gas was released from Ms Winfrey's handbag and the first tears were shed, as he revealed that he suffered from a skin disorder and wailed about cruel tabloid speculation. A strange disease, vitiligo: it not only lightens the skin but makes it extremely thin as well. Whatever the tabloids say, black, white, brown or puce, who cares? Nobody seems to have spotted that the real transformation he has made is from male to female. Perhaps that's why he keeps grabbing his crotch. It's Phantom Limb Syndrome.

It soon became obvious that this was not an interview with Jackson, but an audience, and his private funfair was an appropriately sinister location in which to be taken for a ride by an extended commercial masquerading as a documentary. Any pretence at objectivity rapidly gave way to unrestrained fawning, and Jackson's armband seemed appropriate dress for the chilling propaganda that followed. Oprah dispelled the rumour that she was contractually obliged to call him the King of Pop – 'I wouldn't call you that . . . it's too limiting a title for your genius' – as Winfrey plc formally merged with Jackson Inc. As for Liz Taylor, she just opened her *Roget's Thesaurus* at 'grovel' and started to read: 'Giving, caring, sympathetic, wonderful, super, good and funny.' Just like a funfair, after the ride, I wanted to throw up.

I don't trust a man who strikes so many false notes. Anyone who announces on global television that he is 'essentially a very shy person' should be given a wide berth. If he's very shy, then why does he keep making world tours and releasing videos? It must be that gun to his head. And if he *really* loves his family, why does he never see them? Worst of all, after refusing to give interviews for fifteen years, why does he then complain about 'nosy people' and the misinformed speculation that has inevitably replaced fact? He may try to play the vulnerable, unworldly child, but his calculating introspection gives the lie to that innocent role. Jackson is a real showman, a smooth operator, adept at using the media for his own commercial ends, and my heart cannot bleed for him.

This was a moonwalk of an interview: continually appearing to be moving forward but never making progress. For all that, Michael Jackson is a remarkable singer and dancer, and maybe he should team up with McCartney again and re-record the old Stevie Wonder hit. One drawback – it'd have to be retitled 'Ivory and Ivory'.

The Hypnotic World of Paul McKenna

Gone are the days when the billing 'As seen on TV' was synonymous with quality. No more does the phrase 'Did you see . . . ?' buzz about pubs throughout the land. And was there ever a time when we didn't all watch television in a permanent, moronic trance, only regaining full consciousness when the announcement 'Some viewers may find the following scenes disturbing' is made?

At first sight, *The Hypnotic World of Paul McKenna* (Carlton) is curiously reminiscent of that bygone era. It's a throwback to the mesmerists of vaudeville, those charlatans who once made a good living by exploiting impressionable audience members, inducing them to make embarrassing exhibitions of themselves on stage, before such acts were banned in the early 50s. Paul 'As seen on TV' McKenna seems to be from another age too, one of those 'laygennlemen' presenters with the sort of unconvincing mid-Atlantic voice you usually only hear when your car radio accidentally strays on to a commercial station called something like Cleethorpes FM Gold. But, from the moment that last night's show began referring to members of the public as 'our stars for the night', and introduced us to ten participants who looked like refugees from *Blind Date*, the pro-gramme's true credentials became clear. Strip away the pseudo-psychical preamble and the pseudo-scientific trappings, and under-neath this was simply another example of 90s, lowest-common-denominator people television: by lumpen, for lumpen.

What ensued was doubtless not fake, but it might as well have been. 'These members of the studio audience all want to enter the Hypnotic World of Paul McKenna,' said the voice-over, and they certainly knew exactly how they ought to behave, in order to gain admission. 'Sleep,' said McKenna, clicking his fingers, and the chins dutifully dropped down on to the chests, often before he'd even said the word. Whether it was auto-suggestion, peer pressure, or group hysteria scarcely seemed to matter, because the host's real role was not to mesmerize, but merely to sanction displays of crass exhibitionism by the audience, who performed a series of infantile sketches, like a kindergarten version of *Whose Line is it Anyway*. Watching them French-kissing frogs, talking to hecklers in their bras and acting out the usual variations on the eat-this-apple-which-is-really-an-onion-ha-ha routine, it was obvious that they actually had been hypnotized, only it wasn't by Mr McKenna. No, they'd been hypnotized by the cameras, and the chance to show off on network telly.

Divested of its spurious mystique, the show was inane and dull, with routines that clearly involved an element of scripting but were unfunny enough to have been entirely improvised. Some pretended to be TV announcers, while another was told to act like a lager lout (although I don't think that hypnosis was necessary in his case). Since 'the stars' were now flagging, the 'celebs' were wheeled on and, as Richard O'Sullivan picked up his gavel for an auctioneer's sketch, I could almost hear the entire nation simultaneously utter the phrase 'Ooh, he's aged.' Then, for a *Food and Drink* parody, up popped Gavin Campbell, a man who spent a decade being a 'star' on *That's Life!* and therefore knew all about giving up free will and unquestioningly performing humiliating tasks in public. At least he was a suitable choice for a food show. The man exuded enough oil to keep the presses of Lucca busy for decades.

If you think this show is genuine, then you probably think that professional wrestling is genuine. It's not overtly fraudulent, but there's a collective desire to collude that goes far beyond mere audience suggestibility, and strays deep into the realm of group self-delusion. Don't get me wrong, I'm no prig – I'm so wild, every time I make French toast I get my tongue caught in the toaster – but the entire show is poorly conceived and executed. Carlton's own brand of randomly placed canned (and over-compressed) laughter only serves to highlight the numerous inadequacies. In fact, Carlton's entire output has gone so far beyond a joke that it might as well change its name to Club 18–30 television. Still, at least the programme lived up to its title in one respect. I admit it: I nodded off several times.

TV Heroes

When you shoot at a TV icon, beware of ricochets. After writing about Thora Hird in less than fulsome tones this week, the WRVS has been on to my office (presumably the paramilitary division), insisting that I leave their Führer alone and muttering darkly about retribution. God alone knows what form it will take, probably force-feeding me like a Strasbourg goose with coconut macaroons, or holding me down in a swimming pool of hot sweet tea. Whatever they devise, it's bound to be horrific; after all, they're expert at arranging fêtes worse than death.

To avoid similar reprisals, Danny Baker cunningly uses irony from the titles onwards in *TV Heroes*, leaving those who can recognize urine extraction with a wry grin, and the rest with a blissfully ignorant smile. Like a Mafia assassin, he clasps his victim in a warm and loving embrace, while simultaneously thrusting the knife in and twisting the blade. Last night, he introduced his tribute to Rolf Harris in grandiose mockumentary style: 'The late nineteen-sixties. Woodstock, anti-war riots, the underground press . . . and Australia's former junior backstroke champion is at the very peak of his powers.' There followed an archive orgy of vintage, hyperactive Rolf – gesticulating in wild spasms, slapping paint on to giant canvases, hurling himself around the stage, bouncing like a kangaroo – a human hokey-cokey, continually putting his whole self in. As he watched, Baker could only marvel at the unlikely success of a man who performed 'an act based on Aboriginal tribe music and eight tins of emulsion'.

'It's curious how few television beards have lasted the course,' Baker pointed out, commenting on the longevity of Rolf's lunatic fringe. True, but although 90s Rolf has grown into his face, 60s Rolf looked strangely unconvincing as though, if you removed the glasses, the nose and beard would come away too. Sporting a nippy Italian suit, we saw him surrounded by The Younger Generation, a set of Fenn Street Gang lookalikes who stared at him adoringly with fake stage-school attentiveness, and moved so awkwardly that, by comparison, he seemed to be able to dance. More than any other entertainer of his generation, Rolf understood the importance of gimmicks, and Baker focused on 'the bizarre musical arsenal with which he has widened our narrow island horizons'. We relived them all: the Stylophone, a pocket electronic organ sounding like a cat chewing a bluebottle; the didgeridoo (I'd have prefered the didgeridon't); the wood blocks; the wobble board; not to mention such visual gimmickry as Jake the Peg with his extra leg, diddle diddle diddle dum. He made them all his own, and they all shared one trait: all were fascinatingly dreadful.

Finally, Baker turned to the paintings, those huge, ludicrous, slapdash affairs that kept the nation glued to their sets each Saturday night, watching paint dry and excitedly guessing what it might be, although you were rarely sure even after Rolf told you. By the end it was difficult to say whether Mr Harris had been hugged or mugged, but then his whole career has teetered on the edge of self-parody, from the earliest days right up to his recent version of 'Stairway to Heaven'. Frequently lampooned, he has none the less stayed on our screens, one way or another, for four decades. So who's having the last laugh?

Caroline Wright has produced a perfectly formed bonsai programme, and Danny Baker's writing and delivery was, as usual, effortlessly sharp and perceptive. We are entering a fascinating period in TV, as the baby boomer generation take over the reins of power, and relive their childhoods by plundering the archives. The next few years should induce an epidemic of Proustian moments in viewers, as half-remembered images originally transmitted in an era before domestic VCRs get their first screening since the 60s. Whatever the motives – nostalgia, exorcism, affection or revenge – the results should be fascinating, and this programme is an auspicious start to Alan Yentob's reshaping of the network. Watch out for Johnny Morris, the Craddocks and Pinky and Perky.

Baker put his finger on what has changed in television since the 60s. Then they had entertainers, now we have presenters. In the 90s, instant, transient fame can be achieved simply by sticking your head inside the magic rectangle and reading the autocue, but it was not always so. However absurd they appear in retrospect to our jaded, sophisticated tastes, the subjects of TV Heroes could at least entertain.

The Secret Life of Arnold Bax

With its tongue firmly in its cheek, the opening titles of *The South Bank Show* parade a trendy list of -isms: Individualism, Naturalism, Formalism, Modernism. None of these cultural buzz-words seems quite appropriate to describe Ken Russell's latest film portrait, *The Secret Life of Arnold Bax*, but there are others that perfectly capture its essence: Charlatanism, Philistinism, Vulgarism, a load of old jism.

I had hoped that Russell's tongue would also be in his cheek, but as usual it was sticking out, and blowing an unmelodious raspberry. His appetite for desecrating the shrines of great musicians remains undiminished – over the years he and his actors have danced on the graves of Tchaikovsky, Mahler, Elgar and a host of other decomposing composers – but recently he has turned his artistic sledgehammer to such lesser lights as Martinu and now Bax. The difference last night was that Russell, as well as writing and directing, played the title role himself, looking like Tony Hart on Mogadon and giving a portrayal so dire that I suspect he may have had to perform sexual favours for himself on the casting couch in order to get the part.

The portrait is set in 1948, shortly after Bax's wife has died. His pianist lover Harriet Cohen wants to marry him but Bax does a Sir Adrian and Boults. After failing to seduce a music student, he hangs around the Bijou Cinema where he picks up Annie, a tarty ice-cream girl who moonlights as an exotic fan dancer and speaks like Eliza Doolittle: 'Cor blimey, you're Master of the King's Musick ain't ya?' Their attempted dirty weekend in Cornwall is ultimately aborted when Bax discovers that Harriet's right wrist has been very badly cut (not, however, as badly cut as the film itself) and returns home to compose the Concertante for piano (left-hand) and orchestra.

The script proved to be unfathomably arch, full of luvvies saying, 'What have you got there? Good God! My Symphonic Variations' and 'You must write a fanfare rather like you did for Princess Elizabeth's wedding, darling.' This attempt to put prosaic information into dramatic form often occurs in music documentaries, but the result is invariably as awkward as mixing up recitative with aria. I fully expected to hear Bax, sitting in a Lyon's Corner House, say, 'I'll have a cup of tea with two sugars. Do you know what I did today, dear? I pushed chromatic harmony to a point beyond which classical tonality finishes and a custard cream please.'

The problem with such films is that they start from an incorrect premise. A composer's music may be exquisitely ravishing and romantic, but composers themselves are usually as dull as trainspotters. They do not write symphonies by walking through forests, but by sitting at a desk for six months, bent over a thick pile of sixty-stave manuscript paper. Even when a composer's life is fascinating, there is seldom any direct correlation between biography and music. The distortion and exaggeration required to make a Don Juan out of such a dull man suggests either an indifference to the truth or that Russell doesn't know his Bax from his elbow.

The standard of acting was simply execrable. As an actor, Russell makes a great director and, on the basis of this performance, Glenda Jackson makes a great MP. Russell may argue that the stilted B-movie acting, anachronistic shots of 1990s cars, and the lumbering script were all part of a deliberately stylized portrayal of a dirty old man who produced sublime music. If it was, then it didn't work, although the denouement was certainly a grotesque parody of *Death in Venice*, with Tadzio replaced by a fan-dancing usherette. But the only time the script showed real insight was when Annie turned to Russell and said accusingly: 'You're very fond of getting other people to do your fantasies, but not so good at acting them out yourself.' Couldn't argue with that.

One thing we can be certain of is that Bax was a drinker who, like his music, frequently made irregular movements from bar to bar. Oh well, if Russell can deconsecrate an artist, so can I.

Beyond the Clouds

Forget *Emmerdale*, *Brookside*, *Coronation Street* and the rest of the soaps: *Far-EastEnders* (aka *Beyond the Clouds* (CH4)) outranks them all. This everyday story of Chinese folk is sinology in every sense of the word, with all the sex, drugs, crime, drunkenness, violence and murder anyone could want, not to mention plenty of true love, family celebrations, gossiping grannies and an execution or two thrown in for good measure. Five years in the making, Phil Agland's documentary of life in a small Chinese city has, for the first time on British television, made the people of that huge but remote part of the planet seem fully comprehensible to the rest of us. For decades, the China that most Westerners encountered seemed to be either inscrutably Taoist or stridently Maoist but, by ignoring mystical rhetoric and official pronouncement, and focusing instead on the everyday lives of ordinary citizens, this series has presented contemporary Chinese civilization in a surprisingly accessible light. Even so, there have been occasional sharp reminders of the profound differences between the systems under which we live, and last night saw the clearest presence yet of the forbidding might of the state; a state which, for the supposed benefit of the masses, can at times be almost incomprehensibly brutal with the individual.

Down at Lijiang disco, the music scene had barely caught up with Susan Maugham, but the drug culture was *very* River Phoenix, with heroin freely available, and trafficking on the increase. In scenes chillingly reminiscent of *The Prisoner*, a jolly official tannoy announced, sing-song fashion, that anyone caught blowing their mind would also get their brains blown out (courtesy of the government), while a stash of confiscated drugs was publicly burned, with hardened addicts doubtless vying for places downwind of the bonfire. At a rally in the People's Cinema, the main feature turned out to be rearranging the features of the unfortunate Hu Weixiong, recently convicted of trafficking. Like a hundred others across Yunnan province that day, he was denounced and led away to the execution grounds, where Mr Frontal Lobes had an appointment with Mr Bullet at three o'clock.

It was just deserts up in the hills too. Ten to three and there was honey still for tea, courtesy of teacher Lu's bees. Down in the city, Mr Mu was treated for toothache by an aged dentist (whose own teeth looked like a bombed graveyard), while colleagues told encouraging tales of a previous patient who had almost suffocated from a swollen face after surgery. At Dr Tang's, the mother of Little Swallow continued with acupuncture for her daughter's cerebral palsy, despite the advice of friends 'to forget her, and have a healthy baby instead'. Gangs of disaffected leather-jacketed youths boasted to each other about sex and drugs, while Mr Mu harangued his dead nephew's friend, who'd recently taken to chasing the dragon. Across town, love was blind – literally – since the blind masseuse had fallen for a blind pen-pal in another province, neither of them knowing nor caring that she had the glasses of Elton John, the looks of Cardew 'the cad' Robinson and the couture of Edna the inebriated woman. In China as in Britain, it seems that the sighted get a sadistic kick out of dressing the blind in ridiculous clothes.

But the stars of the series have undoubtedly been the grannies, fearsome oriental Ena Sharples and Dot Cottons, with one tooth between six of them, who believe that the young should either be extremely respectful to their elders, or else dead. The frequent cries of 'Those hooligans, they should shoot them all' and 'Hanging's too good for them,' in between gossip about neighbours being 'hairy pigs who eat from trash cans' and 'the prices you pay for mung beans these days', demonstrated once and for all that grannies are the same the world over.

Exquisitely shot on film, and sensitively accompanied by George Fenton's sparse but cerebral score, this is a jaw-droppingly stunning series, proving yet again that real life (when faithfully recorded) provides us with the best stories. The narration is unaffected, simple and informative, the translation is colloquial without being crass, and these seven episodes are doing more than any officially negotiated détente ever could to ease mistrust between nations. Along with the BAFTAs, gongs and statuettes he'll undoubtedly win by the dozen, Phil Agland deserves a Nobel prize for taking the lid off a culture, and showing the West that, in reality, the Chinese never were inscrutable; it's just that, until now, we never viewed them through the correct scrute.

Blockbusters

In the halcyon monochrome days of 1962, TV youth quizzes like *Top of the Form* and *Take a Letter* were civilized affairs. Sixteen-year-old neurotic Ruth Lawrence lookalikes with plaits and bottle-bottom glasses pitted their wits against their male counterparts – baked-bean-faced Brylcreem boys in short trousers – in an orgy of pointless general knowledge. Losers jolly-well congratulated winners who took home a tacky pewter mug which would languish, unloved, in the school trophy cupboard. Hurrah!

Much has changed on TV in thirty years but Bob Holness, former host of *Take a Letter*, is still here to bring vestiges of old-world chivalry to *Blockbusters*, insisting that contestants shake hands before asking them which school they attend. Take away the high-tech opening credits, where squashed sexangular UFOs pass through a twilight necropolis disturbingly similar to Birmingham, and the true nature of *Blockbusters* is revealed. It is *Top of the Form* on acid.

The game still involves a succession of middle-class teenagers answering general-knowledge questions posed by a gentleman of a certain age trying his damnedest not to sound like a Scout master. Bob has no time for the transitory street cred of a Paul Smith jacket or Nike trainers; he prefers to appear in a pair of sensible, smart Hepworths elasticated trousers with matching shirt, tie and handkerchief, the whole ensemble fetchingly topped off with Glenn Miller glasses. But behind this conservative attire is a man who clearly feels a kinship with young people, demonstrated by frequent lapses into a hip patois quite unknown elsewhere. When he tells us what the kids are 'into', one suspects they are really into calling him a silly old git behind his back, a temptation they can hardly resist, but do since he holds the key to making them rich beyond the dreams of bingo halls.

There are always problems with adolescents on quiz shows, with anarchy never more than a surly silence or a fit of the giggles away. Who can forget the *University Challenge* fiasco when Bamber became puce with rage as a team answered every question 'William Shake-speare'? But Bob is an old hand who has dealt with a legion of difficult youths in his time – the boorish, the taciturn, the flippant and the truculent – and presumably can take revenge on the cheeky ones by making them do the humiliating dance during the end credits. Nevertheless, some still try it on, seeking fresh smutty nuances from the meagre twenty-six letters of the alphabet: 'I'd like a P, please Bob ... I'll have an F, Bob' or, worst of all, 'I want U, Bob.'

Yesterday Chris took on Christian and Andrew, tackling such curiously worded questions as 'What M is a large ostentatious pendant *disported* by men wearing open-topped shirts?' (answer: medallion). In between the rounds of a 'ding-dong battle' Bob persuaded Chris to imitate a seal, something he will sorely regret if he ever becomes a Cabinet minister and Central have not wiped the tapes. Eventually Chris was given the right to 'put himself on the hot spot', won a day with the RSC and looked thoroughly cheesed off in an I-may-be-a-grammar-schoolboy-but-I-wanted-a-Nintendo sort of way.

Last night's edition was show 40 of series ten. *Blockbusters* appeals to almost everyone and for nearly a decade has attracted huge audiences. I suspect the young watch to view their peers and their fashions. Women of a certain age probably watch to pass the winter evenings fantasizing about moonlit fandangos with the dapper Bob. And, more sinisterly, lonely gentlemen in bedsits almost certainly tune in to watch teenage girls perspiring freely and nervously under pressure. Me? I was converted the day Bob told me that a hawsehole is the hole through which the anchor of a ship is pulled.

Whicker's World: the Absolute Monarch

ITV is broadcasting a new endurance game, a trial of strength and will-power tougher even than *Gladiators*. One man flies out to a hot, humid country with a film crew, sits in the presence of the richest man in the world, and tries to act completely normally, as though conducting just another TV interview. The ultimate test of his self-control is to refrain from crawling right up the potentate's backside, but last night Alan Whicker failed to restrain himself so completely that Yorkshire TV will surely have to send a rescue party up the Sultan of Brunei's colon in order to retrieve their star.

Lovable though he is, time has been taking its remorseless toll on our Alan, and his vague, unfocused performance last night reminded me of Accrington Stanley's legendary centre forward, who had to be turned round by his colleagues at half-time and pointed towards the opponents' goal. After decades of being a British institution, he is now starting to look as though he should be in one and, when he began his interview by asking the Sultan how he managed to be so wonderful, it was clear that we had strayed on to Monty-Modlyn-meets-Idi-Amin territory.

The publicity blurb promised 'a fascinating blend of *Scheherazade* and *The King and I*', but what we got was a torrent of grovelling genuflection from our Uriah Heep of a host, while the Sultan looked on with the tranquillity and inner calm of a man who knows that his overseas investments are earning him $6,000,000 dollars a day, while his oil wells are busy sucking up another six. Whicker was positively salivating as he itemized the man's possessions: his fleet of jets, his yachts, his twenty-five palaces, his 153 Bentleys, his Rolls-Royces. Of course, the descriptions work best in a Whicker voice: 'This bashful millionaire . . . this working king . . . an almost mystical aura surrounds him . . .' By now, there was no doubt as to the exact location of the biggest oil slick in Brunei.

As the programme unfolded, I began to suspect that I was watching a man who had sold a sixty-minute programme idea to ITV, but had then only been granted a ten-minute interview with his subject. The rest of the hour was padded out with a potted history of the country and some genial observations about how prosperous it is, how much they like the British, and how well the Sultan looks after his countrymen. But we heard nothing from political opponents, or those imprisoned without trial, and every shot had the acrid whiff of an APPROVED rubber stamp about it. Whicker's questions to the Sultan were bland and fawning throughout; for one instant he summoned up the nerve to ask about a $10,000,000 donation to the Contras, but when he was fobbed off with an evasive answer he kowtowed obsequiously. In the Sultan's Palace you may start by speaking of Oliver North, but what you end up with is Fawn Hall.

We saw the Sultan winning at polo (he always wins), and telling jokes which I didn't understand but which were obviously very funny because everyone around him laughed like drains. We also learned that 'He gives a lot of money to charity but doesn't like anyone to know about it.' Whicker was fearlessly prepared to spill the beans on that one, but more reluctant when it came to delicate questions of censorship, lack of democracy or the growth of Muslim fundamentalism. The Sultan's wealth is so colossal that it would induce financial vertigo in anyone; given that, he seemed a decent enough, level-headed, fine figure of a chap, the sort who might well, on a whim, send $1,000,000 to a journalist who said something nice about him in a

London newspaper. But we were promised an interview, not an audience with the world's richest man, and I would much rather have seen Robert Robinson fronting the programme and bringing some depth and insight to it. I am usually keen to see Whicker's work. But truly, on this occasion at least, the Whicker man proved to be a man of straw.

Next day Mr Whicker wrote to the editor of the *Evening Standard*, describing the article as 'insensitive lavatorial juvenilia' and saying that he felt it was 'deeply unpleasant to feel oneself watched by this sort of obscene peeper'. He also accused me of 'shouting loutish obscenities'. Mr Whicker's wish to be rid of this peeper has subsequently come true, since he's barely been seen on television for some time now.

Ivor the Engine

Whatever the PR people from British Rail may tell you, rail travel isn't what it used to be. The days of elegant, courteous and punctual public transport seem far away when you're sitting in a recently vandalized, urine-scented, freezing cold waiting room, hoping for a non-existent train. Or standing in an InterCity buffet bar, paying Chez Nico prices for a soggy microwaved bacon bun (scalding to the point of inedibility) served by a maniac with spider tattoos on his neck, while a silicon-chip voice relentlessly intones, 'Attention guard, disabled passenger alarm activated,' conjuring up images of a coprophiliac's remake of the shower scene from *Psycho*.

But the perfect little railway still runs every Wednesday on CH4. Originally screened just over thirty years ago, *Ivor the Engine* first hit the screen when the age of steam was drawing to a close, and as the mad axeman, Dr Beeching, was about to close thousands of stations just like Ivor's mythical home of Llaniog in north Wales. Bearing the smart green livery of the Merioneth and Llantacilly Railway, Ivor was the personification of gentleness, totally committed to public service. Unlike most modern children's cartoons – where intergalactic Thargs endlessly quest for magic swords, which they then insist on ramming up other Thargs – the only time Ivor ever let off steam was when he accompanied vocal performances of 'Cwm Rhondda' at the Eisteddfod. Indeed, aficionados will remember that his C, E and G whistles were originally donated to him by a fairground calliope owner, after there'd been a bit of trouble with some stolen pipes.

Yesterday was a typically mixed day at Llaniog Station. First, Jones the Steam and Dai Station received some pretty grim news from a toff in a top hat. 'We're concerned at the lack of revenue,' said Mr Williams the Head Office, 'and the directors want to sell the line to the Welsh National Railway Commission.' Worse, diesel trains were coming and Ivor would soon be sent off to that most ignominious of fates, shunting at the depot. To be fair, it was hard to argue with the directors' point of view: an entire branch line devoted solely to taking Bluebell the donkey on sightseeing trips and delivering the occasional free parcel does not exactly look like a blue-chip investment to potential shareholders. Having delivered his bombshell, Mr Williams departed in his pink Rolls-Royce. No sign of Superglue in the locks or a keying job on the panels; they were respectful to their superiors in those days.

Dai was concerned. So concerned that, without stopping for tea, he set off with Ivor to deliver a new pair of boots to Mr Dimwiddy down in the valley. The lone hermit (despite being cut off from the rest of society) had somehow discovered flared trousers several years before they became fashionable in London. Dai explained his problem and, as luck would have it, Mr Dimwiddy suddenly remembered several thousand bars of gold bullion, languishing in the cupboards under his stairs. 'I dug it out of the ground and melted it down,' he explained, generously offering to buy up the entire railway, despite its lamentably inefficient working practices. 'I could buy the whole of Wales, England and Scotland . . . and after all, what's the use of having a bit of money put aside if you can't help your friends.'

Ivor the Engine hails from the days before TV became self-conscious, and it remains the archetypal children's cartoon. No elaborate script conferences were needed, no child psychologists, just Oliver Postgate and a few mates in a potting shed in 1962, with a camera and some imagination. The beautifully uncluttered drawings have an aesthetic appeal totally lacking in most computer animations, and the simple, atmospheric bassoon score by Vernon Elliott is a model of economy. *Truly* childish nonsense (such as *Pebble Mill* with Ross King) can be found occupying the adult daytime slots. Children's daytime scheduling is much more suitable for we grown-up kids, as well as the younger audience it's primarily aimed at.

Of course, I'd be the last to suggest that young viewers should grow up watching only the cosy programmes. The real world can be cruel and vile, and it's unfair to bring children up without their being made aware of that. But fantasy is essential to life as well, and in that respect Ivor – even in the early black-and-white episodes – can out-Bambi Bambi.

Hearts of Gold

Be warned. It could happen anywhere. On holiday, in the home, on the way to work. A moment's casual benevolence, a thoughtless charitable gesture and, before you know it, Esther Rantzen will have turned you and your good deed into a ratings-boosting feature on her prime-time, slime-time *Hearts of Gold*.

Appearing on this programme is the media equivalent of being awarded the British Empire Medal, for the Heart of Gold is a patronizing and meaningless decoration given only to lowly 'punters', as a pretext for wallowing in cheap sentimentality at their expense. The show is a grotesque Frankensteinian affair, constructed from bits of other successful formats, crudely stitched together; the dubious worthiness and crass humour of *That's Life!*, the incontinent tear ducts of *This is Your Life* and enough tragic medical cases for an entire series of *Your Life in Their Hands*. Yet in spite of all that life, it would still need an almighty thunderbolt from on high ever to animate this moribund monstrosity.

On came the hosts, the hushed-to-the-point-of-reverential Mike Smith (living proof of the need for ejector seats in helicopters) and St Esther in her Edith Cavell mode, telling us that they have 'told terrible lies to wonderful . . . ordinary people' to get them there under false pretexts. Most TV executives are of course expert at spotting 'ordinary people' because they themselves are extraordinary: extraordinarily

callous, manipulative and exploitative. This programme is the fur-
thest that Esther has yet gone in taking Light Entertainment down the
road of 'Let's take the smoked windows out of the ambulance so we can
enjoy the suffering,' and featured cancer, polio, a broken neck,
chronic alcoholism, multiple sclerosis and muscular dystrophy. After
all, there's nothing like a good old-fashioned Variety show.

Hearts of Gold mixes ordinary people (decent types who face
adversity with bravery and good humour) with a leavening of star
names, veering uneasily between tragedy and showbiz because, when
all's said and done, you want a bit of glamour with your misery. A
delightful ten-year-old who had raised £4,000 for cancer research was
hit over the head by Timmy Mallett. A worthy Portuguese life saver
had his shirt unbuttoned to the navel by Betty Boo. A good Samaritan
was involved in an inept Beadle-esque 'My best man's pissed, will you
stand in for him?' candid camera piece, with Esther as a heavily veiled
bride (though not heavily enough for my liking). This whole section
seemed determined to humiliate the victim for trying to do a good
deed. Later, an admirable woman who worked with alcoholics was
asked to help make a documentary that would undoubtedly have been
well worth seeing but, yet again, it was a trick, and all we got was more
insipid mush. Lastly the ten-year-old was handed a fund-raising book
of poetry that had been secretly published with her picture on it,
although cruelly the 'poems' turned out to be by Paul Daniels, Gloria
Hunniford and Michaela Strachan. When the closing credits rolled,
only the names of the presenters and stars were listed. Sorry, luvvies,
ordinary people don't make the caption roller. Leave through the back
door, don't forget your callipers, off you go, we've another show to
record.

Exactly *what* can you say to someone who has saved your life, and
why say it in public? Scientists are now working on the theory that
Rantzenitis is a mutant strain of Monkhouse syndrome, a terrible
affliction that often struck Bob during *The Golden Shot* when he would
start describing the disability of someone he didn't know, and break
down on camera. *Hearts of Gold* is all about physical courage, since you
need an awful lot to watch it. It is callous and vulgar, and trivializes
altruism by putting a price on it; save a drowning man – win a guitar
('from our friends at Yamaha'). This is not simply tabloidal TV, it is

worse. This is the stuff that local rags are made of – mawkish, sentimental, ignoble junk. The sooner it is axed, the better.

Wish You Were Here . . . ?

There are two unavoidable phenomena the Met Office never warn you about when they forecast sub-zero temperatures. The immediate appearance of ice-cream vans, and the unavoidable glut of travel shows.

Wish You Were Here . . . ? is back and Judith (she's overdone it on the first day again) Chalmers is sporting a suntan that would shame your average Hiroshima victim. Judith must spray the fake burn on beforehand in a bid to gain our sympathy, since otherwise she would be lynched for having the plummest job in television. The peripatetic lobster certainly has the plummiest voice, opening her vowels and intoning in her delightfully patronizing 1950s RADA as though addressing a group of retards. Speaking from the Sierra Nevada, she introduced a revolutionary concept, the Slump Buster: 'We know there's a slump . . . but isn't that the time that you *really need* a holiday?' And as she gave us details, the nation's dispossessed and repossessed must have been uncertain whether to laugh or cry.

Wish You Were Here . . . ? is, I fear, not so much a programme as a freebie trough for presenters to push their snouts into, but the title's question mark is prudent, since I certainly had no wish to visit any of its venues. Judith introduced the first location as 'Andalu-thia' but it was really the Costa del Sol, inhabited solely by OAPs on Thomsons 'Young at Heart' extended winter breaks. These were the thrifty folk whose savings earned them a fortune when interest rates were sky-high: the only buggers who can now afford holidays in Spain. At home they drive Reliant Rialtos smack in the middle of the road with their neck collars on. In Spain they sing, 'Up on a looma blanca – just like a bird in the sky,' endlessly repeat their one Spanish phrase, 'Has it got squid in it?' and live in buildings that make Crawley New Town look like Hampstead. Thanks, but no thanks.

Judith shares the programme with Floella Benjamin and the schoolmasterly John Carter, a trio of vacation junkies who have

overdosed on holidays and demonstrate that too much travel narrows rather than broadens the mind. They also prove that it can give you a nasty dose of the clichés: quaint villages always nestle, mountains always tower majestically, beaches are sun-kissed, nightlife is exotic, and tropical paradises are always unspoiled. One suspects that travel-show presenters resort to such phatic language because they spend the entire visit insensible with cheap local booze, and have to resort to reading out the travel brochure when, six months later in a dubbing studio, they try to piece together their report.

Floella pulled the short straw and got sent to Blackpool, a town which, to paraphrase, looks like it's helping police with its enquiries. She described it as 'the Riviera of the north' and, as I didn't see anyone holding a gun to her head, and I know she is not a pathological liar, I can only presume someone was holding a gun to her kitten's head. People may knock Blackpool, she said, but it's a great place to have fun, to treat yourself and treat the family. Next year, apparently, they're even going to treat the sewage on the beach.

Finally, Mr Carter from Form IVb had been on holiday to Alaska, and decided to tell the whole school about it. The boys greatly enjoyed his talk, especially the home-movie pictures of snow, ice, glaciers and more snow. The whole school hopes he visits Alaska again soon, and stays there much, much longer next time.

This is a predictable programme that has been out in the sun too long, has had a mild stroke and lost its critical faculties. Blackpool equals fish and chips, Spain equals flamenco, Alaska equals the awesome majesty of nature. There is no objective assessment of venues or holiday packages but, with the substantial team (and budget) they employ, they really should be doing better than sitting in the pockets of tourist boards and tour operators. And is the researcher the same Moira Stewart who reads BBC news? I think we should be told.

But the programme must work subliminally because, as I watched it, I began to feel in need of a short break myself. The commercial break signifying the end of the show.

Dear Mr Lewis-Smith

I was delighted with your write-up on Judith Chalmers.
As I am a woman probably old enough to be your great
grandmother I always feel I must be right if somebody
like you shares my views.

For years I have said when I accidentally watch "Wish
You Were Here?"   "You must be joking of course".   I
may be had for obscenity if I write what I really reply.   Although I am anOAP I don't career round Majorca
etc although I have been there and like it - way out of
the concrete jungles.   I don't even drive.

I find her nauseating and if I have ever thought about
going somewhere about which she is expounding I resolve
never to go there.   I was finally put off when I read
in a magazine she said "there is no question of **me** not
going out to work when I was married" instead of "my".

She probably wrote different to instead of different
from but I couldn't bear to read on.   But then I find
so many in the "media" have no knowledge of grammar.

I like to give all performers a fair chance.   Not
being patronising but I find if I watch or listen
to something three times and it irritates me beyond
endurance that's their lot!

Annie Rice is another.   I find her unnerving the way
she focuses those eyes upon the watcher.   Miriam
Stoppard was another though she is seldom on the box now.
I'll pass a thick veil over Des O'Connor.   Give me the
Muppets any time.

But chacun a etc and obviously somebody somewhere likes
these people and I don't have to watch.   I just turn
off the appropriate knob.

Yours sincerely

Agnes Kimmersley

The Day Today

Around about the age when you first realize that university degrees are not bestowed by God, but are dished out mechanically by employees of the lucrative academic industry, it also dawns on you that TV news does not descend from on high either. Apart from the odd natural disaster or political upheaval, most reports are little more than gossip, or coverage of PR events, and only make the news agenda because an editor decided (usually weeks beforehand) to send a camera crew along. Yet, despite its trivial and artificial content, the deluded people who work in the industry continue to believe that, because they shape the news, they shape the world.

The Day Today tackles such arrogance head-on, embodying the eternal satirical principle that, if you don't like the message, then you should shoot the messenger. Unlike *KYTV* (which entirely lost its focus when it moved from radio), the former R4 *On the Hour* team have successfully reassembled their current affairs parody in purely televisual terms, synthesizing elements of *Newsnight*, *Sky News* and US rolling news networks into a glorious fusion of inanity and insanity. After opening graphics so slick that they put the genuine *Newsnight* titles to shame, Chris Morris appeared as a Paxman-style anchorman with the news headlines – 'Sacked chimney sweep pumps boss full of mayonnaise . . . Bottomley refreshed after three days on cross' – neatly capturing the senseless intonation of a newsman who moves words from autocue to microphone without passing them through his brain, and produces a stream of fluent, authoritative idioglossia.

The production budget for this series is, allegedly, bigger than that of many feature films, but the sequence of coruscating news parodies that followed (with a scrupulous attention to detail not seen since *Spinal Tap*) confirmed that every penny had been well spent. Barbara Wintergreen's report on a convicted serial killer who wanted to die like Elvis (stuffed full of drugs and cheeseburgers and electrocuted on the toilet) was shot in authentic, smudgy CNN colour, with authentically crass and insensitive commentary: 'So, as Baxter turns as blue as his suede shoes . . .' Back in the studio Janet Breen, organizer of the London Jam Festival, was subjected to the full Paxmanesque range of sneers and snide asides, bursting into tears while her tormentor revelled in her dis-confiture.

Dressed in a smart new Pringle sweater, Alan Partridge (a man who considers the lyrics of Abba to be the last word in philosophy) took us through the year's sporting highlights, noticing nothing wrong when a diver concussed himself on the springboard: 'There he goes, down, double back twister, bangs his head, and in . . . textbook, lovely.' Why on earth does Rory Bremner persist with his feeble John Motson impersonations, when Steve Coogan has transformed the man, with his nylon hair and nylon mind, into such a glorious creation? But I must be careful not to show any more admiration for Mr Coogan in print, or there'll be talk; as it is, in some countries we're already considered to be married.

On it went at breakneck speed, with not one weak link nor dud performance anywhere. An unmasking of bullying in the C of E, environ-mental scientists in Alaska finding a nine-mile gap between the horizon and the earth, noisy neighbours being given some no-nonsense good-honest-coppering with the aid of a few tigers, amateur camcorder footage of a woman pierced by a shaft of frozen urine from a passing airplane, and Coogan (damn, I've mentioned him again) just wonderful as Elsie Tanner during a two-minute reconstruction of an entire themed archive night on BBC2. Avoiding the obvious news-room jokes, and packing every second full of acute observation and sharp parody, Morris, Armando Iannucci and the rest of the team have produced a brilliantly original show. Their radio origins reveal them-selves continually in their distinguished use of sound, and their bravery in running without canned laughter has paid off: a show this good doesn't need it.

Current Affairs broadcasting has taken itself far too seriously for far too long, regarding itself as beyond reproach, and it's high time that its pretensions were exposed. Many years ago, an unusually portentous Ludovic Kennedy contemptuously dismissed DJs in the celebrated phrase 'Moron shall speak unto moron,' and claimed the moral high ground for TV journalism. He clearly failed to realize that, one day, his own profession would become equally adept at talking gibberish.

Inside Story: Wiped Out

And lo, the City of London is truly a place of miracles. Financiers indicted on serious fraud charges are regularly acquitted on grounds of ill-health (something that never happens to burglars), but the moment the judge says, 'You may leave the court,' the sound of falling crutches and sprinting feet can be heard and the defendant, now fully healed, offs merrily away to mismanage yet another public company. There's even been a complete recovery from Alzheimer's, a disease previously thought incurable: the remedy, apparently, was parole and a lucrative directorship. And as for the miraculous goings-on at Lloyd's in recent years, the place should be renamed Lourdes.

The Square Mile's salubrious effect must be spreading nation-wide because, after watching last night's *Inside Story: Wiped Out* (BBC1) – which interviewed some of the many thousands of ruined Lloyd's Names – I, too, felt on top of the world. There's nothing that makes one feel better than contemplating the downfall of others, especially when they're the sort of county types who used to hold the finest 'high spotties' (house parties), until they grew short of a 'spodder cairsh' (spot of cash). But the greatest miracle of all was that (with a few exceptions) they were still living in the grand style, even though they didn't have a penny to their (Lloyd's) name, proving again the truth of the old adage: owe the bank £100, it's your problem; owe them £1,000,000, it's their problem. These were people who, back in the mid-80s, willingly agreed to unlimited liability because they thought it was a one-way bet: 'I was told I would send no money, and they would send me a cheque every year,' said one. But you couldn't help thinking that, when the world's most exclusive financial group suddenly started asking the only moderately wealthy to climb on board, Groucho Marx's warning apropos of club membership ought to have sprung to their minds.

Groucho's brother Karl could have predicted what would happen next and, as the pitiful stories unfolded, you would have had to have had a heart of stone not to laugh. One chap was so skint he was down to his last Bentley, and all because he'd believed 'in the utmost good faith' of a bunch of insurance underwriters; a man that naïve shouldn't be allowed to wander out of the nursery, let alone into the City. A former deb from Northumberland was so impoverished she'd had to turn the family mansion into a B&B, and I wish we could have seen her skivvying for a party of stroppy oiks, and frying bacon on her Aga. Another woman revealed that her brother (Anthony Gooda, head of the most notorious Lloyd's syndicate) used to refer to each of his clients as 'a Lombard' (Loads of Money But a Right Dick). Still, at least Mr Gooda couldn't be suspected of nepotism: he'd ruined his sister, just the same as everybody else.

There was some genuine hardship. A father's suicide. A disabled Sussex couple whose small vineyard was destroyed by the 87 hurricane (an ill wind that also magnified their losses at Lloyd's). But, when an elderly Irish couple lamented that 'We had to sell up and move somewhere considerably smaller,' and the camera panned to reveal a caravan, I was howling with laughter again. It transpired that most of Lloyd's recent losses were due to tens of thousands of insurance claims from asbestosis sufferers; and, since none of the interviewees (whose anguish has only been fiscal, not physical) expressed any sympathy for those victims, I couldn't muster up too much pity for Names who thought they were enjoying a free lunch, and only started whingeing when they got stuck with the bill.

Philippa Walker's excellently produced programme was as slow and as deliciously exquisite as a Chinese trial. Uncluttered by voice-over, the bowed heads were allowed all the time they needed to make their own confessions – 'In the end, the only person who's lost my money is me, I'm the idiot' – and the result was one of the funniest programmes of the year, far outstripping anything that an LE department could produce. Not that any of us should feel too smug, because these people clearly can't pay what they owe, which is why our insurance premiums are currently going through the roof, to underwrite the whole sorry mess. The truth is that, when it comes down to it, Lloyd's isn't insuring us; we're insuring them.

Omnibus: Freeze

I watched an arts programme last night. It must have been an arts programme, because I remember switching on the TV at 10.25, viewing for two hours, then looking at my watch and it said 10.26. Even the worthiest arts programmes can be heavy going, but they become positively tedious when the sole intention is to outrage. I get all the outrage I need simply by tuning into daytime television, and don't require any extra thank you.

Omnibus: Freeze (BBC1) focused on the work of British artist Damien Hirst, darling of the avant-garde and *bête noire* of the popular press. Preoccupied with 'confronting the big issues of life and death' (wowie), Mr Hirst not only sees the grinning skull beneath the skin, but likes *us* to see it too, bisecting pregnant cows with a chainsaw, cramming shelves with jars of rotting offal and suspending dead sharks in glass cabinets; in short, he's an artist whose *oeuvre* is (literally) a complete shambles and (metaphorically) difficult to swallow. To sweeten such a bitter pill, the programme began with a fantasy sequence in which a sinister dentist (Donald Pleasence) administered gas to young Damien (though not as much gas as many of his critics would have liked) and induced a dream-like state. It wasn't much of a conceit but, then again, the artist was obviously so conceited already that it hardly seemed to matter.

Just as Warhol had the Factory and a load of hangers-on, so does Damien. We saw the East End building where the original 1988 Freeze exhibition was mounted, and where he first acquired his sad legion of acolytes, mostly dressed in the official *Late Show* uniform of buttoned-up black shirt, no tie, and very silly Robert Elms glasses. Someone had built a complete costermonger's stall (a critic described this as a metaphor for capitalism), while another critic wearing welder's goggles told us that Hirst's 'A Thousand Years' – an exhibit involving maggots, a cow's head and innumerable flies being zapped on an insectocutor – was a metaphor for the human life cycle, although it seemed to me more like a metaphor for an Italian restaurant I once ate in near King's Cross. Then we saw Sarah Lucas and Tracy Emin, who were either a metaphor for a failed forceps delivery or had recently been making model airplanes under a duvet. As they giggled, and gabbled on about their latest creations (a selection of T-shirts with obscene slogans), the programme's title suddenly began to make sense: these two were frozen – in time – as first-year art students. I bet in ten years' time they'll be PR girls for something like Quorn, and won't care to be reminded about their masterpiece, 'Sod You Gits'.

On came more of them, I'm afraid. Someone tampered with phone lines and connected art galleries to each other. Someone dangerous said 'fuck' and (as is customary on such occasions chez Lewis-Smith) we gave the TV set a curtsy. Two photographers attended press events 'as artists' but were indistinguishable from genuine press photographers except for the lack of a sixty-inch beer gut. And a woman received an Arts Council grant to build a tower out of salt bricks (no modern art film is complete without bricks) on Brighton beach, sending the local mayor apoplectic with rage. That was the point, of course. This was the same tired old shake-the-Establishment-to-its-foundations stuff that the avant-garde has been doing for nearly a century – from Tzara and Dada to Duchamp and Warhol – and which Galton and Simpson lampooned so brilliantly in *The Rebel*. It's a world where outrage is everything, and nothing is sacred (least of all cows apparently). Until, that is, someone utters the magic phrase 'I'd like to buy it, how much?' when, inexplicably, everyone suddenly becomes very serious and businesslike. All major credit cards accepted.

Shocking? Well, about as shocking as knock-down ginger. These were just another tiresome group of pale youths who've learned the simple galvanic-response trick: give a minor shock – get a knee-jerk reaction. Who knows if it's great art or rubbish? We're far too close to it, and only when the dust has settled will anyone be able to judge, if they care to. Andrea Cornes' flip film displayed the characteristic insecurity the chattering classes always feel when confronted with the incomprehensible. They remember the first night of *The Rite of Spring*, and want to be remembered as the ones who cheered, not rioted; so they applaud everything they see, just to be on the safe side.

I have since come to know Damien Hirst personally, and now regard him as a friend. However, I still think his sculptures stink, especially during the summer months.

Food and Drink

Eating out in Britain can be a grim experience, with jaded food, pumped full of monosodium glutamate, being served to equally jaded customers, pumped full of muzak. Yet, if it's atmosphere that restaurateurs are after, why don't they play sound-effect records in their premises, instead of monotonous background music? Think of the ambience it would create if you wandered into an empty restaurant and immediately heard an animated crowd of Belgian football supporters, sipped your soup to the sound of a dentist's drill, or drank your coffee while listening to two iguanas copulating. You might even be distracted from the terrible food.

Atmosphere is so noticeably lacking from *Food and Drink*, you'd think the programme had been vacuum-packed. In other countries the art of eating well is proudly celebrated, but Britain's longest-running TV food show is dedicated to making this most natural of desires seem like a shameful vice. Last night Chris Kelly began with the portentous phrase: '*Food and Drink* can reveal . . .' before gleefully telling us that 'healthy' polyunsaturated margarines (which his programme has been advocating for years) are full of trans fatty acids, and we'll all have heart attacks and die anyway. An American moustache with leather armpatches was filmed in front of a lot of books and said it was a very important piece of research (he should know, since he'd published it), while an English moustache sat in front of more books and said he wasn't so sure. Reporter Vicky Kimm pointed at tubs of margarine, slowly repeated everything Chris had just said as though she were talking to six-year-olds, and told us we had to pour runny oil over our bread from now on, or we'd all be sorry. At the end of this in-shallow investigation, Chris suddenly contradicted everything we'd just heard, saying, 'The message seems to be "Choose the spread you want",' but anyway the real message seemed to be 'Run yet another food scare story and maybe the show will get a credit in the tabloids.'

'I've got a spectacular way of cooking salmon,' announced Michael Barry. He hadn't. Although, to be fair, it did have the edge on last week's recipe – how to use a toasted-sandwich maker to make a toasted sandwich. As ever, Barry (who bears an unfortunate resemblance to the sort of youth leaders you see in police photofit pictures, wanted in

connection with incidents involving woggles) epitomized the programme's guilty conscience, using fromage frais 'because it's healthy',
although last week he was slopping in double cream without a care,
and telling us not to worry. But my desire for him to finish quickly was
tempered by the awful knowledge of what was coming next: the
weekly 'witty' Barry–Kelly interchange, reminiscent of Wogan and
Young at their worst, guaranteed humour-free and with the added
horror that Chris usually forgets to sample the food before pronounc-
ing, 'Hmmm, tastes great.'

Jilly Goolden (known, chez Lewis-Smith, as 'Miss Ex-Ophthalmic
Goitre 1933') claimed she was going to revive the image of sherry, but
instead nearly destroyed it by drowning it in a succession of garish red
and green cocktails. Then it was time for the weekly advertising break
with Gateway, Oddbins, Winerack and Bottoms Up all allowed to
advertise free on the new, commercial BBC2. Finally, Antonio
Carluccio was in southern Italy, still uncertain whether he was making
a holiday report or a food item. While his producer shot some dismal
That's Life! staged comedy routines, and some fat Calabrian peasants
shot anything that moved, Carluccio briefly escaped the slaughter by
wandering into the woods in search of mushrooms. The only fungi to
be with on this show.

Food and Drink long ago passed its sell-by date, and is now moving
beyond even the point of parody. There is no cohesion between its
various sections, nor is there any purpose to many of them. Its painful
links urgently need removal, the clumsy over-editing is no substitute
for its lack of editorial direction, and it's ironic that a show which
frequently praises the merits of organic production should have
nothing remotely organic about its own structure. With the question-
ably cosy relationship it enjoys with major food and drink retailers,
and its often outrageous use of product placement, the programme
seems to continue not through merit but through sheer inertia, and it's
high time the BBC questioned its *raison d'être*.

Can anyone stomach the thought of another series?

Lipstick on Your Collar

'Bum holes. Bum holes. Bum holes. Bum holes,' Not exactly 'In sooth, I know not why I am so sad,' it's true, but the opening lines of Dennis Potter's romantic comedy convey the speaker's melancholy with equal clarity. And just as the Bard often had characters unexpectedly breaking into Elizabethan ditties of the 'Where is fancy bred?' variety in his romantic comedies, so Potter's cast find themselves suddenly singing along to the New Elizabethan pressings: Frankie Vaughan's 'Garden of Eden'.

I imagine a billion hairs stood appreciatively on the backs of quinquagenarian necks throughout the country as *Lipstick on Your Collar* started with the evocative sight and sound of a jukebox stylus dropping on to scratchy vinyl. This led into a jaw-dropping title sequence, with three girls divesting an army private of both his uniform and his innocence, to the accompaniment of Connie Francis. The glaring primary colours had the feel of old Technicolor stock about them, and perfectly encapsulated the changing mood of Britain in the mid-50s: a society so used to drab greyness that it now wanted its reds and yellows as garish as possible. In the previous two series of Potter's trilogy, the popular songs have injected a bleak gallows humour into the drama, but here they are sudden bursts of sunshine, punctuating the stifling boredom and rigidity of Whitehall in 1956, in those final days before Suez and rock 'n' roll swept away the old Britain for good. The open-plan War Office in which Private Hopper is lethargically completing his National Service is run like a schoolroom, full of nincompoops obediently translating Russian newspapers into English in the service of that curious oxymoron, military intelligence. Two worlds are about to collide: old-fashioned Whitehall, with its belief in Empire and its blinkered, obedient functionaries talking in camp public-school tones about 'drinkie-winkies' and 'giving the Mau Mau a hiding'; and the young, affluent, sexually curious, post-Festival of Britain generation, chomping at the bit against the repressive society. Behind his desk, the bored Hopper synthesizes these two worlds, imagining elaborate sexual fantasies in the office. Bizarre things go on in his head, but nothing as outlandish as what his superiors are thinking; they are imagining that Britain still rules the world.

I don't know exactly *what* happened to Potter in the Forest of Dean all those years ago but it clearly still preys on his mind and we're all paying for it; the tangled plot of last night's episode unravelled itself amid camp depictions of communal buggery, to the tune of 'Little Bitty Pretty One'. Major 'Bum hole' Hedges is bored with his work, as is Hopper, who is counting the days to his demob. His replacement is Private Francis, who behaves like a simpleton yet can (ominously) quote Pushkin in the original. In his Fulham digs Francis becomes infatuated with the girl upstairs: Sylvia, a tightly dressed usherette whose impossibly curvaceous form is a tribute to the architectural skills of the British foundation-garment industry. Sylvia's unpleasant husband is Corporal Berry from the War Office, and Francis spends the night listening to the loneliest sound in the world: energetic copulation by the couple in the room above. The episode ends with a sinisterly pale Humber Snipe containing a sinisterly pale Roy Hudd, snooping on them all.

The attention to 1950s detail is astonishing: period Swan kettles, plaster Alsatians, ship's-wheel barometer, zip-up sleeveless cardigans and the sort of blackheads that only regular applications of Brylcreem can bring on. Only the London accents (clearly acquired at the Dick Van Dyke School of Cockney) let the side down, but the strength of Potter's script, his quirky visual imagination and his exquisite ability to create permanent unease combine to make superb television. Potter is probably the finest playwright that television has yet produced, and it would have been tragic if the ridiculous uproar surrounding *Blackeyes* had persuaded him to throw in the towel. As it is, he has bounced back with a perfectly judged work, reminiscent of Shostakovitch's *Response to Just Criticism*. He may appear to be toeing the party line, but he clearly doesn't mean it, and remains as gloriously subversive as ever.

The response to *Blackeyes* apparently dented Potter's confidence so badly that, at one point during the writing of *Lipstick*, he gave up and sent his fee back to CH4. Not many playwrights would risk doing that, and even fewer would find the company returning the cheque. Whatever CH4 paid him, they've got their money's worth already.

Gladiators

Joe Orton was once imprisoned for sticking photographs of beautiful women's faces on to the bodies of musclemen and secreting the bizarre montages within pages of books at his local library. In *Gladiators*, half a dozen of these androgynes have now sprung to life and, accompanied by six men with thighs as thick as tree trunks and brains to match, have been given a series on prime-time television. *Gladiators* is *It's a Knockout* on steroids, a modernized version of the fairground boxing booths that once toured the country, inviting the public to 'Go three rounds and win ten shillings' and greatly expanding the potential market of the then nascent British false-teeth industry in the process. These modern gladiators, however, are professional musclepersons, great hulking brutes with a physique and a general demeanour that screams out 'missing link'; they fancy themselves enormously, but their simian antics make you think not so much of Chippendales as Chipperfields.

On Saturday night they towered over the comparatively puny members of the public (aka contenders), who spoke gamely about David and Goliath, although I could not help but think that what I was about to witness would be more like an arm-wrestling competition with Stephen Hawking. As someone whose direct experience of athletics is somewhat circumscribed – the only weight loss I have ever obtained from the exercise bike I bought three years ago was when I carried it upstairs from the car – I watched the first show in a state of exhaustion and confusion.

It soon became clear that whoever devised the games was obsessed by balls. In 'Atlaspheres', people rolled around inside balls for several pointless minutes, occasionally colliding like cumbersome wobbly fat men as a geyser of CO_2 gas shot upwards. In 'Danger Zone', balls were shot from crossbows and bazookas, and in 'Swingshot' contestants bounced up and down on ropes gathering more balls while a gentleman called Wolf narrowed his slits to mere eyes in an unsuccessful effort to look menacing. But, as if to show us that the programme was not entirely balls, there was 'Duel', a dull updated version of the slippery pole with combatants hitting each other with giant cotton buds, and a climbing game involving a lot of women having a catfight half-way up a wall, which the referee unsportingly stopped just as it was getting interesting.

The saving grace of *It's a Knockout* was some sense that the participants could recognize their own ridiculousness. The costumes and the events in *Gladiators* are even more ludicrous, but the irony that is so desperately needed is utterly missing; and the presenters do nothing to improve matters. Where Eddie Waring had presence, John Fashanu and Ulrika Jonsson have absence, conducting post-event interviews guaranteed to sap whatever remaining energy contestants and viewers still have: 'Was it hard?' 'Yes, it was hard.' 'Right. Well, make no mistake, these are hard things to push around.' Oh Wogan, thou shouldst be living at this hour.

The show is a carbon copy of the American version, but the extrovert spontaneity required to make it work sits as convincingly with the British as does 'Have a nice day, y'all come back now' on the lips of a McDonald's waitress in Grimsby. Even the pros are suspect; Wolf is balding, Hawk's one claim to fame is as 'a former Mr Wales', and only chivalry and the *Evening Standard*'s legal department prevent me from naming the cross-eyed gladiatrix. If this programme is a success and these hulks become cultural icons, then I fear for the children. Come the millennium, infants' schools throughout the country will be resonating to the sound of teachers calling out: 'Jet, you're milk monitor . . . Shadow and Hawk, let's hear your six times table . . . Cobra, stop pulling Flame's hair.'

As the credits rolled, I noticed that the programme was the responsibility of Sam Goldwyn Productions. To paraphrase one of the great man's sayings: *Gladiators?* Include me out.

QVC

Good news: the age of consumer durables is finally over. Bad news: we've now entered the era of consumer unendurables, thanks to QVC, the twenty-four-hour-a-day, 365-day-a-year, shop-till-you-drop satellite paean to the great god Ratner.

On QVC, they like to boast that the real stars of the shows are the inanimate bits of metal and plastic on sale and, once you've watched the presenters inaction (one word, not two) for a few minutes, you can't help but agree. Although the faces change periodically and each hour is themed – jewellery, car care, D-Day memorabilia, World Cup souvenirs – the sluggish, laboured pace of the programmes never varies, and the result is curiously like stepping into a televisual paternoster, where nothing ever seems to start or finish. So it was that I spent a month last Friday watching the *Personal Hi-Tech* hour, presented by Julian Balentine (a human Mogadon dressed in the sort of gingham number once favoured by Bobby Bennett on *Stars on Sunday*). He's doubtless worked in local radio too, because he displayed a talent only valued there: an ability to move his mouth completely independently of his brain.

Sitting in a cosy World of Leather set that even GMTV would deride as embarrassingly downmarket, Julian was already operating at incoherence factor 3 when I tuned in, describing item H10347: 'Literally, it's fantastic.' He called it an infra-red massager, but the phallic shape of this plastic vibrator carried the same dubious subtext that surrounds teenage girls' deodorant containers. Someone who'd bought one spoke on the phone, announcing herself as 'Heidi from Austria', but Julian wasn't thrown, effortlessly displaying an encyclopedic lack of knowledge: 'So you speak Austrian then...?' Moving on to H10238, he caressed a swivel-lamp clock radio, a truly appalling piece of cack that, if it were a can of beans, would have carried the Harlequin brand label and be found rusting on the top shelf of a corner shop. 'The volume control has maximum and minimum,' he told us, highlighting its best features, 'and there's a manual tuning facility' (cutting out that automatic tuning misery). 'I like it and I'm talking from personal erm... personal erm... personal erm... I'm just talking from my point of view.' The word he'd forgotten was 'experience'. The person who'd booked him had forgotten it too.

Each product was separated from the next by the sort of sleazy music which (I'm told) usually accompanies films involving Swedish models and donkeys. J11137 was a radio-controlled clock that 'only works within nine hundred miles of Rugby', a somewhat unusual marketing feature. 'You won't believe what I'm doing now,' squealed Julian apropos of J11077, 'I'm operating a TV with a watch.' But sadly it was all too believable that this ersatz General Jumbo would try to flog us an ugly watch-cum-remote-control (with buttons so small even an ophthalmic technician's screwdriver would be unable to operate it) yet, moments later, be praising the huge buttons on H10595 (another remote control) which were 'literally much better than the fiddly little buttons you get on some units'. You could automatically solve the word games on the H10671 databank by buying the H10557 spellcheck to do it for you (alternatively, you could buy neither). Meanwhile he peppered his speech with 'literally' – 'I'll literally turn the power off. . . I'll literally increase the volume . . . literally we're out of time . . .' – as only the illiterate can. Another caller proudly announced that she could order in Spanish, said one word, 'Holà,' and got stuck. Like most callers, she was constantly buying things from QVC. The only thing she hadn't got, apparently, was a life.

Julian reappeared with H10347, the 'literally, it's fantastic' infra-red device, but by now I'd got the massage. What I'd been watching was an Innovations catalogue with its own TV series, a dismal procession of personal organizers bought exclusively by those with no lives to organize, and personal shredders by those with lives so empty they have nothing confidential to dispose of. The channel's regular audience of dysfunctional, crisp-eating cathode-ray onanists presumably believe that endlessly buying consumer durables will improve the quality of their lives, yet, if they really want life to get better, the off switch might be a better option. It's easy as pie with H10595, the One-for-all-One remote control.

'The infra-red massager has a swivel-head,' said Julian, as I swivelled mine away from the set, wondering what the channel's acronym stood for. They claim it's Quality, Value, Convenience. Not a bit. Quarantine for Vile Crap is nearer the mark.

Daws Butler: Voice Magician

One of the best-kept secrets in television is that the choicest and most secure jobs are those behind the cameras. Presenters are mere cannon fodder, thrown into battle only to be mown down by wicked critics and a fickle public the moment they put their heads above the trenches, while the producers and technicians behave like World War One generals, sitting well behind the line of fire and ordering their troops into action. And, when the sniping stops, they simply find new presenters and carry on.

Amongst these sensible but anonymous folk are people whose voices are recognized by everyone, but whose faces remain unknown. These artistes are free to ply their trade without the irritation of constantly being recognized in Tesco and asked to 'say their catchphrase' or being instructed to 'do your funny walk'. You might be living next door to Basil Brush, Gordon the Gopher or the man who says 'soft, strong and very long' without ever realizing it, and they like to keep it that way. But occasionally, TV lifts up its safety curtain and reveals such people, as on yesterday's award-winning documentary *Daws Butler: Voice Magician*.

During a career spanning fifty years, Daws has been the voice of dozens of world-famous cartoon characters, including Snagglepuss ('exit stage right even'), Yogi ('smarter than the average') Bear and Mr Jinks ('I hate you meeces to pieces'). The programme neatly juxta-posed biographical details and interviews with Daws and his col-leagues to produce an analysis of 'voice-over artistes', that extraordi-nary group of people who gather together in dank, subterranean dubbing suites and get paid to anthropomorphize. Daws served his apprenticeship in vaudeville, before moving through radio and on to MGM where he voiced many of the Tex Avery cartoons. He teamed up with Stan Freberg (of 'Banana Boat' – 'Day O' – fame) on a TV puppet show *Time For Beany*, a knockabout, semi-improvised panto-mime involving a serpent made from a pair of his kid's pyjamas and a papier-mâché kid with a propeller growing out of his head, the whole show looking like Sooty on Benzedrine. But, for all the anarchy, Daws was a dedicated and serious artist who believed he was not just voicing but acting; the characterization started with the brain, then the heart, and only *then* emerged from the mouth.

His range of pitch, accent and timbre was stunning, and his ability to switch instantly from one voice to another was so complete that he often recorded both parts of a dialogue simultaneously. He would adopt the physical posture of a character in order to find their voice, throwing his shoulders and arms back and broadening his chest cavity to become Yogi Bear, or moving his jaw continuously for Quick Draw

McGraw. Huckleberry Hound's unmistakably laconic drawl was modelled on a lugubrious neighbour he heard at his wife's house in North
Carolina during the war; he had stored the voice away in his head for
a decade, until the perfect creation popped up from his subconscious.

Most remarkable was seeing his colleagues, Bill Hanna and Joe
Barbera (for whom he did his best work), along with such contemporaries as Don Messick and June Foray. Although we didn't see
them at work in the studio, it was extraordinary to watch this group
of sober, aged, leathery actors suddenly change gear and become Boo
Boo, Mrs Jetson, Barney, Wallygator, Chilli Willi and everybody's
favourite, Snagglepuss, with his elongated delivery borrowed from
Bert Lahr's cowardly Oz lion. All in all, a faultless and enchanting
hour that never once repeated itself, unlike Mr Hanna and Mr
Barbera's thrifty backdrops; tree, post, telephone box, tree, post,
telephone box, tree . . .

Sadly, Daws died in 1988, but this low-budget, high-quality film
serves as a suitable memorial to a highly respected member of an
unsung but noble profession. They are a sensitive bunch. When Jim
Henson (the voice of Kermit) died, the little frog sat alone, forlorn and
mute, throughout the memorial service. By all accounts, grown men
wept as they passed him to leave and read the little sign around his
neck: 'I've lost my voice.' Ahh.

Good Morning . . . With Anne and Nick

There are only three reasons why anyone would smile and say 'good
morning' to a traffic warden: 1, they are a traffic warden themselves;
2, they are parked on a double yellow line and are making a futile plea
for mercy; or 3, they have just been given a pre-med, and have entered
that woozy state where everything is blissful and Hitler wasn't such a
bad chap after all. When, in the opening sequence of *Good Morning*,
Anne Diamond strode along a high street smiling at traffic wardens,
policemen and just about anyone in uniform, 3 seemed the most
probable explanation.

This preliminary diagnosis was confirmed once the show got under
way. Only people on a pre-med would stare continuously, blankly but

amiably into the camera lens and say 'good morning' forty-two times in the first hour the way Anne and Nick did; presumably this is the special chemistry which they are said to share. At least ITV's husband-and-wife team (Richard and Judy) display a certain naturalness in each other's presence, but the ersatz marriage between Anne and Nick is curiously empty and unconvincing, just a few nervous touches as though they were two first-year university Christian students, keeping themselves pure for Jesus. He's a nice boy. Bit of a card. Probably tells jokes with the occasional 'bloody' in them. Yesterday, they began by discussing the problems of TV personalities getting recognized in public – a difficulty that could never befall them since, clearly, neither possesses a personality.

Daytime shows are the last refuge of psychobabble and pseudo-science, and we soon had both. Robert Holden, 'a stress-buster from the laughter clinic', warned us against 'hurry sickness' (but ran out of time before he could say more), while Lori Reid told us we could discover if we were mentally well-balanced or not by looking at the angle of our thumb, something only the mentally unbalanced would consider doing. But also, on morning TV, you're only ever a minute away from a makeover, so on came a group of fat, butch women rugby players to complain about the way people stereotype women rugby players as fat and butch. A viewer called Christie phoned in simply to tell everyone 'I feel great and sparkling and I'm not on drugs,' so presumably her medication needs changing. Dishy doc Mark Porter did a 'Remember small children can choke on peanuts'-type item; I'm never sure whether that's a warning or a handy hint. Next, the only man ever to be upstaged by a dustbin, Ted Rogers, popped in for coffee. 'Ted's just finished in Cleveland,' Nick told us, although, to be fair, Ted's finished just about everywhere nowadays.

Suddenly, Mr Rogers shouted, 'I'm alternative,' and launched into a dangerously unfunny routine about Cabinet ministers buying packets of three and being 'politically erect': an ignominious spectacle to behold, rather like catching Grandad playing with himself. Someone told us to clean out the budgie's cage, a weatherman said it was cold (so *that's* what was turning the rain white), and two half-baked camp cake makers, Greg and Max, showed us how to ice a heart-shaped sponge; fruit cake might have been more appropriate. When Will

Hanrahan ('TV's Mr Local Radio') and the Felixstowe coffee group climbed into a thirty-eight-ton army tank, crushed a car and claimed, 'We're relieving stress' I confess that something snapped inside me. 'Tanks a lot,' quipped Nick shortly afterwards; 'now, please call us about stress' and, blow me down, I came on. Anne, Nick and Vic. Using the soubriquet Major Finnigan (a tribute to ITV's Judy), I said, 'Hello, do you really think the average housewife, suffering from serious depression, can go about crushing cars with Russian tanks? The only thing that stresses me out is the sight of your inane faces grinning at me every day, and all the off-camera chortling. Can't you put the Test Card and Music on instead?' The pair said nothing, but grinned inanely through clenched teeth, and chortled as I was unceremoniously cut off.

Finally, Lowri Turner, Queen of the Makeover, brought her human fatty Tressie dolls back on. But somehow, the feature missed the point, because it wasn't the guests who needed a complete makeover, but the presenters and production staff. An eighth of the broadcasting day is given over to this meaningless pap, which represents nothing except the world as viewed through the eyes of the nineteen-year-old dizzy ex-Roedean researchers who compile it. Somebody should do for this slot what *The Big Breakfast* did for *Channel 4 Daily*. Now that would be a worthwhile makeover.

Anne Diamond and Nick Owen's solicitor, Ian Bloom, sent me a long letter in which he described my article as intemperate, abusive and defamatory, and pointed out that Anne and Nick are very professional and experienced television presenters. He also sent me a transcript, and berated me for editing and paraphrasing the telephone conversation. Despite seeing these comments written in a document emanating from one of London's leading and reputable firms of solicitors, I still stand by my review, except to concede that, whilst Anne and Nick did not say 'nothing', they said nothing worth repeating. I have the transcript to hand and although I have no permission to reproduce it the copy is held by my publishers for inspection.

The Essential History of Europe: Belgium

I refuse to make old cheap jokes about Belgium. It's just too easy to say that when you book into a Bruges hotel and switch on your electric toothbrush the streetlights dim. Or that Belgium is merely a depot where the French and the Dutch keep their spare citizens. True, perhaps, but far too easy.

It's doubtful whether a series entitled *The Essential History of Europe* needed to devote an entire programme to a region with ten million inhabitants and no sign whatever of national culture or identity. As if trying to compensate for the nothingness of the country, the programme began in outer space, with the opening bars of *Also sprach Zarathustra* triumphantly accompanying recent footage of the first Belgian astronaut (who wears short, white cotton socks). Getting a man into orbit thirty years after everybody else did not seem like much of an achievement to me at first, but then the penny dropped: he is a national hero because the lucky sod managed to get out of the country.

The programme soon nose-dived back to earth, as a couple of Belgian Sealed Knotters, who had turned being herberts into an art form, introduced the history of what is not so much a country as a doormat. Over the centuries, Belgium has been invaded more than three dozen times, by the Romans, French, Germans, Austrians and anyone else looking for a convenient short cut or battlefield. Too small to raise an effective army, the Belgians hit on a novel method of self-defence: they made the place so mind-crashingly dull that before any invader started to do anything *really* unpleasant to the population they lost the will to live and left crestfallen. The defence worked and, even when the Nazis occupied Belgium during the Second World War, the standard torture at the SS concentration camp (called Breendonk – what else?) was, we were told, being swung on a rope with no trousers on.

Once peacetime came, Belgium invited all its neighbours to invade it at once, and has since grown rich as the centre of the European Community, the terminus of the gravy train. A country of Eurocrats and chocolates, so ridiculous that Leon Brittan has chosen to live there, its lack of identity was nicely underlined in a sequence revealing that none of its citizens even knows the national anthem. Although this bland, bourgeois country has produced some memorable visual artists – Magritte, Brueghel, Bosch – their work was a reaction against the soporific dullness of the place; Belgium has not so much produced them as thrown them out, like a body ejecting poison. Baudelaire's description of the place – 'insipid fruit, food, eyes, hair . . . everything is sad, the physiognomy is vague, sombre, unformed, pallid, obscure' – highlighted every Frenchman's worst fear: if they are very bad in this lifetime, they might be forced to come back as Belgians.

This was a heart-warming film for a British audience. Ever since Suez, we have been reduced to a ridiculous insignificant pinprick in western Europe, so it was delightful to see a nation even more ludicrously irrelevant than ourselves. As usual, the direction was superb, the categories neatly delineated and Bernard Hill's narration economical and clear, although it's a pity that he made no mention of Joseph Jongen, former director of the Brussels Conservatoire and possibly the world's dullest composer. But it is not surprising that the programme makers left Belgium until the end of this excellent series. Each film has been made in a way that reflects the identity of the country – France was stylish and pacy, Portugal nostalgic and reflective, Italy loud and passionate – but what can you do with Belgium, except offer a dull, heavy truffle? Although Belgium might like to see itself as the prototype for a united Europe, who would want to give up the glorious pride and folly of being French, Spanish, Italian or British to embrace such wretched drabness?

Forgive me, I cannot resist it any longer:

Q: What goes *bang* (twenty-second pause) *bang* (twenty-second pause) *bang*?

A: A Belgian machine gun.

The Big Breakfast

'Here's *The Big Breakfast* you ordered, sir. Big eggs, big bacon, big sausages. But a word of warning about the mushrooms. They're magic mushrooms, and I'm afraid the next two hours might prove to be a little peculiar, sir.'

Charlie Parsons has done it again. For years, in programmes like *Club X* and *The Word*, he has been allowed to follow his Parson's nose and produce, let us say, somewhat exotic television. Now CH4, having abandoned its hopeless attempt to woo the serious-minded Radio 4 audience away from *Today*, has entrusted its early-morning schedule to his tender mercies, appointing him executive producer of *The Big Breakfast*, two hours of 'in yer face entertainment'.

After a decade of TV-am we have wretchedly low expectations of the breakfast format: the smooth inanity of Mike Morris, the relaxed early-morning 'slow blink' affected by Anne Diamond and her successors, the face-painted gyrating stick insects in body stockings pretending not to be desperate for oxygen, the incessant baby talk, the whole studio resembling an AGM of funeral directors. Now thankfully TV-am is itself almost dead and buried, and CH4 has produced a programme that doesn't have the smell of formaldehyde about it, a show where stasis has become twitch, and where the only baby talk you might hear would be if they decided to deliver one live in the studio, right there – plop – on the breakfast table.

Presenter Chris Evans, with his thick NHS glasses, prominent earpiece and two-shilling haircut, looks like a cross between Eric Morecambe and the boy on the 1950s Dr Barnardo's envelope. Together with Gaby Roslin, they hosted a sort of *Tiswas* for grown-ups, a kedgeree of bizarre, trivial, grotesque and fascinating items: two dogs played the piano; a man on the A58 asked passing motorists to let an accordionist into their car; a woman exhibited a giant hissing cockroach; Brian Gould advised us to strike a match in the lavatory to disperse unpleasant smells; a Liverpudlian policeman was asked to fit a new doorbell; a fountain made entirely from milk bottles was switched on; a woman who had recently set fire to her husband was given a two-minute interview; the Banana Splits appeared, presumably in homage to Janet Street-Porter for whom Bingo is a dead ringer;

a man begged Jeyes to manufacture toilet paper with one side hard and one side soft; and Chris revealed a *Sun* headline about Paula Yates dodging the TV licence, while everyone cheered.

There were more serious moments. Bob Geldof interviewed the Australian PM Paul Keating, who told him, 'I didn't touch her, I was only trying to guide the Queen,' a desperate defence heard all too often nowadays in magistrates' courts throughout the country. It was delightful to see a politician in a $10,000 suit put on the spot by someone resembling a bearded bag lady who had just passed through a wind tunnel, but it also made me realize what millions of women must suffer each morning, waking up next to crumpled hairy wrecks. After his in-depth interview, Paula Yates gave Joanna Lumley an in-shallow probing, and periodically we went to the 'newsroom', apparently a converted wardrobe. How refreshing to see news treated with the contempt it deserves, the joky low-tech credits accompanying each story making it look not so much CNN as ESN. The little toys that always pop out of cereal boxes proved to be a pair of alien puppets, Zig and Zag, two anarchic furballs overdosed on tartrazine, the spitting image of Douglas Hurd and Shirley Williams. They upstaged Evans (no easy feat), ate the cameras, screamed into the lens, and generally stole the show.

Doubtless *TBB* will get a mauling from TV critics, miserable, cranky, difficult swine that they are. But it will survive if it continues to be as inventive and arresting as this. However, Parsons could make room for an additional presenter. How about Frank Bough? Now that would be really perverse.

Budget 93

His critics say that his annual budget performances lack conviction, that he looks increasingly jaded nowadays, and that he ought to go for the sake of the country. But, against all the odds, David Dimbleby somehow manages to cling on to the job, and yesterday presented his fifteenth *Budget* programme to the nation.

As with *Election Special*, what is ostensibly political coverage is really an extended ego trip for the presenters, and the first team were all there yesterday, neat and scrubbed like schoolboys embarking on a day trip: Jay major, Dimbleby minor and the class swot Peter Snow. As usual, Snow had been given the key to the toy cupboard, and was ready to provide instant computer analysis of the sort that so memorably secured a landslide victory for Ross Perot last November. Jabbering and gesticulating like a maniacal cross between Basil Fawlty and Patrick Moore, our Peter was dressed in a jacket and trousers that seemed appropriate for budget day – they screamed out 'panic buy'. Put simply, the man was wearing a *brown suit*. Enough said.

Budget 93 began funereally. No opening credits, no sympathy please, just a coffin-shaped table around which sat the suitably moribund representatives of vested interest – economist, union rep, business director, political analyst – looking like a batch of unreconstructed photofit pictures gathered together to take part in an absurd annual ritual worthy of *Gormenghast*. The clichés came trotting out as neatly as dressage ponies – 'We hope this will be a budget for jobs . . . Government borrowing must be reduced . . . Help for small businesses . . . Must retain the confidence of the City . . .' – filling the traditional hour of speculative foreplay. As usual, any attempt to finish a sentence was interrupted by Dimbleby's periodic cry of 'I must stop you there.' Then, a meaningless shot of a battered red box held aloft. 'That's the budget box, now let's see the PM leaving number ten,' said our anchorman and, for reasons that he never adequately explained, through the door walked a black man with a cellphone trailed by someone holding a pot of builder's putty. Then back to the studio, and more irrelevant conjecture about what we might soon hear. 'I must stop you there . . . we're going over now to the floor of the House.'

'Green shoots . . . blah blah . . . most vulnerable members of society blah . . . implementation . . . blah . . . closing the GDP gap . . . blah . . . I therefore propose . . . blah . . .' On and on went our beloved Norman, rearranging the deck chairs on the *Titanic*. And when it was all over, Dimbleby told us that it was the longest budget speech by a chancellor since the last longest budget speech, and asked his guests for their reaction: 'a missed opportunity', 'got it just about right', 'political time bomb', 'the man's a genuis'. Peter Jay said that the budget details were all precisely as he had forecast them, although curiously he hadn't shared those details with his audience beforehand.

'I must stop you there, we're going over to Westminster.' Beneath Big Ben, politicians debated what you should or should not do to green shoots, as though this were *Gardeners' Question Time*, while a disaffected youth made his hardy-annual V sign behind their backs. Back in the studio, Peter Snow had had his playtime cut short by the Chancellor's verbosity, but still managed to demonstrate graphically that a couple earning £100,000 a year would be 48p a week better off. The champagne corks must have been popping all over the stockbroker belt last night.

Like that other meaningless ritual, the Boat Race, the ceremony surrounding the budget is a quaint relic of a bygone era. The obsession with the price of those traditional proletarian staples, beer and fags, seems a little patronizing in an age when the average working man is more interested in the implications for his mortgage and pension fund, and the unemployed are more bothered about their prospects of getting a job. This year, the presenters seemed tired and lacklustre, with the exception of Snow who rattled on regardless. But even he only truly reaches his peak during an all-nighter, when the combination of lack of sleep and information overload finally unhinge him.

Oddest of all, the budget was running on two channels, yet I'll bet nobody was watching. They were all queuing up outside petrol stations to beat the six o'clock price hike. Oh dear, I'm sorry, we've run out of time – I'll have to stop me there.

Without Walls: Good Morning Mr Hitler

Those of us whose earliest TV memories are black and white will remember the impact of going to the cinema and seeing the Daleks for the first time in colour on the big screen. Red, blue and gold, with amber blinkers, they were larger than ever, yet somehow lacked the menace of their monochrome siblings; in breathtaking but tell-tale colour, you could plainly see they were nothing more than a collection of spare parts from a Morris Minor (indicators included).

On last night's *Without Walls*, another would-be master race suddenly burst into colour, thanks to some recently discovered amateur footage of the Führer. Six years before Herr Schickelgruber decided to ventilate his head the man's way, Hans Feierabend had shot him on celluloid at a Munich arts festival, visiting a vast exhibition at the newly built Haus der Kunst; but unlike Goebbels, who never permitted a moment's informality to soften the official black-and-white propaganda films, *Good Morning Mr Hitler* captured the Third Reich in relaxed mood, a sea of unnerving brown uniforms, blonde women, golden eagles and red swastika flags. Feierabend, who belonged to the local film club, had obtained a security pass permitting him to shoot the Nazi hierarchy from close range. He was an orthopaedic technician by trade and, as his camera dwelt on the leadership – Goebbels with his club foot, Adolf Wagner with his wooden leg, Hitler minus a testicle and Hess clearly missing something up top – the suspicion grew that his interest in them was perhaps more prosthetic than aesthetic.

The film itself was fascinating, but unfortunately there wasn't very much of it. So, to eke out fifteen minutes of original footage, a clutch of blue-rinsed Teutonic biddies (who had once been peripherally involved with the Nazis) were invited to watch and reminisce. Their contribution was an unfocused, slightly macabre commentary on these Aryan home movies: 'There's Goebbels, he was charming . . . that's Minister Wagner, what a womanizer . . . Hitler used to come over for tea; we'd never say "Heil mein Führer," always "Good-morning, Mr Hitler."' One woman, asked why Hitler had organized this colossal festival, won the award for understatement: 'Well . . . he was a bit power-crazy.' Ilse Müller, whose father had published *Mein Kampf*, was questioned about the Jews, and didn't seem to have learned much from the Holocaust: 'I suppose we didn't take enough interest, because, of course, there are some very decent Jews.' Charlotte Knobloch (of the Munich Jewish Cultural Association) looked on in fascinated horror at the sumptuous processions, unaware that such things had ever taken place; in 1939, the Jews were all either in hiding, or crammed into the concentration camp at Dachau, only a few miles outside the city.

Feierabend had captured some extraordinary moments. The final pageant – a celebration of two thousand years of German culture with thousands of Nordic maidens and medieval knights on horseback –

was as huge as it was ludicrous, like a Cecil B. de Mille remake of *Die Walküre*; such an over-the-top spectacle could appeal only to the very lowest taste, but then that was just what the Führer intended. It was odd to observe Hitler speaking in a controlled, rational voice, rather than the ranting scream we are accustomed to hearing; usually it suits us to depict evil men as raving monsters too. Odder still, we learned that Hitler and Chaplin were born on the same day, and that Adolf decided on his moustache after watching one of Charlie's films during World War One.

The programme was nearly a fascinating glimpse of Fascism as the aestheticization of politics, but turned out to be televisual meat loaf: too much bland extender and not enough real substance. With a brief introduction the archive material could have stood alone, without continual interruptions from elderly, equivocating talking heads making the obligatory 'We didn't know what was going on' noises. The use of Mahler and Bach gave exactly the right tone of ominous grandeur to the footage, but the additional score from Rosalie Coopman and a bank of synthesizers was unnecessary and unimaginative. As for the tricky problem of what to do with the surviving legacy of Nazi art, the question was raised but not resolved. Display it and risk exciting the neo-Nazis? Store it unseen for decades at great expense (the current policy)? Or commit the ultimate irony and destroy the lot, condemning it as diseased?

The Haus der Kunst is a disco now, and the only pure Nordic art you'll find there is a copy of *Abba's Greatest Hits*. So much for a Reich that would last a thousand years.

Choir of the Year

Being 'in a kwa' is a medical disability affecting many middle-aged, middle-class people, usually from the Home Counties. First symptoms include dressing like librarians and attending Richard Baker musical evenings at the town hall, but those with the full-blown virus soon experience an overwhelming urge to head for cold, damp church halls and perform four-part cacophony and distant-harmony singing in them. A unique feature of the disease is that the patients themselves do not seem to suffer, although anyone unfortunate enough to be in the audience almost certainly does.

As part of the government's new emphasis on care in the community, BBC2 has been running a Choir of the Year competition, where kwas can find mutual support and understanding among others of their own kind. The typical mixed amateur kwa works on a very simple premise. First, a 'dishy' male conductor is appointed; his presence tempts numerous prissy women with floral frocks and Esther Rantzen teeth to join the kwa, whereupon a lot of bearded men with velvet jackets and dandruff also sign up. The kwa meets once a week, and soon becomes a hotbed of unrequited passion which, in theory, the conductor can channel into the music. Unfortunately, as we discovered during last night's quarter-final, the theory breaks down at this point and the performances usually remain as flat as pancakes.

The likeable Howard Goodall introduced the programme, standing in front of a set that resembled the façade of a heavily bombed 1920s tube station. Two separate competitions were being held in tandem, one for youth kwas, the other for adults. The kids performed delightfully and enthusiastically on behalf of their schools, and any technical shortcomings could be forgiven since you knew that, before long, they'd either get better or give up. But it soon became clear that this was as good as the adult kwas would ever get, and that they are destined to wallow in mediocrity for all eternity, never improving, but probably never having the sense to pack it in. Surrey Harmony were a female barbershop chorus and, as you would expect from the name, they had soon turned their dressing room into a barbershop, with curling tongs and heated rollers being expertly applied. Sadly, no such expertise showed in their rendition of 'Old Man River', which sounded like an indifferent male barbershop ensemble on helium. Meanwhile, the Oxford Pro Musica Singers' twee version of 'Go Take a Train' totally failed in its attempt to capture the mood of a late-night jazz club: they sounded not so much like people who go to all the hip joints, more like the sort of people who might have plastic ones fitted.

The organizers' insistence on theatrical gestures and 'amusing' performances is sadly misguided, and trivializes choral singing, which should be about perfection of sound, not appearance or facile choreography. It is all part of the current insidious Nigel Kennedyization of

classical music, which has now reached the point where basic technique and serious performance are being sacrificed for image and
novelty. The programme makers seemed to have little confidence in
the performances, constantly interrupting them with irrelevant, be-
hind-the-scenes items that marginalized the music and prevented us
from ever hearing a complete piece. There were some fine moments
– Farnham Youth Choir's Pergolesi (conducted by the almost perfectly named David Victor-Smith) was controlled and assured, and
South Hampstead High School brought off an excellent but difficult
piece by Nicholas Maw with panache and style – but the programme
was preoccupied with the competition, and insufficiently interested
in performances.

The overall winners (who will presumably each win a pair of
overalls) will not be announced until next month. However, one of
the judges, David Thomas, has already won my award for Most
Hogwash in a Single Soundbite, for his statement that 'Communication is the most important thing, even if it is at the expense of
technique.' Fine sentiments, except for one thing: without technique,
there are no means of communication.

Beadle's About

Is there any indignity that people will not submit to, so long as it
guarantees them admission into the magic rectangle? I doubt it. Only
recently I witnessed a people programme on US TV which featured a
sad case called Mr Mazzeo. The man was so desperate to appear that
he was prepared to set light to his own genitals in the studio, holding
a pan above them and frying an egg sunny-side-up while singing, 'I
don't want to set the world on fire.' Bet he was a laugh a minute in the
burns unit.

But for really thorough bottom-of-the-barrel-scraping, you need
look no further than *Beadle's About*, with its low-budget set, its no-
budget titles and a sig tune so crass that even Chas 'n' Dave would
consider it a touch plebeian. A fitting introduction indeed for Mr
Beadle, a man with a truly marvellous insignificance, part Seymour
Bunz, part human oil slick, decanted into a double-breasted suit to

match his double chins, with a synthetic smile to match the synthetic laugh track that greets his every feeble pun. Wherever there's alliteration there's usually an illiterate and, sure enough, the great man was soon inviting us to 'tickle yourself with tonight's top treats'.

The top treats that followed – low on wit, high on sadism – could best be summarized under the collective heading 'A Group of Burly Men Intimidating a Lone Woman'. Michelle, delighted to be attending her first day of work at a hair-restoration clinic, applied lotion to three men's heads. They left, had their heads promptly shaved, then returned and claimed their hair had spontaneously fallen out, shouting abuse at the (obviously distressed) girl while she tried to protest her innocence. 'What a hair-raising experience,' squelched Jeremy, telling Michelle she was 'just wonderful' before dispatching her back to join the other three million on the dole queue from which she presumably thought she'd just escaped. Then to Hythe for more shouting men and a girl. Here, a group of bogus council workmen removed the shop sign from Sally's bakery, trespassing on her property and harassing her until she was reduced to screaming profanities at them. Back in the studio Mr Beadle told us, 'Sadly, Sally can't be with us tonight'; he might have added, 'But luckily we got her to sign the release form while she was still in a state of shock – never fails.'

Finally, we had a real-life Sharon and Tracy, the former with a passion for showbiz celebs. Consequently she had no problem with Jeremy, but there was 'hell toupee' in a wig shop where Sharon sold the wrong rugs and then had to field telephone calls from Terry Wogan, Bruce Forsyth, Ronald Reagan, Prince Charles, John Major and Michael Caine, all made within three minutes by a man whose impersonations were slightly less convincing than Elton John's fringe. Some might have called this stretching a joke, but there was no joke to stretch. Sharon was obviously well aware that this was a feeble prank, the obvious line 'Am I on *Beadle's About*?' appeared to have been cut from the final tape and anyone who thought that what they were watching wasn't faked probably believes that the enthusiastic orgasm of a Soho prostitute is genuine too. But then that's precisely the same audience that this show caters for. So, no surprises there.

It's fake. All fake, from the implausible set-ups and the post-production re-reaction shots to the unconvincing acting and the canned laughter. Fakest of all are the targets of the japes. Expose a few con-men, pederastic vicars, bent High Court judges – that would make great and worthy TV. But, of course, such people are professionals and have access to lawyers, so they are best left well alone by TV companies. Better by far to pick on the uneducated and the credulous. It's the same fertile soil that has been ploughed for years by Esther Rantzen in *That's Life!* and Noel Edmonds in *House Party*.

The remedy is in our hands. At the end of the show, Mr Beadle told us, 'Remember, we couldn't make the show without your help.' Readers of the world unite. As Karl Marx nearly said, we have nothing to lose but our brains.

Hale and Pace

The matching pair of ancient Greek masks, Tragedy and Comedy, together form the world's oldest double act. Yet their close similarity is seldom appreciated by television executives, who recognize tragedy as a rare and precious art form, but assume that comedy can be produced as easily as turning on a tap. Every year, they ask their Light Entertainment departments for more and more programmes to fill the schedules, in the belief that jokes can be endlessly hammered out, just like any other consumer durable. But, inevitably, what these joke departments produce is chiefly tragedy, and their jokesmiths turn out mostly rusty old clangers.

As far as I know, Hale and Pace are the world's only double act consisting of two straight men, and LWT's joke department should, by rights, face immediate prosecution under the Trade Descriptions Act (1972). Back for a seventh series, Gareth (the unfunny one with the moustache) and Norman (the unfunny one without the moustache) brought a curiously stunted, adolescent atmosphere to the screen last night, as they embarked on yet another half-hour of random, puerile references to sex, without a genuine comedic target in sight. Within seconds we were hearing about Hale's homosexual lover, and how Hale had screwed Pace's wife and granny, followed by references to 'dogs licking their cobblers . . . toss pot . . . prick . . . wank', and even a comparison of penis sizes. As for a sketch which included the exchange 'U is the twenty-first letter of the alphabet,' 'Well, *ewe* is a sheep, baa,' 'Well, *you* have got so much cheek you could be Roseanne Barr's arse,' I can only bow my head in shame and embarrassment.

Following the tiresome fashion of recent sketch series, the show was peppered with one-dimensional Viz-style caricatures, such as 'The Sports Mad Dads' ('My son's got a bigger todger than yours') and 'Sven and Benny, the Sauna-loving Swedes' ('Great big sexy dildo vibrators'). Not remotely funny, but never mind because, as always, Hale and Pace augmented the skits with their limited range of facial expressions – the quizzical gaze, the cross-eyed stare, the grimace – which they used as a substitute for comedic invention (in the same way that R1 disc jockeys still point at records whenever they're having their photo taken). But that was hardly surprising, when one of the sketches (which, they proudly announced at the start of the series, were almost entirely of their own invention) spent two tedious minutes discussing canine *haute couture*, just so the title 'Doggie Fashion' could be flashed on screen. These were scripts so thin that even Kate Moss would think them anorexic.

Hale and Pace regularly claim to be 'pushing back the boundaries of comedy', but their targets, on those rare occasions when they focused on anything at all, were invariably as weak as kittens (indeed, kittens in microwaves are something of a speciality for this pair). Every imbecile long ago noticed Sister Wendy's buck teeth and Chris Eubank's idiosyncratic speech, so that's presumably why Hale and Pace highlighted them. As for a parody of *Oliver*, and an embarrassed father explaining the facts of life to his son, these targets were expertly dealt with thirty years ago, and have long since been obsolete. Most sketches just petered out inconsequentially but, when there was a punchline, it was so clumsily and laboriously set up that you could almost imagine Tonto with his ear to the ground, telling the Lone Ranger: 'Two white men come with pay-off, Kemu Sabi. Long way away. Here in ten minutes.'

I'm all in favour of vulgarity (be it Rabelais or Rab C Nesbitt) but let's have a little wit with our smut, not this brainless, adolescent, nervous tittering, born of sexual inadequacy and (I presume) uncertain sexual orientation – the type, in fact, one might hear at (I also presume) a pornographic movie. There may have been a live studio audience for the show, but it was clearly embarrassed to be there because a hysterical, desperately over-processed laugh track had obviously been dubbed on afterwards, and executive producer John Kaye Cooper must feel immensely proud of this plucky attempt to turn television into the lava lamp of the 90s. The only consolation is that, if these two ex-teacher-training college students weren't on the box, they'd now be instructing our kids in the GCSE syllabus, so things could be worse. Marginally.

Coincidentally, I was rummaging through an old tea chest the other day, and I found a torn yellowing fragment of this very newspaper, containing the beginning of a three-year-old review by my distinguished and perspicacious predecessor, Jaci Stephens. 'Anyone who does not think Hale and Pace are hilarious', it read, 'must be a) thick, b) brain-dead, or c) stupid.' If I'd been her, and a sub-editor had added a 'not' to my review like that, I'd have sued.

Sykes

It's a peculiarity of our education system that, although colleges teach hundreds of subjects for which there aren't any jobs, not one offers a course in the art of comedy. Television channels commission hundreds of situation comedies each year, most of which turn out as situation tragedies because the writers have never learned their craft. Meanwhile, the media are full of imbeciles claiming that 'Comedy is the new rock and roll,' although most performers are one-chord wonders who clearly couldn't pass their comedic Grade 1. Can't some rich philanthropist step forward and endow a comedy college? I've already got the Latin motto: *Per ardua ad risum.*

I've found our chancellor too. Eric Sykes. While Benny Hill, Tommy Cooper and Eric Morecambe are belatedly acknowledged as geniuses, we all seem to overlook the genius still among us, but the daily repeats of *Sykes* on UK Gold, introduced by the brass band and the big bass drum, confirm his status as one of the comedy greats. Beginning in 1960, and continuing until the death of Hattie Jacques in 1980, his shows always had a strangeness and absurd innocence that set them apart from others of the period and, a generation later, they still stand up extremely well (certainly far better than the walls of the ultra-cheap BBC set, which wobble whenever a door is slammed). Some of the jokes are so old that they can barely stand either, but they're only old because they're good, and Sykes uses them to brilliant effect. Blending Christmas-cracker gags with farce and slapstick, he gently undermines the cosy domestic world with a manic streak of logic, and ultimately produces that rarest of hybrids: a surreal sit-com that's actually funny.

Last night's archive episode began harmlessly enough, with Eric and Hattie visiting Mrs Rumbelow, their cello-playing neighbour, to use her bath. Hattie listened politely to a dreadful rendition of the 'Dying Swan' (no mystery about who the murderer was), answering the query 'Did you recognize it?' with 'Oh yes, it's a cello,' and mentioning that 'Eric was at the Royal College of Music for two years, you know . . . he was the caretaker' (I told you the gags were old). Meanwhile, Eric was upstairs in the bath and in his element, surrounded by plastic boats and planes, reconstructing the Battle of the River Plate, the Battle of Jutland, 'and, when the water gets cold, it's the Russian Convoys'. A one-man com ᵤₜ zone, he strafed, bombed, mined, torpedoed and sank himself, even giving us a Churchillian victory speech into the bargain, in a brilliant tour de farce.

Then, like a thread coming loose, Eric's world started to unravel, and he began deconstructing the genre, years before Derrida had even thought of such a thing. A toe stuck in a tap may be an old routine, but this resulted in an official warning for parking a bath on a double yellow line. Downstairs, Hattie predictably sat on the cello, but her hopeful, hopeless attempt to sellotape it back together again – 'There, I think that's as good as new' – was the stroke of brilliance. And in Casualty, there was an epidemic of people getting stuck in things (a classic English obsession), one man turning up with a silver chamber-pot rammed down over his eyes. 'Ever had one of these on your head?' 'No.' 'You've missed nothing, mate.'

The main performances were quirky and spectacular, especially Deryck Guyler as the benign PC Corky, asking Eric to help him out: 'Go on, let me arrest you. We've got a new inspector, he wants plenty of arrests . . . you could get off with a caution.' Even the minor characters' fluffs only added to the charm of a show apparently recorded in a single take, without pauses or retakes. As for Sykes, almost stone deaf, his timing still knocked spots off most of today's performers. Given the dismal state of most present-day comedy, I find myself subsisting more and more on UK Gold's diet of tried and tested comedies (what could be funnier than the nightly reruns of DLT on *Top of the Pops?*) not seen for many years on the major networks. Of course, not all 60s and 70s comedy was as good as *Sykes* – *Mind Your Language* and *On the Buses* disprove that contention – but so far the station is successfully winnowing the gold from the dross. The funniest thing of all is that, while terrestrial channels spend fortunes commissioning new comedies, which are mostly stale before they hit the airwaves, UK Gold pays considerably less to transmit old shows which, by and large, remain as fresh as the moment they were first broadcast. If I were them, I'd be laughing my socks off, twenty-four hours a day.

Go Fishing

A curious station, Anglia. Like something out of *Awakenings*, it slumbered quietly for decades, suddenly went berserk with the gaudy razzmatazz of *Sale of the Century* in the 1970s, and then fell asleep again. Its rare contributions to the network usually involve dumb animals – cows, pigs, sheep, Nicholas Parsons – and its excellent *Survival* documentaries ensure the station's own survival at each franchise renewal. It somehow seems right and proper then that the angling series *Go Fishing* should be made by Anglia.

In last night's opening titles, an animated Colossus strode purposefully around the globe: Africa, the Pacific, the Great Lakes, all manner of exotic locations for the series were hinted at. But then, just fancy, we homed in on a road map of Norwich (which just happens to be Anglia's home town). Worse, we were greeted by an unnamed bearded gentleman (let's call him Herbert) dressed in the sort of Army surplus clothing favoured by people who 'honestly can't remember what happened' when they are arrested with a smoking gun in their hands, surrounded by scenes of carnage. All became clear. The programme's budget was low, and a drawing of Africa was the best we could expect. It was so low, in fact, that the entire thing was going to be shot in

Herbert's back garden, and promised to be as dull as ditchwater.

The ditchwater running into Herbert's private pond was extremely dull, the colour of thin pea soup, and therein lay the show's major problem. Anglia couldn't afford expensive underwater cameras, and your average fish is notoriously reluctant to venture above the murky surface of its pond. So, naturally, Herbert didn't talk to us about fish at all, but instead catalogued all the wild flowers in the vicinity, 'betony, dandelions, lilies, lovely yellow irises', while a pianist who had just discovered the glories of the interrupted cadence played a crass version of 'English Country Garden'. Herbert also showed us his collection of trees – unremarkable clumps of willows, conifers and poplars – but he remained by far the most wooden thing on screen. Blow me, ten minutes in he began talking about the dreadful weather we'd been having lately, and there was still no sign of a fish. An awful thought struck me: perhaps he hadn't really got any fish, and was stalling.

Finally he set about catching some carp, explaining the complex procedure to us in minute detail: 'I'm using this, it's a hook on a line.' Armed with trout pellets, a catapult, a landing net and a huge rod with a clutch-action reel, you somehow couldn't help admiring the sight of a twelve-stone man preparing to engage in mortal combat with a two-pound fish. Very Ernest Hemingway. For ages, very little happened but then suddenly, there it was. Nothing. Just a bit of splashing beneath the pea-green surface. After a lot of thrashing, Herbert landed his catch: some algae, half a dozen lilies, and not a carp but a catfish which he proudly held up to the camera. This was one of the ugliest specimens I've seen on British TV for some time, all gaping mouth, glassy eyes and dripping whiskers. The fish wasn't too pretty either.

After six hours, I checked the scheduling in the *Radio Times*. Yes, this was only a half-hour programme, but somehow it was managing to convey the full tedium of a day wasted on a riverbank, and was making Warhol's *Empire State Building* look like a Spielberg movie. 'It's quite hot,' the lanky Herbert told us, standing right at the water's edge, 'we've had a drought in Norfolk, the water level is two foot below where it should be.' I disagreed. The water level was precisely six foot two inches below where it should have been.

Eventually Herbert (whom the end credits identified as John

Wilson) caught his fish and said goodbye. I'm not one to carp, but let's put it this way: if I ever found myself sitting opposite him on the Edinburgh-bound train, I'd pull the communication cord and jump off by Finsbury Park. It was all pretty enough – although it would have looked so much better on film than on video – but who is the programme for? Surely fishermen would rather do it than watch it? As for me, I prefer my fish on a plate at Manzi's, where I insist on selecting my own whitebait from a tank: 'I'll have that one . . . and that one . . . and that one . . .'

CountryFile

For many years, television has had its very own Bermuda Triangle, a place where, once presenters enter, they are inexplicably never heard of again. It's called daytime Sunday scheduling, a luckless region of worthy programmes inhabited by past-tense people whose faces stare helplessly out from the screen.

CountryFile's presenter John Craven still manages to retain his old *Newsround* sang-froid. He is now, paradoxically, both much greyer and much greener than before, resplendent in a Barbour and wellies, but underneath he still sports a smart and ridiculous woolly jumper, a legacy of his glory days. Yesterday, the opening rural headlines were introduced by thunderous stings (complete with urgent tickertape effects) as forceful and imposing as *News at Ten*'s bongs. And there were thundering stories to match: 'Sheep scab on the increase . . . we have pictures' (tickety-tick-tick); 'Potato sorters demand pay increase' (tickety-tick-tick); and 'Ducks may have to be culled' (tickety-tick-quack).

If wide-screen television pictures were being transmitted, then Libby Purves would have been the logical choice to present the first item. Instead a considerably slimmer (but equally gung-ho) *doppelgänger* in regulation Barbour and wellies shouted at us in a hurdy-gurdy of a voice about a topic on which she was extremely well-informed: not stupid old cows, as I had first suspected, but male fish that have been changing sex. This phenomenon was first noticed by Essex fisherfolk, although why these solitary gentlemen should have been taking such a keen interest in the genitalia of trout was never satisfactorily explained. With all the portentousness of Gavin Esler reporting on the situation in Bosnia, she bellowed at us that our rivers are becoming brim- full of transvestite fish. Presumably, at this very moment, there are camp salmon swimming up the Thames, desperate to slip into a pair of fishnets. Liana Stupples, a Friend of the Earth with a voice so dull that I suspect the earth pretends it's out whenever she calls by, came on and blamed micro-pollutants, and a scientist said it was all caused by the faeces of women on the Pill introducing ethinyloestradiol into the rivers via sewage outlets. Strangely, I can't remember Joe Grundy and Clarrie discussing this one on *The Archers* lately.

Until yesterday, a 'Big Green One' was something I had only heard (and seen hanging) from the lips of Glaswegian gentlemen who loiter around King's Cross Station. But these Big Green Ones turned out to be yet more absurd environmental media awards for any kids green enough to compete for them. Finally, we went off to France, to interview a local entrepreneur who has been making a small fortune out of selling bonsai vines to the Japanese; this section may have been only three minutes long, but it gave a better insight into the French mentality that all twelve episodes of *A Year of Xenophobia in Provence* are likely to achieve.

The bonsai vine would be an appropriate emblem for this bonsai programme, with its small budget and its small issues. It's unclear what audience it is aimed at and, if anyone investigated, I fear they would find that the show is really the urban middleclass talking to itself. It's hard to imagine that any farmer is going to tune in on his one day off; no, he's seen quite enough thank you and will be feet up, teeth out, watching the footer. *CountryFile* conforms to the folk myth of rural England, all Constable's babbling brooks and Wordsworth's hosts of daffs, when the reality is grinding poverty, solitude and suicide, with a few gentlemen farmers creaming off a fortune while claiming, 'I'm as poor as a church mouse.' This is the countryside as viewed by people 'gone bush' – Shepherd's Bush – misty-eyed townspeople, who'd like to move out there if only it weren't so damned primitive; if genuine country folk were involved, it would be one long paean of praise to the city.

As the credits rolled, I dozed off and had a strange dream in which the Wessex Young Farmers Dyslexic Group came on and sang, 'Old MacDonald had a farm, L, M, L, M, X.' Does odd things to the imagination, daytime Sunday TV.

Open Space: Full Frontal

It's always amateurs that spoil things for everyone else. Amateur musicians who can't play in tune. Amateur drunks who can't hold their booze on New Year's Eve. And amateur nudists, those portly, middle-aged men and women who insist that the body is the temple of the soul, even though theirs resembles the Ayodhya mosque as of last Wednesday. On *Full Frontal*, it was wobbly-jelly time again as Sue Piper of British Naturism introduced a sad pageant of sagging buttocks, wrinkled bellies and pointed floppies obeying gravity by drooping down to the navel. It was a sight to make you wish that the Corby Trouser Press people would invent a model for humans.

As I watched, I regressed back to my sniggering schooldays, fully expecting a smack round the back of the head for impudence: 'Grow up, boy, it's perfectly natural, nothing to laugh at.' But, clearly, I have refused to grow up, and carry on sniggering at the naked snooker, the naked ping-pong and the naked exhibitionism of these people who have so much to cover up, yet rush to bare all for the cameras whenever a crew turns up. And why not? We laugh at people in ill-fitting clothes because they look absurd, and the effect of ill-fitting skin is equally ridiculous.

Piper, a human oxymoron sitting gloriously, ridiculously naked in a heavily-clad chintz armchair, told us that 'Nudity is, after all, my natural state,' although her flat, monotonous presentation suggested her natural state might really be a coma. She was puzzled that 'Naturism is always being made a figure for comedy,' but the people she introduced us to gave us a thousand reasons to laugh. One by one they quivered by, tubs of lard encased within acres of gooseflesh, shrivelled genitalia swinging like pendulums on miniature grandfather clocks, varicose veins bulging red and blue on legs that looked like road maps of Italy. They fixed a false smile as they volleyballed, cooked sausages and frolicked (never any light engineering, accordion or chainsaw work) and proved the truth of the old adage about nude dancing. Not everything stops when the music stops.

Oddly, the least flabby couple made the most unpleasant viewing: Caroline and Christian Knott, the reincarnation of Keith Pratt and Candice Marie. Arrogant, self-assured and self-deluded. My spirits sagged when she told us that 'Naturism is a way of being able to see that everyone is unique, but everyone is the same,' something that did not seem to me to justify the annual subscription. She barked while he listened obediently – it was clear who didn't wear the trousers in *their* house. Then . . . it happened.

Eleven minutes in, somebody said (as they always do in naturist films), 'All this nudity . . . it's not at all sexual, you know.' Is that something to celebrate? What an appalling state of affairs. Most of us are capable, on occasion, of finding erotic stimuli in a queue at the post office, and for a group of people, naked or not, to be in a permanent state of non-arousal suggests that something is seriously amiss. Frankly, open day down at Deptford Crematorium sounds a more stimulating prospect than joining in with this lifeless, detumescent cultish bunch.

There was some wonderful private archive footage of the Speilplatz naturist club taken in the 1930s, with the quaintly pagan avant-garde having the decency to keep their eccentricity to themselves. And the clips from the 1958 film *Travelling Light* (which ran for eight months in cinemas throughout a sex-starved, pre-*Lady Chatterley* Britain, and deserves to be shown again in its entirety) were a pure delight. But overall the programme was tired *Health and Efficiency* stuff, a marriage of insane exhibitionists and prurient producers who like to get a bit of sanitized rumpy-pumpy past the Board of Governors. Still, at least Jeremy Gibson's Community Programme Unit produced an excellently shot programme, with a fine (uncredited) score.

I remain unconvinced by the challenge of naturism and shall continue to trust my initial schoolboy response. One obese, unlovely gentleman haughtily announced, 'I think some people are frightened of their own bodies.' The truth is, me old cock, they are frightened of *yours*.

Bobby Davro: Rock with Laughter

I've said it before, but I'll say it again. If the likes of Bobby Davro are really so desperate to see themselves on TV, then can they please just go and stand outside Dixons shop window? That way, the rest of us would not have to endure the weekly sight of this overgrown, hyperactive show-off of a schoolboy making desperate and futile bids for adult attention.

When a performer utters the ellipsis 'laygennlemen', you know you've strayed into lumpen territory, but *Rock with Laughter* takes you further, deep into previously uncharted regions of imbecility. Other 'artistes' have a discreet cross or mark on which to stand, but Mr Davro clearly requires something less subtle – a twelve-foot circle with his name emblazoned across it – from which to announce that the theme of the show was 'Saturday night'. Inexplicably, he then promptly launched into a routine about fighting: 'Me dad was a boxer . . . and me mum was a whippet.' He followed this up with a thoroughly patronizing impersonation of a pidgin-speaking West Indian, which he claimed was Chris Eubank, although Eubank's diction and syntax are, in fact, vastly superior to Mr Davro's. If he must imitate boxers, why doesn't he stick to Michael Watson? He could do him without trying.

For thirty minutes there was non-stop laughter, all of it coming from Mr Davro who corpsed continuously, as befitted a man dying on stage. He joined The Grumbleweeds (world-famous in Manchester) for an interminable sketch about beer, and was so amused by the line 'Me mouf's as dry as a camel's jock strap' that he was unable to continue for some time. Perhaps the cause was desperation, fear or self-indulgence, but more probably he was simply overcome with laughter at the thought that the BBC was actually going to pay him for this dire performance. And still no sign of anything to do with Saturday night. Next, he donned a bald wig and impersonated Right Said Fred, giggling uncontrollably as he sang 'Shave Your Head', and not waving but drowning. Presumably that's why Duncan Goodhew had been booked to partner him; only such a strong swimmer could survive.

Wafts of formaldehyde filled the studio as The Grumbleweeds returned with a Bee Gees *Night Fever* routine, already stale in 1978, interspersed with fossilized topical gags. You could imagine the boys in rehearsal, taking a pencil to the yellowing pages of their script, crossing out the word 'Callaghan' and substituting 'Major'. After one punchline – 'I drive a pantry ... no, it's a Lada' – I looked at the list of scriptwriters, and saw mention of a Mr Simple. Need I say more? Mr Davro slapped on another bald wig and tried to 'do' Victor Meldrew, which is not unlike watching Douglas Bader trying to 'do' Fred Astaire. At one point we even saw a Japanese soldier who 'didn't know the war was over'; it must be fully twenty years since that gag last saw active service. Finally, still sticking to the Saturday-night theme, several roller-skating men in tights did a low-budget version of *Starlight Express*, while Mr Davro (dressed as Ringo Starr during the *Sergeant Pepper* era) told Thomas the Tank Engine stories, queer jokes of the '"Poof poof," said the little gay engine, "I've got a tender behind"' sort. The entire production team must be very proud of itself.

Don't get me wrong. I like non-PC jokes. Offend them all, regardless of race, creed, colour, sex or species, that's my motto. When comedy works, it's usually cruel, but what it should never be is infantile. Contestants in pub talent nights perform dated material and do lousy impersonations because they don't know any better, but to allow such bilge on to TV is an insult to the audience. This series, commissioned before Jim Moir's departure, has been the last feeble gasp of the old Light Entertainment guard at BBC1. Thankfully, I can't see this, or anything remotely like it, getting back on air. Ever.

Mr Davro saved his very best performance for last: he portrayed someone who could not sing, performing a soulful, doleful, send-in-the-clowns, deep-down-I'm-sensitive song. Ironically, this was the funniest thing in the show. As the credits rolled, I decided to phone the BBC to enquire who was responsible for the show, and whether they were, perhaps, unwell. 'Head of Variety,' the switchboard told me. 'Can you put me through to him?' 'I'm sorry, we don't have one at the moment.' Now there's a funny thing, laygennlemen.

Rab C Nesbitt

For decades, BBC Scotland has been synonymous with bland, anodyne, inoffensive humour. So much so that I admit to having felt an
uneasy sense of relief when I learned that the man who used to die on
our screens each Hogmanay while hosting the inane White Heather
Club and singing 'Donald Where's Yer Troosers' had recently died on
a permanent basis. At a time when even Billy Connolly has sanitized
his act and taken to dining with the Royals, only *Rab C Nesbitt*
provides a suitable antidote.

Rab C Nesbitt. Say it loud and there's music playing, say it soft and
it's almost like praying. With his fetid, griseous string vest, his pallid
complexion and his dishevelled graveyard brown teeth – eloquent
testimony to the virtues of the Glaswegian diet – the King of Giro
Valley is a celebration of all that is vile, disgusting and honest in
Scottish life, and a powerful reason why scientists must never be
allowed to develop smellyvision. When Glasgow was busy marketing
itself as the European City of Culture, you can be sure that the only
culture to be found chez Nesbitt was the green stuff growing inside the
fridge of his Govan slum. Gregor Fisher's *alter ego* first assaulted our
screens as a lone drunken philosopher, raging briefly and incoherently
into the ether, but when he acquired his own full-length show he also
acquired a wife (Mary), two kids and a modicum of sensitivity.
However last night, from the moment that Nesbitt minor stuck his
chip into his brother's ear for flavouring before eating it, it was clear
what sort of a family we were dealing with; this was sit-com, Hieronymus
Bosch-style.

The first programme of series three found Mary (not so much a
peroxide as a Domestos blonde) languishing in the intensive-care
ward of a Glasgow hospital. She was suffering from acute peritonitis,
but an even worse pain was the insufferably prim Mrs Monteith in the
next bed, a 'pucker-mouthed, scrag-necked old bitch' forever reading
The People's Friend. Her bottle of Lucozade and Mary's bottle of Tizer
neatly summarized the unbridgeable gulf between their classes, as did
the consultant's diagnosis that 'In Govan, until something actually
turns black and drops off, they think it's bad form to bother the doctor.'
Meanwhile, Rab was walking the beaches of Blackpool with his

motley progeny – 'Blackpool is LA for scum' – too anxious even to
drink, while a friend tried to raise his spirits with some macabre Govan
humour: 'The Lord giveth and the Lord taketh away – your wife's
critical but, on the other hand, you won a table lamp at bingo.'

Suffering from the heady effects of sobriety, Rab began an unlikely
flirtation with Cath (Anita Dobson), in whose face (courtesy of some
rather tired morphing) he saw an image of Mary. Death, infidelity,
wife-beating and the futility of existence were all touched on, with the
programme frequently veering nearer to drama than conventional sit-
com. Rab's embryonic New Man tendencies allowed him some
poignant moments, but his essential recidivism was never far below
the surface.

There are problems with the show for southerners. Not since the
days of *Roni e Ryan* (the only humorous show in Welsh ever broadcast
on London transmitters) has comedy been so linguistically demanding. Heaven knows what the Ceefax subtitler manages to make of lines
which often seem to have the phonetic structure 'Ochty bastar nachty
blooin.' But that may be the way that writer Ian Pattison manages to
get so much black, slick and sick material past the censors, and the
show repays the extra effort it requires. Rab is becoming a rounded,
three-dimensional character, the supporting characters are strong,
and they could well dispense with the safety net of dubbed laughter
that occasionally supports their dialogue. Where else on British TV
would the line 'Your stitches have broken, Mrs Nesbitt' be followed by
the response 'Thank God, I thought I'd pissed myself.' Somebody at
BBC Scotland has some guts, and four cheers to them.

A Cook's Tour of France

Nowhere is the dichotomy between those who eat to live and those
who live to eat more apparent than on television, where ads for
McCain Oven Chips mingle with programmes featuring chefs pains-
takingly preparing *Coquilles St-Jacques à la crème*. Food shows obviously hit the spot with the audiences who switch on in vast numbers,
which is why the TV schedulers continue to eat them up. But, in the
process of chalking up Light Entertainment-sized viewing figures, the

presenters have frequently felt obliged to add not just a soupçon of humour, but a huge and overpowering dollop. Like sex films, food programmes often try to disguise the overtly sensual nature of the subject matter by hedging it around with nervous laughter. Keith Floyd's recent series on Spain took this approach to its limit, concentrating so hard on boozy gags that you were never vouchsafed a complete recipe for any of the dishes. Thankfully, in *A Cook's Tour of France*, crudities have given way to *crudités*, and food is once again treated with the respect and the seriousness which it deserves.

The first programme in the series began with what sounded like an elegant remix of the Floyd-Stranglers waltz theme, but all similarity between the two presentational styles ended thereafter. To be fair to Floyd, my preference for Mireille Johnston is not exclusively culinary (I confess that there is something about the sight of a mature and attractive Frenchwoman roughly handling endives that invariably turns my knees to wobbly aspic), but I preferred her programme, waltz and all. She began her journey along the Atlantic coast in Marennes, musing over those slimy things served in ashtrays known as oysters which, it emerged, are expensive not because they are rare but because they spend several years at an exclusive finishing school, absorbing minerals and purifying themselves before being harvested and graded into various sizes: small, medium and bloody huge profits. Ms Johnston asked a man who made his living from selling these bombastic bivalves whether or not they *really* had aphrodisiacal properties. Quite unexpectedly he told us they did, and moreover that we should all buy lots of them; they contain glycogen, and therefore, 'scientifically, they *are* an aphrodisiac'.

She visited a market in Nantes, a town so backward they do not have the shredded bits of green crêpe material used by British greengrocers since time immemorial to display their shrivelled bananas, and have to make do with fresh, unblemished and beautifully presented fruit and vegetables. Then on to the banks of the Loire River, home of Muscadet, the wine that helps you work, rest and play. Inevitably, a display of frogs' legs was shown (something I am certain the French do simply to shock the British, since I've only ever seen them displayed, never eaten); a *beurre blanc*, the classic butter-and-wine-vinegar sauce, was prepared; she visited a salt farm, made *cassoulet* and *chou farci* and observed a housewife making goat's cheese. This beautifully photographed series, discreetly accompanied by Jacques Brel songs and impressionistic harp music, looks like being the definitive TV monument to French domestic virtue, that miraculous Gallic ability to make the very best out of inexpensive and readily available ingredients.

Gliding slowly across an algae-covered backwater in a flat-bottomed boat with a professional fisherman, after having eaten and enjoyed everything she had encountered, Mireille Johnston suddenly revealed her Achilles eel. 'Yugh. I hate eels. Is it true they mate with snakes?' Call me impetuous if you will, but I suddenly felt the urge to whisk her away from all this, off to my regular haunt, the Wood Street Pie, Eel and Mash Shop in Walthamstow, where I would introduce her to the true subtleties of classic British cuisine. There, amongst the Formica-topped tables, we would sample the eels, prepared in a rich succulent liquor by the *patron* himself, with only a slice of bread-and-marge as accompaniment. Then we would rip open a fresh can of Tango, switch on Radio 2, and dance to the strains of the BBC Big Band, while the gumming septuagenarian clientele exhaled seductive wafts of Woodbine and murmured appreciatively at our frenzied passion. After such delights, why would she ever want to return to France?

Next day, I received a letter with 'Re Cook's Tour of France' written on the envelope. The letter itself made reference to an earlier review of another programme, headlined 'Rolling the Vice' in the *Evening Standard*, but still, imagine my surprise when I read the letter, reproduced on the opposite page.
     I replied:

9. ii. 94

Dear Joseph Kumeroa,
Thank you for your letter of 24 January. I am not a medical man, but it seems to me that a long cold shower might do the trick.
     Yours sincerely,

Victor Lewis-Smith

To Victor Lewis-Smith,
Evening Standard.

A response to your article 'Rolling the Vice'.

24 January 1994.

Dear Reader,

I am writing this in an attempt to get beyond the establishment figures to whom I have been writing in vain.

I want to educate the general public to the fact that it is cultivating a planetary disease,literally breeding the social and economic disasters with which it is having to contend. The root of the problem as I see it is the LIE that Nature has made no provisions whatsoever for men's sexual needs,therefore opposition to Nature - who has assigned only one natural function to vaginal intercourse - is to be encouraged and indeed savagely upheld by Laws,etc.,to break those who love the Good Life.

In reality Nature has imparted breast-like qualities to the paternal penis, rendering men highly susceptible to two closely-related sexual contacts as Nature intended : (a) vaginal intercourse which offers sexual access to the baby they want to bring into the world and (b) fellatio,the paternal equivalent of breast-feeding and nursing,which offers the essence of intercourse during pregnancy and the fatherly interest or affection it arouses. The penis breast image is not a perversion because it exhibits the characteristics of a 'given' phenomenon,Nature having reinforced the image in various ways. By contrast, no natural provisions exist for sodomy which is a true perversion,as is vaginal intercourse for recreational purposes only.

I attack the twisted sense of values to which men are being forced to conform in the name of medical science or whatever. Everybody is entitled to know the simple facts of life which,until now,I have been giving only to establishment figures.

The attached documents will put you fully into the picture.

Yours sincerely,

Joseph Kumeroa

The Complete BBC Diet and Fitness Show

This TV-critic lark has some strange side effects. Ever since they fitted closed-circuit cameras down at my local supermarket, I've found myself staring for hours at the screen, transfixed in reviewing mode. Live and in colour, Tescovision is far more gripping than most broadcast programmes: see how ugly you are from exciting new angles; enjoy the *frisson* of head-on collisions between delinquent trolleys; and thrill as security guards swoop down upon some shoplifting OAP caught in the act of secreting a tube of Steradent and an iced bun in a place not recommended by the manufacturers.

Iced buns are off the menu on *The Complete BBC Diet and Fitness Show*. Aiming itself at sad fatties who'll try anything to get thin, so long as it doesn't involve eating less, it's the latest in a Niagara of series promulgating the comforting myth that slimming can be achieved without pain. On waddled Jeni Barnett, perky and porky, her relentless jollity strangely reminiscent of the cackling fat girls you see in pubs – life-and-soul-of-the-party types who laugh raucously all evening, then go home alone and cry themselves to sleep. You know me. I don't want to cause offence but, if this woman is serious about wanting to lose ten pounds of ugly fat, then she ought to consider the method Henry VIII used so successfully on his wives.

When you hear the phrase 'Our special guest is Roy Walker,' you can be certain that you're watching daytime TV. After a generous plug from Jeni for 'Prue Leith's salubrious west London restaurant', Roy confided that, despite having given up salt, he was still a trifle overweight (beginner's bra job, I thought), and had to be informed about 'hidden calories' – a wicked practice whereby chefs add butter, eggs and cream to your food before they serve it, on the feeble pretext that it tastes better that way. Poor Roy was horrified to discover that the 'fish with curried butter sauce' listed on the menu had butter in it, almost as horrified as I was by his atrocious acting and feigned stupidity (or was it genuine?). In the kitchen, the head chef (of Prue Leith's restaurant, we were reminded again) told us that a good way to ingest fewer calories was to eat less, or alternatively to have soufflés made without eggs. I believe they're available in the shops, under the brand name Soggy Cardboard.

Dr Barry Lynch showed us how to dry-fry some lamb, carrots and onions, all without a gram of fat. While my eyes will believe anything (it certainly looked good), and even my taste buds might be tricked, my stomach wouldn't be fooled for an instant. It wants the artery-hardening buzz that only comes from great mounds of suet, and won't be fobbed off with anything else. Exercise was next and, as Jennifer Chinn led Jeni Double-Chin through a bending exercise, I felt the deep sadness I always feel whenever I see anyone over thirty-five (age or waist) wearing lycra. Me no lycra. Executive producer Barry Lynch left just enough time to tell us to buy the BBC diet book, written by Barry Lynch. Finally, we interrupt this review to remind you once again about Prue Leith's restaurant because, sure enough, there was a long, lingering close-up of the restaurant sign as Roy and Jeni departed. I wonder if dinner was on the house?

Of course it's easy to make fat jokes. Very easy. But there is something unsettling about the programme's underlying assumption that losing weight is automatically a good thing, and that slimming is fun. It's not. Slimming is slow, miserable torture for those that attempt it, the more so since it usually ends in guilt and failure. The only people who genuinely find it fun all work in the diet industry, where they've made a fortune persuading the rest of us to indulge in senseless masochism, and frankly it would be more appropriate if guests on these shows came on wearing horse-hair shirts and whipped themselves instead. If the fat end of the wedge is some poor kid contracting anorexia after being told she ought to look like Mandy Smith, then programmes like this are the thin end of the wedge, and ought to examine their own motives because, essentially, slimming is starvation. And starvation is scarcely the province of cheap, flip, ersatz Light Entertainment shows.

Still, Ms Barnett did convince me of one thing. Jaw-clamping isn't such a bad idea.

Face to Face: Ken Dodd

There are some stories which, although patently untrue, nevertheless deserve to be officially authenticated. I can therefore confirm that when Brigitte Bardot appeared on *Desert Island Discs* back in the 60s, and was asked by Roy Plomley to make her next selection, she replied, 'I want a penis.' After a stunned silence (during which Mr Plomley was heard to murmur, 'We'll come to your luxury later, dear'), an innocent explanation finally emerged. In her strong French accent, the poor woman was simply requesting one of her favourite records: 'Happiness' by Ken Dodd.

King Doddy was the guest on last night's *Face to Face* (BBC2), his teeth appearing in such tight close-up that I became distracted, and couldn't help wondering whether poisonous snakes ever accidentally bite their own tongues; and, if so, do they die? Mr Dodd may be one of the least venomous entertainers in the country but, with half his dental equipment fanned out like a peacock's tail, it's a miracle the man doesn't take half his head off whenever he sneezes. 'Ken Dodd is one of our funniest stand-up comedians,' said Jeremy Isaacs, a phrase which (some would say) should be followed by 'and next week, we'll be showing you how to nail jelly to the ceiling with a china hammer,' but Isaacs clearly believed it to be true. His guest's ability to brandish a tickling stick while regurgitating one-liners was deemed proof of profound philosophical insight, and he interviewed Dodd as though he were talking to the comedic Dalai Lama, instead of simply another skilled tradesman, like a plumber or a garage mechanic.

The early questions and responses were little more than a string of antiphonal truisms, drawn straight from the I-Spy Book of Comedians' clichés. 'No two audiences are alike,' Ken told us, who admitted to feeling 'very excited, and a little bit scared' when about to go on stage, and said that 'Comedy's all to do with timing' (which, at different points in the interview, he insisted was instinctive and learned). Isaacs raised the platitude level higher still with some mind-numbingly banal enquiries – 'Are you essentially sad? . . . When did you first find you could make people laugh?' – reading the questions straight from a clipboard with little attempt to respond to anything Dodd said, and no willingness to go with the flow (a world away from the deceptively conversational, yet ultimately far more penetrating, technique of Anthony Clare). The two men agreed that timing was all-important in a performance, but there was precious little of it on offer in this juddering, stumbling interview.

The probing stuck firmly to Dodd's professional life, with taxing personal questions strictly off the agenda and, as it progressed, the programme increasingly invited unfavourable comparisons with the famous Tony Hancock edition. Like Hancock, Dodd was overly keen to present himself as something of an intellectual (which he clearly isn't) when, if he'd only relaxed more and not worried so much about his grammatical slips, he might have revealed a more human, likeable side. As it was, when he began to talk about his collection of books, and his research into 'trying to find the secret source of laughter', he soon wandered way out of his depth, becoming so vaguely mystical that even a medieval alchemist would have dismissed it as mumbo-jumbo: 'Everybody's tried this, from Aristotle to Schopenhauer . . . everything runs in twos, it's like the perception of incongruity . . . plurals, parallels.' There are few sadder sounds than a comedian inarticulating his craft.

I shall pretend I never heard 'Are you a loner?' and 'What's the real you?' leaving Jeremy Isaacs' lips but, even if I do, I'm still left thinking that this was a 'Wheels Cha-Cha' of a programme. Full of frothy, disappointing stuff, it never got below the surface of a rather strange man, and forty minutes was far too long for such insubstantial fare. Like Rolf Harris, Dodd has had the native wit to reinvent himself every few years, thereby managing to stay firmly in the public eye for four decades, but he emerged from this encounter looking, frankly, a bit thick. Certainly, he should have resisted the temptation to utter one-liners because, on *Face to Face*, they simply don't get a response, although (to give him his due) he did crack one excellent joke about his old mentor and agent: 'He died at ninety . . . I always think he was a hundred and kept ten per cent for himself.' That aside, the gags fell as flat as the conversation and, while we're all used to seeing comedians dying, last night we witnessed a rarer sight: an interviewer dying.

Beam and Da Silva

Why is it that the name Carlton, once synonymous with quality, is now associated with cack? First that rustbucket of a car appeared, and I raised an eyebrow. When the cheapo cigarettes followed, I raised the other one. By then I looked fairly startled, but not as astonished as I was when that Ratner of the airwaves, Carlton Television, started broadcasting, with its bargain basement crammed full of cheap and nasty programmes: in particular, last night's *Beam and Da Silva*. Ladies and gentlemen, I would be prepared to bet that, for sheer misjudgement and laughable incompetence, it will one day become a TV classic to rival *Triangle*.

Any crime show that kicks off with the phrase 'The darkened streets of London conceal many a secret . . . and much crime' is either employing the late Edgar Lustgarten, or else its producer has marshmallow for brains. As for the presenters, Roger Beam and Denise Da Silva claimed to be private detectives, and soon proved beyond doubt that they were, indeed, a pair of genuine dicks. They aimed for *Dempsey and Makepeace* sophistication but behaved so much like two over-excited children – leaping out of cars shouting, 'Let's go for them,' wearing spy headphones, using secret cameras (and probably carrying a *Man From U.N.C.L.E.* invisible-ink pen) – that I wanted to smack the backs of their legs and send them up to bed early.

Beam and Da Silva had vowed to clean up Crime City, so naturally our first port of call was the hub of the vice capital . . . Sidcup: 'I'm a hairdresser and I want you to investigate these raffle tickets.' What followed was a series of non-stories, each ending in a meaningless confrontation with sad con-men who had been organizing bogus charity appeals: a competition that offered a motorbike to the winner but had taken people for a ride; a moron who ran an animal helpline yet didn't know the difference between tapeworm and ringworm; an Aids charity that hadn't donated as much money as promised. While the secret camera (by the looks of things operated by a blind Parkinson's disease victim) gave us close-ups of an isolated ear or nostril, Beam snapped at the villains' heels with all the ferocity of a rabid hamster, squealing fatuous and illiterate remarks: 'Our vet phoned with one of *the most easiest* questions.' Is it any wonder that crime is on the increase, with programmes like this? Not only are you confident that you could do better than *any* of the con-men on show but, if Beam and Da Silva should ever catch up with you, it wouldn't matter.

The show claimed to be exposing the cynical manipulation of the public, but its own moral standards seemed even more questionable, exploiting the ill and the handicapped in a quest for ratings-boosting footage, and demonstrating a breathtaking combination of crassness and loutishness. Issues of right and wrong are complex, and it is irresponsible for a programme simply to point a camera at someone, proclaim their guilt, and attempt to provoke a violent response. In a week when we have seen crowds baying for blood in Liverpool, TV has a duty not to encourage such a simplistic mentality.

As for Beam, he would like to be the next Roger Cook but, in his black shirt and raincoat, he looks more like what my mother used to call 'a bit of a large boy', conducting his interviews at a school-playground level, with name-calling and insults substituting for serious investigation. Worse, he does not even possess the fearlessness of Cook, who likes nothing better than barging into the villain's office and getting a satisfying smack right at the end of his nose and the programme. Last night's show culminated in the farcical sight of a crook actually trying to drag Beam in through his front door, while the nervous reporter tried to run away. If he and Da Silva really *were* responsible for combating crime in London, then God help us all.

The darkened streets of London do indeed contain much crime, but half-baked, sordid, sensation-seeking shows like this are a piffling irrelevance that will do nothing to combat it. As the closing credits rolled, we were asked, 'Do you know of anything that needs investigating . . . ?' I can name something: the programme itself. Its ill-informed, ill-considered and sleazy presentation has left a tide mark on my TV screen that even Mr Sheen cannot remove.

I received a postcard from the duo shortly afterwards, reworking the old Mrs-Lincoln-at-the-theatre joke and asking whether, apart from that, I had enjoyed the show. A year later, I heard from their editor that, alas, Beam and DaSilva were no more. Not literally dead, just dead as far as television was concerned. According to their editor, they were unable to agree between themselves which of them was 'the 100 per cent all-time shit' and, while they were arguing the toss, their series was axed. An appropriate end to a truly terrible show.

Mr. Victor Lewis-Smith,
The Evening Standard,
2 Derry St,
London.
W8 5TT

REUSE THE POST CODE!

That Victor,
Did you like it?

Love

Roger + Denise + Ø + Ø

Beam and DaSilva - London's newest Prestige
Every Thursday on Carlton at 6.30 p.m. beginning
February 4th

WALKER PRINT LTD London 071-253 1200

Beam and DaSilva is produced for Carlton by
Chrysalis Factual Programmes P.O. Box 1018 London
W2 6ZY.

The Fast Show

Even humble television critics like me are occasionally allowed to meet the stars of this wonderful business of ours we like to call 'the show', and a rum old bunch of stars they usually turn out to be. The late Roy Castle (who seems to make more media appearances *post mortem* than pre) once advised me, seconds after we first met, to do something with a swannee whistle anatomically impossible for a man of my age. But stranger still was the time I bumped into Paul Whitehouse at an awards ceremony and found, moments after collision, that a casual discussion had veered into such deep, dark perversion that the Marquis de Sade himself would have blushed.

The casual discussion that veers into deep, dark perversion is a recurring theme in *The Fast Show* (BBC2), what with references to handcuffing, blindfolding, pearl necklacing, bondage, latent homosexual trysts and bull-dyke lesbians; and that was just the trailer for last night's programme. Although Mr Whitehouse's appetite for depravity must surely trouble his puritanical mother Mary, at least the man has a grasp of economics that even John Maynard Keynes would envy – he's written one show but, through speed and sleight of hand, he's fooled the BBC into thinking he's written six. Indeed, I briefly thought I'd been sent the wrong advance tape of last night's programme, because the sketches involving Bob and Ralph, Professor Denzil Dexter and Ron Manager were not merely similar, but virtually identical to the previous week's show. And yet, despite recycling his raw material so assiduously that the Green Party ought to elect him president, and despite numerous stretches so murky that FOG APPROACHING signs ought to be flashing, the show contained several moments of such comedic brilliance that, hours later, I can still see the teeth marks in my carpet.

Much of the success is due to inspirational performances, not just from Whitehouse but from the entire cast. 'Chanel 9 Neus', for example (the Mediterranean television not-work familiar to every package holiday tourist), is not so much a sketch as a ritual, its fluent *gobbledegook ploblematiko tecknik* patois interspersed with fragments of a language tantalizingly close to English ('Chris Waddle . . . Picketty Witch . . . Boutros Boutros Ghali'), and aleatoric phrases of recognizable smut. The unconsummated relationship between lowly gamekeeper Ted and his aristocratic, latently gay boss (a sublime spoof of the social mores underlying Lady Chatterley) gains poignancy from the inevitability of its cyclical return, while rustic Bob Fleming (an expectorant Jack Hargreaves who is, as the French would say, a complete and utter *tousseur*) would disappoint if ever he failed to cough throughout his entire script. As for 30s comedian Arthur 'Where's Me Washboard?' Atkinson, each week is a ninety-second *tour de force*, deliciously skewering those hallowed comics of the Max Miller generation like so many kebabs. And yet, in the very act of lampooning the fatuous catchphrases of yesteryear, isn't *The Fast Show* guilty of exactly the same thing itself, with its endlessly repeated 'Hi, I'm Ed Winchester,' 'I'll get me coat' and 'You haven't seen me, right?'

Up to a point, Lord Copper. It's true that the series owes much to radio comedies of the 40s and 50s, to an era of 'Can I do you now, sir?' and 'Don't forget the diver,' when audiences liked to know in advance when they were supposed to laugh, and what they were supposed to laugh at. It's true, too, that the observation of social embarrassment owes much to Mike Leigh, and Alan Bennett's ear has clearly been purloined in sentences like 'We're big fans of Berni Inns, but now there's Harvester's, what can you do?' But such carping seems mealy-mouthed when you hit upon a gem like the 'Suit You' sketch, which explodes like a Scud missile on the screen. It's inspired, utterly evil, and profoundly funny.

The Fast Show has its feet in Dick Emery, its brain in Monty Python, its groin in Benny Hill, and its heart in *Viz*, and the result is a monster of a show. The performances are excellent (John Thomson and Robin Driscoll are a particular joy), Arch Dyson's direction is superb and, while I ration myself to one use of the word 'genius' each alternate blue moon, I believe that Paul Whitehouse may be touched by it (and, by a simple process of elimination, we're getting some idea of how much Harry Enfield owes to him). Michael Jackson is now getting BBC2's comedy into the best condition it's ever been in and, in an era when the likes of *Hale and Pace* are given airtime, it's our privilege, nay our duty, to raise this programme shoulder-high.

Eldorado

The cruelty taking place every day in Spain is shocking. It's unfair, the way poor dumb animals are forced to walk up and down beaches to the point of exhaustion and, when their useful life is over, are then sent to the knacker's yard. Only a media campaign can save them: End This Torture Now – *Eldorado* Must Stop.

I have spent six months not watching this programme. After its disastrous début, when Jonathan Powell pleaded, 'Give it until December,' I have behaved impeccably, like a juryman locked in a hotel room so the accused can have a fair trial. While other critics gorged themselves I stayed aloof, so that when the time came I could offer a clear and impartial analysis. But now it is December. And I have watched it. And it stinks.

It's fake from the opening credits. You do not write a Spanish-style theme tune simply by adding castanets to a remix of the *EastEnders* sig. Nor do you create convincing characters by dressing them like members of the Hitler Youth, with dead caterpillars, masquerading as sideburns, dangling from their faces. And why do they all wear the sort of sunglasses you normally only see hanging dejectedly from a plastic carousel in the chemist's in winter, the last few pairs in the shop that no one wants to buy? When a Spanish policeman (appropriately named Alberto Junco) can come on and steal the scene by saying (and I quote), 'Izal lemmit cogriffi lamma?' you know that this is a show in its death throes. As to the plot, I am still not clear what was going on.

First, a barrowboy shouted at a man I last saw in a McCain Oven Chip commercial (he acted badly then, which I suppose is why *Eldorado* snapped him up). An old woman was fearful of rape and wanted to buy a dog, although she was a bit of a dog herself and probably needn't worry. A man called Freddie said 'hello' and I instantly shouted out, 'I bet he's a homosexual.' I do it with wig wearers too: 'I bet that's a wig,' I say, and it usually is. Anyway, I was right about Freddie. Dieter, who has the looks of Jason Donovan, talked about surfing. A blonde teenage girl with huge breasts floated in a pool and turned out to be a paraplegic, although her real disability, it transpired, was in the acting, rather than the leg, department. It became clear that the village had been designed by Escher, since no matter where she went she always managed to travel downhill in her wheelchair. Meanwhile two Sikhs held a Spanish girl helpless in a tower. It was all so much like a school play that I expected a fit of giggling to break out. I have read that a certain Kathy Pitkin – aka Fizz – had been sacked from the show for not acting well enough, but it is obvious to me that she left, seduced by the offer of a Christmas panto in Leeds. She now has a real acting job and must be laughing heartily (though probably unconvincingly) at those she left behind.

This is a drama built on quicksand, though not quick enough for my liking, and how the network responsible for *EastEnders* could have created it amazes me. Soap watchers don't want sun and sky, they want cold, misery, grime, drizzle and derision, they want Manchester and *Coronation Street*. Six months in, there is a total collapse of confidence in Spain. Robert Chartham remarked, a propos of sex, that 'There must be no fear.' The same is true of drama, and therein lies the problem: these actors have lost their nerve. Last night, a pair of horses couldn't walk down their ramp convincingly and even the typewriter was dubbed because it wasn't being a typewriter properly. When actors have to deliver such lines as – 'I'm not getting any younger.' 'None of us are' – it's small wonder they're scared.

In July, the critics gave *Eldorado* a summary execution. In December, I am calling for a wintry execution.

Without Walls: Hells Angel

One of television history's most delightful moments occurred in 1975, when Jason King appeared in court and was fined after an incident in a gentlemen's lavatory in Gloucester bus station. It wasn't the sordid details that were so exquisite, nor the phrase 'I had had a good lunch and merely slipped on some stray paper, straight through the cubicle door, Your Honour,' unconvincingly offered by way of explanation. No, what was so sublime was the discovery that the heart-throb actor's real name was not Jason King, nor Peter Wyngarde, but *Cyril Lovis Goldbert*.

I experienced a similar thrill last night, while watching *Without Walls: Hell's Angel* (CH4) and learning that Mother Theresa's real

name is Agnes. Television has always had an attitude problem with
nuns, being fascinated by the eccentric ones (flying, singing, toothy
art-appreciating), but feeling distinctly uneasy about the religious
variety, who receive obligatory murmurs of approval but are rarely
given airtime. Hitherto, Agnes has always received uncritical praise
from the news media, but last night Christopher Hitchens decided
(now that she's eighty-four and apparently not litigious) that it's safe
to start putting the boot into the shrivelled brown nun. 'Mother
Theresa's rise was television's first miracle,' he told us at the outset.
That this was aired at all was television's second.

As a potential assassin, Hitchens preferred the sawn-off shotgun to
the telescopic rifle, blasting away indiscriminately in hopes of inflicting as much damage as possible on anyone within range. Malcolm
Muggeridge was dismissed as 'that old fraud and mountebank' because
he'd once made a programme extolling Mother Theresa's work in her
Calcutta hospice, and what sounded like an irreverent Muggeridge
joke about her divine powers was presented as though he'd really
claimed she could work miracles. Her Home for the Dying was
compared to Belsen, and condemned for its lack of basic hygiene,
although the only alternative for many terminally ill patients in one
of the poorest cities on earth would be to die in the streets. And when
we saw her shaking hands with President Reagan, Hitchens regarded
it as definitive proof that she was an ardent supporter of US foreign
policy, and of Central American death squads.

'The great white hope takes on the big black hole,' fulminated
Hitchens, almost foaming at the mouth as he reran the sort of
simplistic arguments used years ago to besmirch Albert Schweitzer's
reputation. Mother Theresa's mission was nothing more than an old
colonial outpost, he said, salving the West's conscience about Third
World poverty, claiming to be apolitical while supporting the status
quo, and helping heartless multinationals evade their responsibilities
by preaching forgiveness to the survivors of Bhopal. True enough, but
this is one little old woman we're talking about, a Vatican patsy, not
an imperialist force for evil. The manufactured sense of outrage had
more than a whiff of the sixth-form debating society about it, the more
so since the presenter's name, appearance and intellectual capacity
were all worryingly reminiscent of Christopher Biggins. Paradoxic-

ally, the programme arrived both half-baked *and* stale, since Hitchens accused Mother Theresa of helping to keep the military dictatorship in Haiti in power, when of course they've recently been replaced by the Marxist leader Aristide. And who returned Aristide to power? Why, the US, whose foreign policy Mother Theresa supposedly supports, and Hitchens roundly condemns. Now, there's an irony for you.

I've never believed in altruism, and I'd trust Mother Theresa about as far as I could throw her (quite a long way, actually, since I won a silver medal for nun-throwing at the Barcelona Olympics). Her mission currently has outlets in 105 countries, like some spiritual version of McDonald's, she spends far too much time being presented with gongs, and her ability to pop up anywhere in the world, the instant there's a major disaster, sometimes makes me suspect her of causing the floods and famines herself. All the same, this was supposed to be the case for the prosecution, and yet I ended up disliking her less. Hitchens' real contempt clearly stems from her condemnation of contraceptives, and that's understandable because he himself is a dire warning of the dreadful consequences that can follow if their free availability is ever restricted.

The programme was as dubious as its subject but, at the very end, I swear I saw a miracle. The producer's name was Tariq Ali, and his conversion into a public limited company and capitalist entrepreneur beats walking on water any day.

Natural Neighbours

It is delightful to know that television bosses occasionally suffer unexpected shocks, especially when the weekly viewing figures come in. In 1964, BBC1's *Election Special* was trounced in the afternoon ratings by BBC2's Test Card and Music. In 1983, TV-am's audience once became unmeasurably small (until the station was saved by Roland, the only rat ever to swim *towards* a sinking ship). But more remarkable still was a South Carolina channel which opened last year. Its pre-launch test transmission – a single live shot of a fish-tank – gained such massive ratings that, when the station finally went on air, its controller had no option but to give the aquarium its own nightly prime-time slot.

Marine life makes soothing viewing, so the ratings for last night's *Dolphin Dreaming* (which concluded BBC1's *Natural Neighbours* series) were doubtless pretty healthy too, certainly healthier than the minds of most of the participants. 'Be uninterrupted in your thoughts for thirty minutes,' advised the narration (a state that usually only occurs when watching *Neighbours*), as we were introduced to a boatful of earnest New Agers, embarking on a swimming-with-dolphins holiday in the Bahamas. I grew suspicious the moment I heard the word 'body' pronounced 'bardee', but when the group leader told us, 'We've got a broad spectrum of people here, therapists, dancers, a didgeridoo player . . .' I knew we were in for a half-hour of unadulterated, organic psychobabble, and so it proved to be. There was plenty of talk of life-changing encounters and out-of-body experiences, but no thanks: the only out-of-body experience I either need or want is the one I have each morning, after a cup of strong coffee and some stewed prunes.

To this group of misty-eyed, self-satisfied smilers (the sort of people who advertise their alternative services on the windows of wholefood stores), dolphins were 'highly intelligent creatures . . . who give unconditional love' (although, considering that humans have been wantonly slaughtering them for centuries, dolphins must be as stupidly loyal as dogs if they still love us unconditionally). 'I want to find myself,' said one woman and, thanks to a husband who'd paid her fare, she found herself in the Bahamas. A second spoke of 'a kindred spirit beneath the waves', while others serenaded their new-found aquatic friends with glockenspiels and didgeridoos. They claimed to be communicating and receiving kindnesses but (as with most animals) a dolphin's expression cannot change, so how could they tell? After all, the entire species permanently wears the same benign grin, whether they're frolicking harmlessly with New Agers or devouring an entire shoal of fish at lunchtime.

Meanwhile, off the coast of southern Ireland, teenager Ruth Conder was suffering from ME, that pernicious disease which cruelly attacks the well-to-do, rendering them incapable of physical effort (curiously, ME never seems to strike, say, subsistence farmers in the poorer parts of Africa). With her mother at the helm, their small craft ploughed the waves in search of Fungi, a maverick dolphin who's been cruising the shoreline for the past decade, because Ruth believed that 'swimming with him gives me energy'. Whenever they sighted him, their pet dog began to howl uninhibitedly, but it was clear which members of the family were really barking. A lone voice of reason came from a scientist, who said that swimmers tend to misinterpret the creatures' behaviour: 'People think they're playing, when really they're pursuing a female behind the swimmer.' As I watched, I remembered the dolphins that swam with me once, in Santa Barbara. I felt no communality, nor did I spot any intelligence, because not one of them whispered in my ear that I should be wearing sun-block factor 14 in that heat. I ended up like a lobster. Thick or what?

Frolicking with dolphins is harmless enough and, if ME sufferers think it helps them, then I suppose it does. But, like many other pleasurable yet undignified activities, people really shouldn't allow themselves to be filmed while they're engaged in it. Griff Rhys-Jones's narration was splendidly economical, and wisely resisted the temptation to make the swimmers seem ridiculous: why bother, when they were making such a good job of it themselves? The photography was stunning, with excellent post-production, and the entire series has brought a fresh style to wildlife programmes (too often a rather jaded, formulaic area of television). Even so, if these people really wanted an experience that would get their metabolisms going, I'd rather have seen them starring in a film about swimming with sharks. Unconditional love with blood, a playful maul here and there, a severed limb or two: then they really *would* feel just fantastic, as they're hauled out of the sea to safety.

This is one of many dozens of letters I received on the subject of myalgic encephalomyelitis, far more than I have ever received on any other subject. The ME sufferers claimed that their disease made it impossible for them to so much as get out of bed or put one foot in front of the other, yet dozens of them had nevertheless managed to type or write extensive letters (in most cases, six or eight pages long), and walk down to the postbox to mail them. My articles seemed to have great therapeutic value for ME sufferers, provoking them to feats of physical exertion of which they had no idea they were capable, and I therefore considered it my duty to write deprecatingly about ME on a regular basis in my column, in a bid to boost their energy levels and get them firmly on to the road to recovery. Few of them contacted me again, though, so I can only suppose that there was a mass relapse.

ME
Myalgic Encephalomyelitis
ASSOCIATION

Mr Victor Lewis-Smith
TV Reviews
Evening Standard
Northcliff House
2 Derry Street
Kensington
LONDON W8 5EE

Stanhope House High Street Stanford le Hope
Essex SS17 0HA   Telephone: 0375 642466
                              Facsimile: 0375 360256

December 7, 1994

Ref: VA/ES/2780

Dear Mr Lewis-Smith

We read with some dismay your article on "Mystics in the swim", dated Wednesday, 30 November, particularly your reference to Ruth Conder suffering from ME "...that pernicious disease which cruelly attacks the well-to-do, rendering them incapable of physical effort (curiously, ME never seems to strike, say, subsistence farmers in the poorer parts of Africa)."

It is clear that you have only a limited knowledge of this illness - are you aware that it is not only the well-to-do that contract this illness? It can hit anybody from the highest in the land to the poorest and seems to be associated with "civilised" countries where hygiene has been a priority issue. Physical effort is only part of the problem since the illness creates   a significant   amount of pain and affects the hypothalamus which controls all of the autonomic parts of the body. ME can, as many serious illnesses, have a devastating effect on peoples' lives.   Thus, statements   such as   your's merely contribute to misunderstanding and ignorance about the illness rather than helping patients receive the respect and support that they deserve.

We have taken the liberty of enclosing further information for you about this illness and hope that you will find this of value.

Yours sincerely

Vicki Airs
CHIEF EXECUTIVE

Enc

Registered in England ● Company registration no: 2361986 ● Registered charity no. 801279 ● Registered office: Stanhope House, High Street, Stanford le Hope, Essex SS17 0HA

Neighbours

As teachers endlessly tell children, 'You can't talk and listen at the same time.' In my time there seemed to be no disputing such a self-evident truth, but nowadays kids have an unanswerable response: *Neighbours*, the show you can listen to while talking on the phone, while reading Bertrand Russell, while decoding the genetic information in a DNA molecule, all without missing a single nuance of the plot. Yet the Aussie soap that can be understood using only one per cent of a normal brain also has a huge following among the cerebrally challenged, and at 5.35 each evening the sound of millions of knuckles can be heard scraping against the carpet as the nation's imbeciles gather round their TV sets to watch the latest episode.

Neighbours is recorded in a studio the size of a Lilliputian Telecom phone box, with furniture that looks like MFI rejects, and walls that wobble whenever an actor picks up the phone. The designs may be cheap and wooden, but not nearly as cheap and wooden as the acting and the dialogue; it soon becomes clear that the most moving thing on this show is the scenery.

The 'creative team' are not so ambitious as to attempt characterization, but content themselves with cardboard cut-outs of crass stereotypes. The males are either empty-headed, surfing macho men, or naughty boys who play japes, while the women are kindly grannies, stern harridans or sex dolls with mouths gaping open and vacant expressions. Those in authority speak like English governesses while anyone caught misbehaving lapses into a broad local accent, a telling atavism suggesting that the legacy of transportation is still buried deep within the Australian psyche. But they have the last laugh because, after years of persuading the British to emigrate there for twopence halfpenny, they can now export their tuppenny ha'penny actors back to the old country.

There must be a mass outbreak of ergot poisoning in Erinsburgh, because nothing else satisfactorily explains the abnormal goings-on in Ramsay Street. In the short time I have been watching (check my knuckles) there have been two brain tumours, sudden blindness, a broken back, six road deaths, a shooting, several murders, a suicide and a rape. Worse, the low budget rarely allows location shooting, so most external events have to be narrated by the actors, in the manner of a chorus in Greek tragedy telling us there's been a bit of eye trouble in Thebes. Amongst the calamities peppering this Australian tragedy are simplistic moral exhortations to keep on the straight and narrow, combined with comic scenes and practical jokes so feeble that even the groundlings at the Globe Theatre would have felt their intelligence was being insulted.

It is pointless giving names to characters without personalities and, until the rest of the cast reach the high standards set by Bouncer the dog, I shall use the technique perfected by John Motson when commentating on football matches in Eastern Europe, and refer to them by their position in the team. Yesterday, in what looked like a televised version of the *Dandy*, Macho (father of Jason Donovan, and living proof that thespian idiocy is congenital) was visited by his sister Harridan. Son of Macho said, 'I'll take her surfing, she'll scare off the sharks.' Tee hee! Granny cleaned her glasses while Governess placed a don't-employ-underage-children moral into the script. Son of Macho planned a jape on Macho. Yaroo! Granny told Dolly she'd never get on in life if she was lazy. Naughty Boy played a jape with snails. Lummee! Dolly II played another jape on Harridan II, inviting 'drongos to call on the old chook' (which meant sending the local rapists to the house of a middle-aged spinster). Cripes! Lastly, Naughty Boy II put a bucket of custard over a door hoping to cover Dolly III, but ended up soaking Harridan III. Ho ho!

More skill goes into the logistics of making five episodes of *Neighbours* each week than goes into the writing, acting or directing, and the inappropriate library music is laughable. But apart from that it's great. As the end credits rolled, Reg Grundy Productions informed us that 'All events depicted in this photoplay are purely fictitious' and that 'Any similarity to persons living or dead is purely coincidental.' Come on, Reg, any similarity would not just be coincidence. It would be a miracle.

Omnibus: Sir John Betjeman

It's hard to believe that a humble ex-Radio 1 disc jockey could be responsible for a seemingly impossible sci-fi journey to the centre of the earth. Yet I'd be prepared to bet that, when Maestro Mike Read first performed his masterful setting of John Betjeman's 'Myfanwy' in public, the late poet laureate began spinning in his grave so rapidly that, even as I write, he's probably still corkscrewing his way towards the earth's very core.

There wasn't much spin on last night's *Omnibus: Sir John Betjeman* (BBC1). Not because the subject wasn't fascinating (I'd be engrossed by a tribute to the man if it were in Morse code) but because the material was presented in such a conventional bio-documentary fashion, with truncated archive snippets sandwiched between sound bites from a dozen talking heads, all offering unsubstantiated snippets of praise or criticism. And what criticism. Like the composer Malcolm Arnold, Betjeman's popularity with a non-specialist audience has precluded recognition of his significance by the legion of minor academics (regrettably well-represented on this programme) who compile reference books, and who like their art to be exclusive. Heroes only to their own first-year students, they queued up to dismiss Betjeman's poetry as a mere succession of well-worn rhymes, alternating lines of eight and seven syllables, relying solely on suburban allusions for effect. But fortunately there were plenty of admirers too, to marvel at the genius's gift for using orthodox forms to express a most unorthodox view of the world.

His lifelong friend Joan Kunzer remembered his childhood as troubled and unhappy, with miserable years wasted at the Dragon prep school and at Marlborough, uselessly pursuing sporting excellence when even sporting mediocrity was far beyond him. Only at Oxford did he find his poetic voice, and Richard Ingrams (who, judging from his posture, had either just been given an air-enema with a foot pump or else was suffering the agony of piles) believed that his young fogey image was born there, as a conscious rejection of the Modernism around him. As Philip Larkin pointed out, 'He should by rights have been writing about pylons and politics, but he preferred churches, places and girls.' His love of churches, 'centuries of faith reflected in flint and stone', was matched by a scholarly and comprehensive knowledge of architecture, and a burning contempt for commerce when it ran roughshod over beauty. 'Never rave on too much about buildings you love in front of the wrong people, or they'll pull them down,' he warned and, although he could understand why Goering wanted to destroy London, the British eagerness to do the same thing after the war filled him with despair.

Although he treated his television career as 'hack work', he had an unparalleled gift as a presenter, coming across as an amateur in the best sense of the word. 'He made the difficult look so easy,' said Barry Humphries, 'whereas people like rock stars make the easy look difficult.' Betjeman conveyed enthusiasm and wore his learning lightly, qualities that made him equally engaging as an interviewee on *Parkinson* (I'm hardly one to talk but I'd forgotten, until I saw an excerpt, that the host used to present the show in those days with a dead poodle on his head).

This was a workmanlike and long-overdue film from Rick Stroud, but Betjeman understood the medium of television far better than most, and I'm glad to see that a retrospective season is in the schedules. Still, at least Jim Parker's music was everything that Mike Read's isn't, while John Hurt's narration (sounding like a post-tracheotomy Jack Hawkins) proved yet again that the man surely gargles with broken glass before recording sessions. Even so, we could have done without some of the more senile ramblings of Betjeman's contemporaries, and there seems little point in devoting airtime to interviewees who give contradictory information – did Betjeman have an unhappy childhood or not? – unless their differences are resolved. In any case, whatever his childhood was like, it's certain that he didn't have a happy old age, being tragically gripped by Parkinson's disease in his final years. In fact, when you consider how many former guests have subsequently bitten the dust, that 70s chat show clearly has a lot to answer for.

One Man and His Dog

In childhood, we often misconstrue, as only children can. For years, I believed that Mr Banda was not only the President of Malawi, but also made duplicating machines. My favourite hymn was the one about a teddy with a squint: Gladly, my cross-eyed bear. And the day the BBC announced they were going to televise sheepdog trials, I was utterly convinced that the poor mutts were being put up against a wall and shot.

Almost two decades later, *One Man and His Dog* (BBC2) is still going strong, with yesterday's edition looking little different from that first programme. The original presenter, Phil Drabble, has recently given way to Robin Page, but otherwise it's exactly the same show, from the contestants' haircuts and Barbours, right down to the opening titles, with their 70s typeface and *Robin's Nest*-slewing synthesizers. That's hardly surprising, because the programme's real function is to celebrate the unchanging, idyllic televisual haven called 'the countryside' (a mythical place, strangely at odds with the reality of rural life, where crime and suicide rates are soaring, unemployment and poverty are endemic and drunkenness is often the only refuge). The show is a canine *Archers*, placating the atavistic agrarian urges in its urban audience. You've heard of TV listings; well, this is a Grade I-listed programme, and no one's allowed to alter it: if it *were* ever taken out of the schedules, I suspect the whole network would collapse.

The Lake District setting for yesterday's sheepdog trials was undeniably majestic but, as is often the case with the countryside, it somehow lacked sustained dramatic impact. Robin Page and commentator Gus Dermody (looking like the elderly models you find in thermal underwear brochures produced by adventurous gentleman's outfitters in Tewkesbury) tried to instil some enthusiasm – 'We've had seven days of tension . . . the Young Handlers competition is the most important date in the calendar' – but for this lot to be called 'exciting' one of the contestants would have had to have whistled up his dog and made its eyes water. The collies had more personality than their owners, running around with tongues hanging out like party squeakers at nearly full blow, their black lips resembling the rancid rubber around old fridge doors. As for the sheep, their faces were so expressionless, they could have been knitted out of wool themselves. 'There's one sheep that could well lead them in,' said Gus as the flock approached the pen, 'he's the one at the front.' And, sure enough, it did. Uncanny, the rustic wisdom of these country folk.

'Outrun, Lift, Fetch, Drive, Shed, Pen.' It may mean something to shepherds but, to the rest of us, it's Mornington Crescent on four legs. A quartet of youths (all with dour farmer-fathers faintly reminiscent of John Laurie in *The Thirty-Nine Steps*) competed, signalling frantically to dogs that did exactly what they damn well pleased. 'Out come the seven Herdwick . . . bit loose on the flanks,' said Gus (part John Motson, part Jack Hargreaves) as Callum directed Cap by blowing the sort of whistle that usually accompanies a coffin slipping from beneath a flag and into the sea. David and Glen scored ninety-four with (we were told) an excellent Shed. Then came Maralyn, One Person in Her Own Right and Her Dog, who was studying science (a sort of shepherd's *pi* r squared), and whose performance was congratulated by Robin with patronizing touches of 'Clever little filly' in his voice. Lastly, David told us that 'My dad learned me a lot about dogs, sheep, cattle': everything, in fact, except English. And, in between, we were treated to readings – 'paths immortalized by the poets, Wordsworth and Coleridge . . . Wainwright Country . . .' – taken straight from the local tourist-authority leaflets, thoughtfully left in hotels offering concessionary rates to the BBC.

Nothing about this programme should be changed. Like the *Long Range Shipping Forecast*, its immutability and impenetrability are its strengths, and it's comforting to know that the show is there, even if one seldom bothers to tune in. All the same, it would be delightful, one week, to see a single rebellious sheep round up seven sheepdogs. David and Glen won, and were told, 'It's really good to see you young whippersnappers keeping up the tradition,' but David looked to me like the sort of rural kid one sees hanging around the village-square phone box, telephoning the talking clock for kicks and dreaming of the city, where life would be less crashingly repetitive. And, watching the sheep trotting obediently into the pen while the dog frolicked merrily behind them, they went like lambs to the slaughter (the fate that has probably already befallen them). Only the BBC has realized

that, simply by removing an S, you can turn that slaughter into
laughter. Or, at least, into light entertainment.

Come Dancing

I've never really got to grips with proper grown-up, joined-up dancing.
Some years ago (during the punk era), when I attempted the pogo, I
only succeeded in knocking myself out against a low ceiling, and
cavortings of the *Come Dancing* sort have always left me cold. After all,
the standard, awkward gyrations of its participants – writhing bodies,
grimaces, flailing limbs, noses thrust into armpits – you can watch
every day during rush hour on the District Line. The only difference
is a noticeable lack of sequins and the Andy Ross Orchestra.

Come Dancing is a living fossil in the TV schedules, a show frozen
in the 1960s, and what more appropriate venue could there be for Eric
Morley's ageing brainchild than that geriatric Mecca of the south
coast, Bournemouth? The Andy Ross Orchestra provided 'live' music
of the sort that once accompanied local cinema ads for carpet shops,
while presenter Rosemarie Ford's black and white outfit was not so
much a frock, more a 60s TV engineer's test pattern. The audience
(seated at tables) seemed frozen in their sixties too, and you could
almost hear the gummed requests to 'Set me up another double
Wincarnis, and a nip of Doctor Collis Browne for the good lady wife's
spastic colon.' As London North and London South took to the floor,
and the band's sax section played with a vibrato so wide you could fit
a double-decker bus between the notes, I swear the exotic whiff of
Dentufix wafted through the air.

In ballroom dancing, as in war, the old send out the young to fight
their battles, and the floor was soon awash with youthful hopefuls,
slogging it out in the Latin section. Simone and Cara performed what
they said was a samba but looked more like the 60s game Twister on
speed, wearing the sort of fixed, glacial smiles normally only encountered at cosmetics counters in second-rate department stores. A judge
said 'it didn't look at all contrived' and we moved on to the Modern
section. I was not aware that the foxtrot and the quick step were
particularly modern, but down Bournemouth way these can still

presumably provoke rioting in the streets. On bounced two nineteen-year-olds (going-on-fifty), looking as though they were suspended by bungee ropes in the last stages of twang. Another judge said 'the South looked more calmer' and 'it was very quick in the sound of the music', and we were on to the tango.

When an Argentinian couple finish a smouldering tango, you sense they'll be going straight to bed afterwards, to finish what they've started. But, when the Penge Latin Team finish a tango, a nice cup of Horlicks and a Hob-nob seems a far likelier bet. Truly, this was passion, English-style. During the Rialto two-step, my cat woke up and fled from the room. Another judge, who presumably had access to an electron microscope, said 'the North lacked the charisma shown by the South' and Penge forged even further into the lead. Next, a 'star cabaret spot' was announced. I had hoped someone would come on and fill the stage with flags, but no, more dance. On trotted two much older dancers attempting a hip routine although, at their age, a hip replacement would perhaps have been more advisable. The gentleman had clearly modelled himself on Michael Jackson during his 'Smooth Criminal' period and, had he been a shade whiter, he might have got away with it. But why do dancers always freeze in a grotesque rictus at the end, when you know they really want to shout out, 'Christ, I've got a stitch' and collapse on to the floor in a heap?

The South won. It's good to have a hobby, but I remain suspicious of the motives of the OAP audience, living vicariously through the young dancers whom they keep so firmly under their thumb. The world of ballroom dancing is intense, claustrophobic, fiercely competitive, very strange and utterly pointless. Further, I that fear one day these dancers may come to resent the way their youth has been sacrificed on the altar of elderly ambition.

One mystery remains. Why, at the end of the tango, do *Come Dancing* dancers always shout out, 'With milk'? '*Au lait,*' they shout, and again, '*au lait.*' It's all beyond me. Perhaps it's for their Horlicks.

Omnibus: Everything You Wanted to Know About Conductors But Were Afraid to Ask

It's curious that Grove's Dictionary omits from its pages the musical phrase that best describes the attitude of most orchestral players – moano perpetuo. Failed soloists themselves, they whinge incessantly about pay, conditions, the shortcomings of the famous soloists they accompany and, above all, the conductors who dominate their working lives.

To judge from the whine list read out on last night's Omnibus: Everything You Wanted to Know About Conductors But Were Afraid to Ask, most musicians clearly think that an omnibus is the only thing most of these maestri are fit to conduct. True, they had a point. Conducting, like film-directing, is an area where ambitious charlatans can flourish, confident that the technical expertise of those around them will disguise their own incompetence. To most musicians, the orchestra is a perfect working model of the capitalist system, with a hundred people doing all the skilled work, while one man contributes nothing yet takes all the rewards. Small wonder, then, that so many orchestral players turn to drink, after years of working for inept conductors who move unsteadily from bar to bar themselves.

The programme promised to answer the question 'What do conductors actually do?', but instead presented us with an unfocused stream of disconnected talking heads, from both sides of the podium. The conductors talked in high-flown aesthetic terms; Georg Solti said, 'You have to re-create what's in your head,' while Zubin Mehta was preoccupied with deciding 'when to pull on the reins and when to let the orchestra play'. Musicians had more practical concerns: 'Conductors have given me a nervous breakdown,' said one; 'They're vicious and sadistic,' said another; 'I spend my life playing for conductors who don't know the repertoire,' snarled a third. Others complained about the way conductors are packaged by the media, and the colossal fees that even the most ineffectual can command once established. And from the brass players – those sad, attention-seeking bovver boys of the orchestral world – came so many stories of insurrection against dictatorship, and calls for freedom from oppression, that the LPO started to sound more like the PLO.

We heard from various experts (and Robin Ray) but, beyond a vague explanation of what all the hand-waving means, there was still no word about what conductors actually *do*, apart from earning huge fees and causing nervous breakdowns amongst the timid. Not that they were reluctant to be interviewed, dear me no. I counted more than twenty, all complaining how few really good conductors there were, besides themselves. Since the orchestral players all agreed there were fewer than ten conductors world-wide for whom they had any respect, it would have been enjoyable to have named names, and unmasked a few charlatans there and then. But then, subito, the programme derailed with a mini-documentary about Karajan, whose obsession with propagating his own electronic image was blamed for the creation of modern superconductors, and the orchestral world's zero resistance to them. Herbie's Nazi past was irrelevantly raked over and, in a moment of sublime crassness, pictures of Hitler saluting were intercut with Karajan conducting. Call me old-fashioned, but I don't think setting an aggressive tempo for a Beethoven scherzo is quite the same thing as invading Poland.

This was not so much a documentary as an opportunity for whingers to settle a few old musical scores with bitchy but unmemorable phrases. By the end, there was more fur flying than in a fleet of jumbo jets packed full of Persian cats, helped not a jot by the interpolation of unfunny snippets from 50s British comedy films. Overall, if the programme were a piece of music, I doubt if there'd be a second performance. Never establishing a convincing theme or developing its material, this was a bagatelle expanded to Brucknerian proportions, and it would have been quite sufficient at half its length. And, astonishingly, it made no mention of the orchestral rehearsal, the place where a great conductor really *does* earn his money. Even so, any programme that employs a cameraman called Damian Eggs can't be all bad. But, as for the whining orchestral players, it's high time they faced facts: they're a bunch of plug-ugly men and homely women with nimble fingers and a charisma bypass, and they'd be sunk if the rich bloke with the stick didn't inject the animal magnetism and popular appeal they all so clearly lack themselves.

Americana

Television can be a vicious one-eyed monster. When Jonathan Ross first appeared on screen in the 80s he seemed to have complete mastery over the monocular beast, taming it with contemptuous and delightful ease. But over-familiarity leads to laziness, and monsters have endless patience. Like Wogan and many before him, Ross seems to have become blasé, and dropped his guard. We can only hope that he does not doze off completely otherwise the jaws will snap tight, and the one-eyed monster will gobble up yet another victim. It nearly happened last night.

Gobbling was much in evidence throughout *Americana*, whose first part was devoted to a celebration of fat. 'I'm not here to knock the well-fed,' said Ross, an official but empty disclaimer preceding an hour's mockery of 'dumpy, fat, dopey simple people . . . with grossly distended bellies . . . and corrugated chins'. The reason for such obesity was, he argued, that 'Americans eat huge amounts,' an impeccably logical deduction which he repeated monotonously until it became part of his punctuation (I lost count after about the thirtieth variation). There was a huge amount of excess fat in the commentary, and the script itself needed massive liposuction far more urgently than even the most grotesque of the gutbuckets we encountered.

Americana began with Ross, alone in a diner, stuffing himself on the eat-the-plate special in the hope of getting a free lunch. This was clearly staged, because in reality it is Channel 4 which has been providing the free lunch ever since they appointed Ross's company, Channel X, as unofficial guides to 'bizarre, off-beat America'. However, what was served up was not remotely bizarre or off-beat, just sadly prosaic: a pageant of poorly researched, bland PR reps from fast-food chains putting a 'home cooking' gloss on mass-produced goo; interviews with simpletons that allowed Ross to get his teeth into his intellectual inferiors (the only time he appeared genuinely hungry); the whole package loosely held together with silly, unfocused links and more than a touch of Woganesque grandiloquent vocabulary, which is humorous without being funny and cannot disguise the vacuity of thought. With six weeks in the States, this series must have been as much fun to make as it isn't to watch. Still, all aboard the CH4 gravy train. Chuff chuff.

At Czimer Foods, Ross indulged his taste for freaks in a shop devoted to indulging freaky tastes – camel, zebra, hippo, bear or rattlesnake and lion – and where we heard the best gag in the show: 'one of the few places where you might see a man put a lion's head in his mouth'. By and large, attempts at humour were on a basic schoolboy level; a van surmounted by a giant wiener resembled a large penis (tee hee), and was juxtaposed with a vagina-like Donut Hole, while a Dr Ruth clone in McDonald's was asked about 'sucking tackle' (ho ho). He met a near-certifiable woman who cooked chicken in her dishwasher, a man who cooked bacon on his car engine and the grandson of the inventor of the hamburger. He took a trip to Fun City, New Jersey, where sad consumers gambled for cans of beans, and the McDonald's Museum, built on the site of the first retail outlet. Here mannikins served up 1955-style plastic burgers and chips, although the food and service still seemed superior to my local branch; so much meat, yet the programme itself was mere froth.

The closing titles were superb, the film glossy and well directed. But overall this was a poor example of the tired old US food doc which has been handled much more observantly by others. Bob Robinson, over ten years ago, came up with the memorable summary 'The national dish of the United States is the menu.' What did we get from Ross? 'The American dream, it seems to me, is to have your cake, burger, hot dog and pizza . . . and not eat it too.' Run that one by us again, will you, Jonathan?

Americana: Fat was hard to swallow. I can only hope it doesn't repeat on Channel 4.

Pebble Mill

Making an over-the-top glitzy showbiz entrance down a flight of stairs on a daytime TV programme is almost as sad as taking a bow every time your fridge door light comes on. But Judi Spiers swanned on to our screens yesterday as though she was about to host a celebrity gala at Caesar's Palace, rather than the forty minutes of flat chat that comprise the daily fare at Pebble Mill.

In the 70s, *Pebble Mill* had one saving grace: it was shot in the foyer, so you could always look over Donnie McCloud's shoulder to the row of houses beyond, where real people were putting on their Pacamacs or parking their Morris Minors. Now, however, there is nothing but a set that looks like an explosion in a paint factory to distract us from the mind-numbing tedium of the show. Only one criterion seems to apply when booking guests – not 'Are they interesting?' but 'Are they promoting something in Birmingham anyway, so we won't have to pay their expenses?' – and the result is predictably dour: a puff for PR companies, watched by an audience presumably waiting for the Meals on Wheels to arrive. The time-lapse opening title sequence (clouds whizzing over the building, with the hours flying by in seconds) is a cruel hoax; inside the studio, each second will last an hour.

Two bobbies from *The Bill* appeared first. They were in Birmingham to promote No Crime Day, and should have made their first arrest in the studio, since the interview they were given was nothing short of criminal: 'What did you do before *The Bill*?'; 'Do you do all your own stunts?'; 'Have there been any funny moments on the show?' (They said yes, but it then transpired that there had not.) Clearly, every effort had been spared on research, and we were only a hair's breadth away from 'What's your favourite colour?' when a jaw-dropping anecdote was told. With the blood-curdling arrogance of TV people, the actors complained that they had once been on location, filming a scene involving an injured cyclist, when a St John's Ambulance man appeared and had the gall to assist what he thought was a badly wounded man. The imbecile hadn't seen the cameras ... *too* preoccupied with the life-saving nonsense. Completely ruined the take, luvvy. Punters. I ask you.

George Melly was playing in Birmingham anyway, so we had a quick ditty from him, in which he proved yet again that he is the Evelyn Glennie of song and the Douglas Bader of dance. Then a template of a middle-class, middle-aged, middle-brow English authoress came on to plug her latest book. Unfortunately, she had a severe attack of the similes, bursting out with such curious imagery as 'Adapting a good novel is like cooking with salmon, cream and truffles' and 'Having one's own novel adapted is like sending one's children orff to boarding school.' Finally Mr Melly reappeared, an old pro prepared to tolerate the indignity of the programme in return for the opportunity to promote his latest album and concert tour. Judi attempted to match the *doubles entendres* of his lyrics with some single *entendres* of her own: 'Do you stuff your ish?' (wink, wink), 'Do you get many big'uns?' (nudge, nudge). Melly somehow preserved his dignity through this continuous stream of schoolgirl innuendo, toying with her ignorance like an elderly kitten toying with a ball of wool.

Pebble Mill is that unluckiest of formats, a personality show without personality, and Judi's attempts to inject some life into it – constant innuendos, hysterical responses to the feeblest remarks of her guests (laughter that is dangerously close to tears of desperation) – rapidly become wearisome. I first saw her years ago on Westward Television, doing bunny hops with her hand stuck right up the back of a children's puppet name of Gus Honeybun, and she has lost none of the searing intellectual prowess she demonstrated in those days. Strangest of all, why does she come on to a TV programme wearing a skirt that stops half-way up her thigh, and then spend the entire programme trying to pull it down over her knees? Like the programme itself, a case of *mouton vêtu comme d'agneau*, I fear.

Give me an edition of *Pebble Mill* and I'm as happy as the day is long. The day in question being in January. Somewhere inside the Arctic Circle, thank you.

Mr Don and Mr George

We hear periodically about the unmasking of some charlatan surgeon or other. He performs operations for years, eventually gets rumbled when he leaves a monkey wrench inside a patient, and then confesses that he's really just a car mechanic who wandered into hospital one day and assumed a surgeon's role. Similarly, I suspect it's only a matter of time before Seamus Cassidy, CH4's commissioning editor for comedy, holds a press conference to admit that he is, in fact, an ex-bingo caller who knows nothing about comedy. Certainly, the number of genuinely amusing programmes he's commissioned over the past four years can be counted on the fingers of a mitten. What else could explain the lamentable standard of his department's output, which reached a new nadir last night with *Mr Don and Mr George*?

Having achieved the near-impossible feat of being the least funny members of the execrable *Absolutely* team, Jack Docherty and Moray Hunter have now, naturally enough, been rewarded with their own show. Their pre-series handout insisted that the programme title must be printed in lower case (a decree that, thankfully, has been roundly ignored by everyone from the *Radio Times* to Ceefax), but it wasn't really advance publicity at all, more of a cry for attention. As indeed is the whole show: silly clothes, silly walks, silly glasses, silly dialogue and a set by a designer still intent on deconstructing the sit-com, a decade after Gary Shandling took that idea as far as it could go. Worst of all, the comedy described itself as 'strange' and 'weird', and we all know what that means: deeply and desperately unfunny.

The show began topically. We were at war with Iraq, and Mr George attempted to parody a World War Two Churchill speech, an impersonation so poor that Winston himself could have done better, even in his present extremely poor state of health. 'I don't want to go to war, I'm too tall to die,' they cried; if only they were as childish as their material, at least you could send them upstairs to bed. Shouting (on the basis that louder was funnier), they moved on to a 'routine' about the middle classes paying a fortune to live in a shoebox, a target that belonged firmly in the 80s, not the 90s. Next, they entered a recruiting office and they shrieked, 'We can't join the paratroopers, the velocity will mean our berets will fly off.' They cried into the commercial break. I cried into the commercial break. That's the problem with this TV-reviewing lark: you lot can change channels, but I have to watch to the bitter end. And I can't cheat, because Sir down at the *Standard* asks questions afterwards.

In part two, Jack Hedley (formerly of *Colditz*) appeared as the Head of Intelligence, and unwound thirty years of a brilliant career simply by standing next to Mr Don and Mr George. He said, 'Few people want to be spies these days, that's where you two come in' and, swelp me, the lads walked out and came back in again. This was material that even Peter Glaze would have rejected for *Crackerjack*. They attempted satire in a rant against the Swiss – 'Why are they so Swiss? Why is their country so slippery? Why haven't they bothered to invent their own language?' – proving that they are that heady mix, unfunny *and* ignorant, since they have clearly never even heard of Romansch either.

Forgive me for quoting the philosophers, but Arthur Askey put his finger on it (they do at that age) when he said, 'As far as comedy goes, every generation throws up a couple of geniuses and a hell of a load of crap.' After watching Docherty and Hunter, I think it's safe to say that the search is still on for the present generation's pair of geniuses. The programme was not sur-real but sub-real, and something is deeply rotten in Charlotte Street when such atrociously written and abysmally performed drivel is given airtime. Mere competence and technique are no substitute for genuine comedic inspiration, but even the writers of *Terry and June* showed some basic understanding of how to construct comedy. For these two to attempt to deconstruct the sit-com genre is like a first-year art student trying to emulate Escher without having mastered the basic rules of perspective first.

It's just not on. But, unfortunately, it *is* on. That's the problem.

Camberwick Green

Here's a scoop. We all know that David and Richard Attenborough are brothers but, throughout history, many other famous siblings have chosen to keep their family links a secret. Until now. Take Denis Potter's sister Beatrix, whose early unpublished novel *The Singing Snake* inspired her brother's obsession with exuviating vocalists. Melvyn Bragg's nasal tones encouraged his brother Billy to sing dreadfully. There's John and Farrah Fawcett Major, Thomas and Françoise Hardy, and now I can reveal a kinship you may find more surprising still: Henry and Windy Miller were brothers.

True to form, while Henry debauched himself in the fleshpots of Europe, Windy preferred the contemplative life and moved to Camberwick Green, a sort of Plasticine Walmington-on-Sea where the people were decent and the sun always shone (because the special effects needed for rain were far too difficult). And, while Henry was in Paris, grinding out a succession of filthy novels, Windy devoted his days to grinding a purer, better substance: corn. Yesterday afternoon, to the accompaniment of a Woolworth's Winfield 'Bambi' glockenspiel (3s. 6d.), the opening credits rolled once again for this 1960s children's classic, set in a village so sleepy that it made Ambridge look like downtown Rwanda. As usual, nothing remotely unpleasant or alarming was going to happen, but that's not to say that the inhabitants know nothing of suffering. From the stilted way they walk, they're clearly all martyrs to congenital piles.

Yesterday, PC McGarry (number 452) featured atop the revolving music box (Camberwick's equivalent of an Oscar nomination). An amiable knee-bender of the old school, he'd have fitted in nicely at Dock Green if he hadn't been born with feet of clay, but he can be a bit of a martinet when it comes to paperwork. Yesterday, he'd heard a rumour that the doctor's children had been fishing without a licence, but Windy stoutly refused to play copper's nark and act as a witness. Thwarted of a nick (and untutored in the administration of invisible bruising), McGarry left the mill and visited the post office, where he publicly accused Subpostmistress Dingle of not having a dog licence for Packet, her puppy (a vile and pointless allegation to level at the woman who personally issues all licences in Camberwick). McGarry was still without an arrest, and the inhabitants didn't seem to take his threats very seriously: still, I suppose it's hard to create a tough-man image when your police siren is a party squeaker.

Then an urgent call was received at Pippin Fort, where the early-morning parade had only just got under way, even though it was nearly lunchtime. So Colonel Snort (who, with his thick moustache and hat, resembled a Californian leather queen) and troops from the King's Own Play-Dough Regiment raced towards town, pausing only to sing a jaunty military ditty. By the green, they found that the cause of the alarm was a docile swarm of bees preventing access to Murphy's bakery and, with a logic that says much about the military mind, instantly decided that the only possible remedy was to build a new bakery. Luckily, PC McGarry found Windy (a keen apiarist, it emerged) fishing near by and persuaded him to put down his rod and collect the swarm. All ended happily, but I was disappointed in McGarry, not even asking to see Windy Miller's fishing permit. No wonder that, thirty years on, he's still pounding the beat.

Plato's Republic? OK on paper. Pol Pot's Cambodia Year One? Not *quite* the success he'd hoped for. But *Camberwick Green* is a Utopia that actually works, the idealized England of warm beer and village greens that turns politicians misty-eyed. No drugs, no vandalism, no Anne

Diamond, no unemployment, no TV critics and no cracked nipples due to dry skin. All right, so it's made out of Plasticine, but it's a damned sight better than our own Cardboard City. In an age when most children's TV consists of local-radio rejects preening their egos while introducing badly drawn cartoons, Bura and Hardwick's delightful series remains as welcome proof of what can (and could again) be achieved with talent and imagination. Brian Cant narrates Gordon Murray's scripts to perfection, while Freddie Phillips' idiosyncratic double-tracked guitar remains a joy. I believe Mr Phillips is still playing professionally so, next time he's at the Albert Hall performing Henze's *Kammermusik*, why not wait for a quiet bit, then shout out, 'Give us "Riding Along in a Baker's Van".' I'm sure he'd be delighted.

J'accuse: Dame Edna Everage

You probably think it's a pretty cushy number being a TV reviewer, but there are times when we deserve danger money. If civilians don't like a show, they simply follow the programme maker's glib advice – 'You can always switch off' – but those of us on active service cannot escape so easily. We have to watch to the bitter end. I emerged shell-shocked from my office yesterday, after witnessing an abortive ambush in which armfuls of dishonest, ill-informed bilge grenades were lobbed at an undeserving victim, and hit everything except their target.

Something went very wrong with last night's *J'accuse* because, while the executioner was trying out the trapdoor, he allowed eagerness to override caution and succeeded in hanging himself. CH4 usually ensures some equality of stature between accused and accuser, but Rory Bremner's inept assault on Dame Edna had all the authority of Richard Clayderman attacking Beethoven. I have seldom seen a programme so palpably fired by vicious professional jealousy. Of course a cat may look at a king but, if you want to start a palace revolution, you need compelling arguments, not just envy. Sadly, when it came to some serious tackling, Billy Bremner might have been more on the ball than was our Rory.

The central accusation was this: Dame Edna once had a talent to amuse, but now only has a talent to abuse, using it to humiliate guests and audiences alike. To flesh out this modest thought, Mr Bremner offered us the worst Everage impression ever broadcast, and an even more terrible impersonation of a logical argument, castigating Humphries for his cruelty. What is a self-styled satirist doing condemning cruel humour? It is the lifeblood of satire, and anyway the criticism rings false when one recalls Bremner's own New Year show, replete with easy jokes about David Mellor's ugliness. He condemned Edna for transforming from a timid Moonie Ponds housewife into an egomaniacal superstar, yet that organic ability to develop demonstrates the brilliance and comic potential of the original creation, next to which Bremner's impersonations are lifeless simulacra, frozen in time and unable to grow.

Anne Karpf, the sort of dull, pious feminist who never laughs until she has thought through the political ramifications, criticized *Neighbourhood Watch*, condemning it as 'a man using the persona of a woman to denigrate women'. Yet the all-women audiences were sent into hysterics by Edna's gynaecological humour and razor-sharp exposé of their personal foibles. As for New Men like Jeremy Hardy, there was something rather tragic about their humourless, narrow-minded attacks on Humphries, and their repressive, no-platform, ghetto-area approach to comedy made them curiously indistinguishable from a bunch of outraged retired generals from Frinton. Criticisms were made of Edna's 'hackneyed' material, yet there is more originality in one of her shows than in the entire careers of most of her detractors, and her ability to improvise with an audience is unequalled. By the time Bremner began drawing parallels with the rise of Thatcherism and the 'free expression of nastiness', he had abandoned any attempt at grown-up analysis, and descended to the level of the fourth-form debating society. No, I didn't much care for the programme since you ask.

There were some positive contributions, notably from Ned Sherrin and John Lahr, who evinced the only warmth in the show and highlighted the thrill and excitement of a Humphries performance. Bremner could spit as much poison as he wanted, but the programme's problem was the overwhelming case for the defence: Dame Edna is effortlessly hilarious. Bremner, on the other hand, is a club act who has developed a taste for satire, Mike Yarwood with an O level. Last night he let his envy get the better of him. When he concluded by citing

Humphries' lucrative contract with Fox TV as evidence of his corruption, we were no longer listening to criticism, merely jealousy.

There's nothing wrong with the wolves occasionally turning in on the sledge and devouring their leader, but such attacks need teeth, and all Humphries got last night was a light gumming. *J'accuse* can be a splendid vehicle for hatchet jobs on sacred cows, but only when they are administered with the clinical precision of a Zola. We expected the mighty intellect of Emile; what we got was Budd.

Through the Keyhole

I recently devised a new game show, *Celebrity Autopsy*. Each week, two dead TV personalities would be exhumed and given *post mortems* by a glitzy female Home Office pathologist, while a star-studded panel examined their internal organs for clues as to the identity of the famous cadavers. Initially I thought it might be unsuitable for family viewing, but having looked at the current ITV schedule I'm not so sure. LWT will probably be piloting it by this time next week, but remember: I own the format.

In comparison, Yorkshire Television's *Through the Keyhole* is a paean to good taste, demonstrating that, although we ordinary mortals may dwell in squalor, in Starland there are only immaculate houses. To music that recalled the heady days of Picketty Witch *circa* 1972, Sir David Frost bounded on to a set that resembled an accident at the Signal toothpaste factory, and promised us a rare treat: a glimpse into the homes of vulgar *nouveaux riches* media types who enjoy parading their dubious taste on the box. On the panel was Tim Brooke-Taylor, a man whose jowls have now dropped so much that he appears to be permanently travelling in a high-speed lift. He has been 'starring' on indifferent game shows for so long that it is difficult to remember what he was ever famous for, so Frost reminded us: he co-sang 'Funky Gibbon' in 1975, and reached number seven in the charts. Eve Pollard was there too, as was the deeply uncharismatic David Mellor, looking more like Emperor Hirohito every day, and appearing so frequently on TV that I suspect his real motive must be revenge: the media ruined him, now he's going to ruin them.

When looking around an unfamiliar house for clues about its owner, there's nothing like an expert in design and social anthropology to guide you. So, cue the prof, Loyd Grossman from the University of Trite, who is indeed nothing like an expert in design or social anthropology, but none the less rattled off a stream of banal adjectives that testified to an impressive lack of technical vocabulary. A High Victorian Gothic lectern was 'very good', a painting was 'wonderful', while an Ethiopian cross and some ecclesiastical stained glass were both 'terrific'. His deductive powers were equally suspect. Faced with a shelf of books and some sports equipment, he proclaimed, 'These people are both passive and active,' while a picture of yachts on the wall meant 'They are interested in mucking about in boats.' If he saw the 'Guernica' print on my wall, I presume he would conclude that I am interested in dive-bombing Basque towns on behalf of Falangists. Oh yes, and Loyd pointed out that T. S. and George Eliot were not related. Three cheers.

Back to the panel. David Mellor thought that 'What comes across is a strong sense of family,' and, let's face it, he's an expert in the strong-sense-of-family area. Mr Brooke-Taylor said they were 'clearly Renaissance people who can read and go fishing'; to our Tim, even Loyd would pass muster as a Renaissance man. The house owners turned out to be Jonathan Dimbleby and the novelist Bel Mooney, who told us she had 'conceived a powerful and very moving story' but, when asked to relate it, chose to outline a rather mundane and banal one instead. Then, after the commercial break, the entire show was re-enacted, although this time there was a clever twist: the celebrities were Mr and Mrs Kevin Lloyd, and nobody had the faintest idea who they were.

Through the Keyhole is *Hello!* magazine on the box, a neat format that capitalizes on the vanity of second-division TV personalities, and the irrepressible nosiness of the British. Grossman – the man with the coathanger-in-the-mouth accent – may have partly devised the show, but he is the weak link in its presentation, his trivial observations suffering from such advanced idioglossia that Linguaphone could usefully produce an instruction course. His favourite remark is that 'This house is owned by people of taste,' yet what people with *real* taste would allow the cameras (or him) into their house at all? I doubt if we shall ever see Arthur Mullard inviting Loyd into his council flat.

Still, for those who seek fame, there are only two ways to know when you've achieved your goal: when the man from *Through the Keyhole* phones; and when people in mental hospitals start thinking they're you.

King of the Road

With lamentably poor daytime programmes continuing to suck the lifeblood out of evening television, the case for the return of the Test Card and Music from sunrise to sunset becomes ever more unanswerable. To prove my case, I'm thinking of marketing a cardboard black-and-white Test Card. Simply clip it on to your screen at seven a.m., bung on my cassette tape of *Holiday for Strings* and hey presto – experience a blissful flashback to the 1950s. No more Richard, Judy, Anne or Nick.

During the day, the biggest egos invariably front programmes with the smallest budgets. For proof, look no further than *King of the Road*, hosted by denim-clad Ross King who, with his James Dean sunspecs and bulging stomach, is BBC1's very own rebel without a corset. He is currently travelling the length of Britain, and yesterday reached Helensburgh, near Glasgow, clearly a town twinned with nowhere but considering a suicide pact with Bhopal. Being in Scotland, Ross was quick to demonstrate the full depth of his knowledge of his homeland: 'In Scotland, you're absolutely surrounded by history, the place is steeped in it.' Next we saw a montage of local views, accompanied by bagpipe music. Unfortunately, they'd unwittingly chosen a piece played on Northumbrian pipes, but one must make allowances. After all, this is daytime television, where, if they're doing a piece about China, Japanese music will be fine; it all goes *chink chonk* anyway.

Anna Walker – one of the proliferation of blonde Mariella Frostrup clones currently invading the airwaves – interviewed the patronizing commander of the local submarine base, who constantly referred to her as 'dear', and seemed close to telling her not to worry her fluffy little head about all that complicated machinery. To be fair, Anna did her best to give the impression that she *did* have a fluffy little head: 'It looks awfully small,' she said, gazing at a submarine; 'That's because most of it is underwater,' replied the commander. Inside a sub simulator, he told her that it was just like the real thing 'except for the smell'; presumably, scientists have not yet synthesized the distinctive fragrance of sixty sailors whose body odours have been fermenting in the confines of a submerged tin can for three months. Then Ross reappeared to host a *Meet the People* quiz, which turned out to be yet another opportunity to meet Mr King. The answer to one question revealed that Helensburgh was the birthplace of the inventor of television, John Logie Baird, 'without whom there would be no *King of the Road*'. Such grim news doubtless had Mr Baird attempting to contact his lawyers via a ouija board, in a belated effort to have his invention suppressed.

Finally, King (who by now I feared was suffering from a severe case of mistaken nonentity) introduced us to 'the funniest man in Scotland', Jack Milroy, but unfortunately this must have been his day off, because the most risible thing he said was 'Ach cooleen nicht grichter fish and chep supper.' Finally our host met a bunch from a Scottish Historic Re-creation Society, a sad army of Roy Wood lookalikes (during his Wizzard days) dressed in authentic medieval gear with authentic medieval 1970s guitars. As the closing credits rolled, the sight of fourteen hundredweight of kilted imbecility dancing a Highland fling confirmed my view that Scots *en masse* are best encountered outside King's Cross Station with several quarts of Thunderbird wine inside them, sprawled over the pavement and examining the cracks for the meaning of life.

The Navy has the right idea. It uses a simulator for training raw recruits, and does not give them control of the real thing until they have demonstrated a high level of competence. It's a pity that, down at Pebble Mill, what would elsewhere be regarded as a simulation of a programme seems to be connected to the transmitters without a moment's hesitation. *King of the Road* may boast a seven-strong production team and five researchers, but the show they put on screen each day might as well have been produced by the sixteen-year-old receptionist down at the local tourist office.

That's Life!

In life, there are some certainties. Tributes always flood in (they never trickle), lucre is always filthy, virtues are always extolled, rises are always meteoric, gauntlets are always run. And on *That's Life!*, no matter how pitifully tragic a story they might be relating, you won't have to wait long for a gratuitous mention of either willies or titties. This week we had both.

It's significant that the first word in the opening titles is 'help', because Esther and her catatonic catamites desperately need some. For twenty-one years they've been getting away with murder – shamelessly repeating the same shallow format of vulgar misprints mixed with tales of stupid people who've given money to clever people – but now their show is on death row, with the execution date already fixed. On Saturday night, the Patron Saint of Patronizers appeared, wearing a startled expression usually only seen on the faces of blow-up sex dolls, and dressed in a yellow number that made her look like a tube of mustard surmounted by Shergar's teeth. She'd even chosen to make her entrance through the studio audience; presumably, she thought ordinary people might like a last chance to touch the hem of her garment before she departs at Easter.

Esther promised 'new ideas' for this series. 'Each week we'll be joined by a special guest star,' she announced (TV-speak for 'Our ratings have reached rock-bottom'), but instead on came June Whitfield to read a selection of unamusing cuttings in all three of her voices: Eth, the Queen and Margaret Thatcher. The other 'new idea' was Killjoy, seven foot of rubber rhino who cynically jumped on to the Mr Blobby bandwagon, and even more cynically jumped on to a cake replica of the Foreign Office, thereby embarrassing a group of dignified World War Two veterans honourably protesting about a ban on wearing foreign medals. What a pity such an expensive cake couldn't have gone to one of those children's homes Esther cares so much about, instead of being destroyed in such a crass, pointless and unfunny way.

June returned with a joke about fat women which, no doubt, will have been forgotten when the programme runs a 'school bullying special', and another obese teenager is found hanging from a rope. Next, Kevin Devine turned on a video recorder and there – quite unexpectedly – was an old clip of Adrian Mills pretending to be Elvis. 'I had absolutely no idea,' said Adrian, playing the I'm-deeply-embarrassed card while secretly delighting in the extra attention he was getting. There's nothing like incisive investigative journalism, and Kevin's report into con-men was, indeed, nothing like it. Our Kevin had discovered that rarest of beasts, a salesman who told lies, and turned up unannounced at the man's premises. He was clearly hoping for a bit of ratings-boosting Roger Cook violence, but was roundly ignored, and I found myself raising three cheers for con-men everywhere. After all, their victims are usually the thick, the gullible and the greedy and, frankly, deserve everything they get.

Gavin produced a photo of a plumber's van belonging to 'Budjit, Grabbet & Leggete', neither knowing nor caring that there's nothing remotely funny about elaborately contrived names. Then the expressions suddenly went from grin to grim as the team embarked on an astounding piece of xenophobia, castigating poor countries like Greece and Portugal for their low medical standards, and condemning a local doctor in Corfu because 'he spoke very poor English'. In a script that managed simultaneously to bully and to sentimentalize, they relayed a sorry tale of procrastination that ended with a holiday maker being told 'Your mother is clinically dead, go home,' with tears aplenty to compensate for the irrelevance. Finally, we met a sad bunch of Barrett House dwellers, who held snail-racing contests and, even sadder, pretended to be Hoorays. For some reason, Adrian had to kiss a snail's backside, after which he placed the gastropods on the edge of a glass of beer. I had no alternative but to phone the RSPCA and report Esther for cruelty since, even in small quantities, ethyl alcohol is poisonous to snails.

Poison has fuelled *That's Life!* for two decades. The programme treats all who enter its orbit with contempt, humiliating anyone who takes part (except for Esther who, like all TV tyrants, writes everybody's script), and thankfully Alan Yentob is putting the show out of our misery in a few months, a decision for which he deserves a knighthood. In fact, if he pulled the plug on it in mid-series, I'd get a petition going for canonization.

Pobol y Cwm

For decades, the most celebrated fictional village in Wales has been Dylan Thomas's Llareggub – 'Bugger all' in reverse. Bugger all was exactly what happened yesterday in Cwmderi, a mythical south Wales village aspiring to even greater fame. Indeed, after half an hour listening to the guttural utterances of the actors, I'd only learned one worthwhile thing: Welsh must be the world's worst language to speak when you've got tonsillitis.

Broadcast in Wales since the early 70s, *Pobol y Cwm* (*People of the Valley*) was initially intended to challenge the stereotype of the Welsh valleys as being full of nothing but thousands of coal miners. Although Michael Heseltine has since overturned that stereotype more effectively than television ever could, the soap has survived and comes to BBC2 claiming to be 'S4C's top-rated programme'. A proud boast indeed. Accompanied by a tune that was more sag than sig, the opening titles gave a clue to the pace of action we could expect: sheep, grass, beer barrels, snooker, more sheep and a lot of 70s-style moustaches driving tractors. Clearly, this was not going to be life in the fast lane, more like life in the central reservation.

My fears were confirmed when the whole opening scene revolved around Eileen's plans for a meeting of the Round Table. Things perked up briefly when Rhydian (the boss of odd-job man Denzil) asked him to perform a very odd job indeed, handing him a full Bavarian costume complete with lederhosen and saying, 'I want you to wear these tonight . . . for me.' For a moment I expected a sheep to stroll in and complete a charming *ménage à trois*, but sadly it turned out to involve nothing racier than a German evening, complete with ethnic Teutonic food (Black Forest gâteau and Liebfraumilch). Meanwhile Beth, a headmistress with the legs and charisma of a Welsh pit pony, heard that a school governors' meeting had been called to discuss her future, and began shouting hysterically at a moustache: 'Are you calling me mad?' she enquired, biting deep into his wrists.

A land that can boast Shirley Bassey, Splot, Ruth Madoc, Harry Secombe *and* Max Boyce has no need of crack, and the locals got all the excitement they needed in the Deri Arms, talking about beer and pool tables, and dropping the sort of one liners that could make

Neighbours sound like Alan Bennett: 'Never mind about Santa Claus, there's another clause I want to discuss.' Keith from the brewery was given short shrift by Jean (she'd probably boil-washed it) before Rhydian reappeared, uttering the most improbable phrase ever to fall from the lips of a Welsh hotelier: 'Are there any problems with the food?' Then Denzil argued with his boss and went home to put the kids to bed, but it just wasn't his day because no sooner had he done so than there was a cot death in the family. Elswhere, Beth had become completely immobile, and Megan took one look at her before lamenting, 'Beth's been acting very strangely lately.' That wasn't the adverb I'd have used, but I suppose she was just being tactful. By the end, I was so enervated I'd almost lost the will to live. Still, never say Dai.

Despite last week's unfocused documentary about the series, it was hard for new viewers to grasp the storylines or empathize with the characters, and it's a pity that the makers didn't follow the example of Meg Richardson, who would stand at reception and record a special intro for new viewers in Nairobi if Kenyan TV had just bought into the show at episode 837. As for Cwmderi, it's a community built on a false premise, since there are no longer any villages where only Welsh is spoken. In fact, what with the high unemployment rate amongst Equity members and the tiny number of Welsh thespians, any actors in search of a steady job could do worse than to invest in a Linguaphone course.

It won't survive in England.* Subtitled soaps never do, because viewers only watch such shows for the luxury of switching off their intellect, and resent having to turn it back on to read the captions. To be fair, though, *Pobol y Cwm* is rehearsed and shot on the day of transmission (though BBC2 is transmitting episodes nine months late) and, in the last analysis, whether a soap is set in Melbourne, Santa Barbara or south Wales scarcely matters, because really they're all set inside a TV studio, hermetically sealed in time and space from the real world. And what meaning do they have? Bugger all.

* It didn't.

Oracle

The death of a TV station is always poignant, whether it goes with a bang or a whimper. For pure drama, it is hard to match Czechoslovakian Television's last night in 1968, when the staff fled the building, leaving a single camera pointing at the door. Ten minutes later a Russian soldier burst in, looked into the camera, hesitated, then smashed his fist through the lens. When they closed a station in those days, it stayed closed.

There will be nothing so spectacular tonight, as Thames, TV-am, TVS and TVSW meekly shuffle off their mortal coils, diodes and transmitters, four unlucky victims of the government's absurd auction. But a fifth casualty departs with few mourners: that Thunderer of the airwaves, ITV's teletext service, Oracle. I thought I'd take one last chance to page the latest news headlines. Shouldn't be long . . .

Although in operation for twenty years, teletext services remain so ungainly and lumbering that few can understand why the system was ever launched. Everything about it seems designed specifically to irritate the user. Pages take an eternity to call up, and are too small to convey much information. Letters go missing when the wind blows. The crude graphic design resembles Lego. Multi-coloured typefaces trivialize serious news stories. Worse, the paternoster system of multiple pages means you might enter a report at page five of sixteen, so journalists have to waste precious words on perpetual summaries of the story so far. Reading extended news items on Oracle is like watching the dance of the seven veils: you keep hoping everything will shortly be revealed, but eventually you give up in frustration, conned yet again (I'm still waiting for the news headline, by the way. Shouldn't take long . . .).

Most of yesterday's penultimate edition was not worth the phosphor it was projected on to, and seem aimed at adolescent, mentally impaired Guns N' Roses fans who wish they had girlfriends. There are pages of readers' 'Top Ten Fave Groups', while prurience and bad language abound, from 'a company full of bollocks' on 'Beatbox' (542) to 'I miss my girlfriend Sharon's perties' in fifteen-year-old 'Josh's Diary' (567). This feeble diary pretends to be genuine, but is actually a fake, written by an employee whose page number is clearly five hundred points in excess of his IQ. You can learn how to make a tart

(614), discover the time in Nairobi or Bogota from the World Clock (329), order a pair of leggings on offer at £4.95 (185), or chuckle at the thought that a caterpillar is a worm with a sweater on (552). Russell Grant (121) told me I would be entering an unsettling atmosphere of change today; obviously I share the same star sign as Oracle itself (still waiting for that headline by the way. Shouldn't take long . . .).

On a racing page, someone called Mark Holder asked me to call an 0891 number, where I would 'have access to occasional quality info which comes direct from the stables'. I dialled, a recorded voice told me that 'all racing was off', and I was charged 38p. Hurrah. The one advantage teletext services have over newspapers is that they are constantly updated, so I was delighted to read (191) what to do should I 'need a loan before Christmas'. I did make one discovery. On page 566, Oracle has its own daily soap opera, *Park Avenue*. Episode 1444 (in which Rev. Benjiy performs an exorcism) read like a novel that the author had sent to his publisher entirely by telegram, economizing on words to the point where there was no longer any style or characterization, just a pointless listing of invented facts. The cast of *Eldorado* must be its biggest fans, delighted to have found a sadder soap opera watched by even fewer viewers than their own.

What will happen tonight as this *ignis fatuus* is finally snuffed out? Will all the letters fall from the screen like snow at midnight, until only SOS remains? Who cares? The original Oracle at Delphi was closed down by the Romans because its pronouncements were so vague and misleading as to be useless. This modern Oracle is no better, and I would rather the extra lines nicked from the top of the screen were used to give a more defined image of Terry Wogan's toupee. I can only hope that Teletext UK – Oracle's successor – convinces me otherwise.

Oh good, that Oracle news headline I paged has finally appeared. I told you it wouldn't take long. Apparently, Mafeking has just been relieved.

Without Walls: Kicking the Habit

I am told that south coast bedsits are filled to bursting with burned-out, past-tense entertainers. Singing postmen, parrot-faced comics, musclemen who performed to the strains of 'Wheels Cha-Cha', chaps who banged metal trays over their heads for comic effect, these once-famous stars now linger on in penury, alone and forgotten. Mean-spirited and fickle nation that we are, we seem to like nothing better than briefly raising aloft one of our modestly talented peers and then, the instant we become bored, dropping them like stones into oblivion.

As last night's *Without Walls: Kicking the Habit* showed, the true patron saint of one-hit wonders was, however, not British but Belgian – Jeanine Deckers, alias the Singing Nun. The opening 1950s footage of volleyballing nuns could have been taken from an early Monty Python sketch but, as her tragic life story began to unfold, any desire to laugh soon died away. A troubled young woman, she entered the Dominican convent at Fichermont in the hope that a religious life might bring her some peace. Fellow nuns recalled how she learned to strum a few chords on the guitar and began composing simple songs, including 'Dominique', dedicated to the order's founder. All well and good, except that the convent authorities – with that unerring ability to smell money that for centuries has characterized the Catholic Church – fixed up a recording contract with Philips, and Jeanine's pitiful rise and fall had begun.

Her recording of 'Dominique' sold eight million copies world-wide in 1963, topping the US charts for six months, and even toppling Elvis from his throne. Not bad for the first pop song in history to deal with the twelfth-century conversion of heretics (with the possible exception of 'Chirpy Chirpy Cheep Cheep'). The distinguished theologian Professor Tony Blackburn, from the University of Talking Bilge, popped up and told us that 'She should have left the convent and had a career, given the other nuns a bit of publicity.' But she chose to stay, and the record company rechristened her the Singing Nun.

Theologian Sara Maitland attributed Jeanine's success to her mysteriousness; at first, she was only photographed from behind 'and that was terribly sexy because it was terribly enigmatic . . . people could project their own fantasies'. Sadly, when Jeanine was eventually photographed face-on, people stopped projecting their fantasies because she turned out to be a dead ringer for Olive from *On the Buses*, something that may explain why she had become a bride of Christ in the first place. It usually does. Still, the noble Philips and the convent (to whom all royalties accrued) had both made a killing from 'Dominique', so everyone was happy.

Everyone except Jeanine, whose fortunes started to spiral downwards. Once the outside world had encroached into her convent life she grew restless, and left the order in 1966, precisely at the point when the public lost interest in her. Cast loose into the swinging 60s, she wrote and recorded 'The Golden Pill' – a hymn to contraception that has probably still never made it on to the Vatican Radio playlist – and set up house with Annie Berchet, amid press rumours of a lesbian relationship. She never received royalties for her one hit but, when the Belgian government demanded huge back-taxes from her, neither the record company nor even the convent wanted to know. Hopelessly in debt and addicted to tranquillizers, she attempted a final and pathetic comeback with a dreadful disco-dance version of 'Dominique' before enacting a suicide pact with Annie in 1985. Her lawyer produced the tear-stained suicide note she had sent him: 'We've made a mess of our lives, Annie and I. We've reached the end spiritually and financially, and now we go to God and hope he'll pardon us.' They were buried together, beneath a tombstone inscribed with words from one of her songs: THE SINGING NUN IS DEAD. It's a long way to fall when you're a nun.

This was a gem of a programme, brilliantly researched, economically narrated and telling a heart-rending story with integrity and without sentimentality. Most performers are egoists who deserve failure at least as much as they deserve success, but Jeanine was too fragile and unworldly to have merited such treatment. Last night the Church and the record company appeared in the worst possible light, while CH4 was at its very best, fulfilling its public-service remit in an exemplary way. ITV take note.

Open Space: Knuckles of Love and Hate

It's obvious why some of our fellow-countrymen choose to have the words LOVE and HATE tattooed indelibly into their skin. They're the sort of people whose knuckles tend to drag along the ground as they walk, and mere paint would wear away within minutes. After watching last night's *Open Space: Knuckles of Love and Hate*, I began to feel that IMBE on the fingers of one hand and CILE on the other might form a more appropriate motto.

As usual, the space referred to in *Open Space* was clearly located between the ears of the contributors, and was vast enough to send any agoraphobic viewers running screaming from the room. Almost any programme claiming 'to dispel the myths' about some long-established practice is doomed to failure, flying as it does in the face of decades of first-hand observation. On came a motley pageant of artistes holding what looked like vibrators attached to ink-filled dentist drills, all trying to defend their profession. Lal Hardy spoke in fluent platitudes, uttering such profound observations as 'I don't mind people who don't like tattoos . . . if we all liked the same thing life would be very boring' and confirming all one's worst fears about these dubious men who permanently have designs on their customers' bodies.

'I am the practitioner of an ancient custom or ritual,' claimed Lal, 'but do you seriously think it's a deviant practice?' Somehow, you didn't need a course in body language to recognize, from his tightly folded arms and abrasive manner, that he already knew the answer to that one. Someone with a metal stud through his lip talked atavistic nonsense about tribal work, another said 'eksetera' a lot, a third explained how he had learned his craft by practising on his own leg, while another looked as though he frequently drank wood polish and had just rolled off a surgeon's slab in mid-op. One tattooist gave us a profound insight into his working method: 'He brought them two pictures in and I draw them up bigger.' Another told us that branding and scarification were becoming popular too, as though pumping ink into your skin was really quite sensible in comparison. And that, Your Honour, is the case for the defence.

Then came the victims, the sort of sad people who have a knee-trembler with somebody called Tracy, then rush down to the tattoo shop to have her name etched in perpetuity on their pectorals, only to discover that, by the time they get home again, Tracy has gone off with Darren. People were paying good money to be disfigured from head to toe, and end up looking like victims of an alien fungus from an early *Quatermass* movie. Terri had two dolphins copulating on her shoulder, a nameless chap had Ronnie Kray on his back (not, I suspect, the first gentleman to find himself in that position), while a divorcee was having a giant picture of his two children embossed on his epidermis 'because I don't get to see them much these days'. A psychopath told us, 'I'm not a particularly violent person . . . though I'm not saying I haven't had my moments,' and clearly revelled in the unease he could cause in public places, simply by rolling up his sleeves. A black man showed us his torso, and it became clear why artists throughout the ages have preferred to work on white canvases, rather than dark brown ones. And an unreconstructed greaser called Hamish spoke lovingly of how Japanese museums were allowed to display tattooed human skins after death; presumably he plans to ship himself to Tokyo the moment he starts feeling poorly.

Ugly theme, ugly people, ugly photography and an ugly score combined to produce this altogether ugly waste of airtime. The commentary tried to present the subject as a class issue, but in truth there are only two classes – the terminally thick and the rest of us – and there are no prizes for guessing which one forms the queue outside the tattooist's shop. Artistically, the work we saw couldn't hold a candle to the storming-elephants print down at Boots, and the real motivation for both perpetrator and victim seemed to be thinly disguised sado-masochism. These are people without foresight, and I often comfort myself with a futuristic scene set in a nursing home in 2060, when a ninety-year-old pensioner has to explain away, to a bemused student nurse during the bed bath, why the phrase MOTORHEAD ARE GOD. BITE OFF THE HEADS OF KITTENS is tattooed in purple across his buttocks.

December 15, 1993

Mr V Lewis-Smith
Evening Standard
North Cliff House
2 Derry Street
Kensington
London
W8 5TG

Dear Sir

I am writing in response to your somewhat scathing article in the Evening Standard on Thursday 9th December 1993.

I am a client of Lal Hardy and find all of your comments resentful to say the least. Firstly, regarding the programme itself, I and many other people tattooed or not found nothing wrong with the content and how it was delivered. However, it is the remarks about tattooed people and their artists i.e myself that I really took umbrage to. Who are you to make the kind of remarks you did ? Do you know me or the thousands of other people from all walks of life who are tattooed ? Would you say that your doctor, dentist, lawyer, Manager, accountant were sad, disfigured, ugly, terminally thick, without foresight ?? No, you probably would not ! Because you trust them and pay them good money. But how do you know that under their shirts might be lurking the odd tattoo here and there (which is rapidly becoming the case with the so called better professions).

I have been visiting Lal's studio for some 18-24 months and would not go to anyone else. Lal has just finished a full back piece on me, which I obviously hold in high regard. Indeed, every tattoo I see him perform is of the highest standard. Have you ever seen a tattoo being made ? It is a pure skill that the artist can produce such good results with ink and blood spitting at you as you work. A great deal of time and effort is put into drawing a design for a customer to his/her specification, who might even come back and have it done.

I know that I am not sad, disfigured, an alien, ugly, terminally thick, without foresight, into sado-masochism and I have never met Tracy. I suggest you retract your comments about tattooed people and their artists as I feel you have offended may people, indeed reading your article the way you have generalised I see only see you as the narrow minded person.

Yours bitterly

T M C Fleming

Sunday Brunch

Regular readers of this column will know that I have no truck with organized religion. I blame my intense dislike on an unfortunate misunderstanding that occurred some years ago, during my one and only visit to a church. Well, how was I to know that the box which said FOR THE SICK didn't mean the same as it does on airlines?

Since then, like most people in this country, I prefer my occasional contact with Christianity to take place via the box. And, if it's memorably hilarious television you're after, forget Light Entertainment departments, and tune instead to the unintentionally appalling outpourings on offer from religious units, broadcast (appropriately enough) in the graveyard slots of the Sunday schedules. A particularly fine example of the genre is *Sunday Brunch* (ITV), a programme as nondescript as the meal itself, its crudely disguised didacticism blending in about as convincingly as an Allied carpet at Balmoral. All TV presenters are born with clip-on smiles, but only Christians have developed clip-on moral rectitude, none more so than Julian Pettifer and Janey Lee Grace. Both were so wholesome that they could have been knitted by someone's mum: him with his amateur Scientologist's smile, her so scrubbed and wholesome she made Mother Theresa look like a slut.

As in a scene from *The Twilight Zone*, where everything looks normal until the camera pans out and the actors are suddenly revealed to be three-foot dwarfs, it was obvious from the outset that something wasn't quite right. And the moment that the presenters began speaking ('We're going to look at Bhangra,' said Janey, introducing the first item, to which Julian replied, 'Bhangra? Hmmm, that sounds like a sort of curry,' and Janey retorted, 'No, you're thinking of vindaloo'), I realized what it was: they were intellectual midgets. The researcher had presumably been told 'Sikh and ye shall find,' because Ninder Johal had entered the studio to tell us about this form of Anglo-Indian crossover music. 'Why did Bhangra start in Birmingham?' asked Janey; 'It didn't,' said Ninder, who then told us that 'Religion plays little part in this music,' so *he* won't be asked back. Dr Patrick Dixon (Scientology smile factor 8) condemned sexual freedom and declared that 'My book has struck a chord in the heart of the nation,' mercifully unaware that none of the viewers had ever heard of him before, and had completely forgotten his name again within seconds of the caption fading. Then Janey moved to the Isle of Dogs where, she told us, people had started wearing rainbow ribbons to counter the might of the British National Party – and it worked. If only the Germans had tried rainbow ribbons back in the 30s, all that unpleasantness after Nuremberg could have been avoided.

Like its secular weekday equivalents, the magazine format continually trumpeted its own forthcoming attractions (with vacuous titles like 'Hot Potato', 'Open Brief' and 'Real Lives') in an endlessly unsatisfying promotional paternoster. On came two Christians wearing earstuds and sporting Mockney accents and I looked heavenwards as they tried the 'Christ was really cool yeah' approach. Then I realized that one of them was Tony Robinson (confirming his Blairite Christian socialist credentials) who had modestly decided to rewrite Jesus' words for him: 'Look, this kingdom of God business may sound a bit impractical, Utopian, but that's no reason to be silly about it.' How true, and so much better than the King James version. Next, Robert Holden (who runs a 'laughter clinic') said he'd written a book called *Laughter – The Best Medicine* and I sincerely hope he'll chuckle when *Reader's Digest* sues him for copyright on the title. He claimed that giggling was 'internal jogging', said he collected drawings of Jesus guffawing, and grinned so maniacally throughout that a nervous breakdown cannot be far away. His whole philosophy was, indeed, laughable.

Watching a religious programme inevitably leads us to ask ourselves serious questions. Why, for instance, was it being transmitted on a Sunday morning, when anyone remotely interested ought to be in church? And do socialists (naturally inclined to the left) who involve themselves with organized religion (naturally inclined to the right) spend most of their waking hours in osteopathy clinics, being treated for spinal disorders? Still, the great thing about Christians is that you can insult them in print and, true to their religion, they have to turn the other cheek. Unlike Shi'ite Muslims, who clearly have an image problem. They should have a show on ITV and really put the fun back into fundamentalism.

Considering how old you are, it's amazing how little you've accomplished.

25th April 1975

Dear Mr Lewis-Smith,

I take great exception to your remarks about Christians in "Sunday Brunch".

May I remind you that JESUS died on the cross, and was crucified for your own. Christ our Saviour took an earthly form and suffered for you that you might have life ETERNAL. May I remind you that those who do not recognize His loving sacrifice will be damned in the fires of hell for all eternity.

Yours sincerely, David Deamer

28 April 1995

Dear Mr Dennison,
Thank you for your recent letter.
I'm afraid that, until I received it, I had no idea at all that Jesus Christ had done all those things on my behalf. I cannot understand why nobody had ever told me about it before, and thank you for drawing the fact to my attention.
Yours sincerely,

Victor Lewis-Smith

Supermarket Sweep

In a quest for *satori*, Zen mystics spend their lives trying to contemplate impossible phenomena, like the sound of one hand clapping. But if it's a *serious* cerebral workout they're after, all they really need to do is to tune in to morning television, and try to imagine something worse that what they're watching. Waiting for GMTV to end, I saw someone outside a prison reporting 'serious rioting, prisoners hospitalized . . . burns, smoke inhalation'. Then back to a grinning Fern Britton in the studio who said, 'Right, well, tomorrow we'll be sorting out your hair and meeting the stars of *Baywatch*. Now here's *Supermarket Sweep*.' Unfathomable crassness like that would have your average savant reaching in despair for the Anadin within minutes.

The sets of most game shows look like they've come from Asda, but *Supermarket Sweep* is the first one that actually boasts about it. Located in a real-life imitation supermarket, it's hosted by a man with a 'There you go' factor of 10, all the panache of a continuity announcer for Anglia TV and the sort of name – Dale Winton – I thought had died out in the early 60s, along with the likes of Troy Tempest and Rory Storm. Yesterday he stood beneath a huge sign that said FRUIT AND VEGETABLE (a description whose accuracy was verified the instant he opened his mouth) and invited three pairs of contestants – Mandy and Julie, Wayne and Dick, Eve and Julie Anne – to 'prove your shopping skills . . . there's prizes in store and much much more'. A great idea. After all, game shows have been getting grosser and grosser for years; setting one *in* the grocer's was the logical next step.

The answer to the first question was 'dog food', and Julie Anne was the lucky winner. Taking a can of Chum off a shelf is not particularly gripping TV, even by daytime standards, so she was told to run as fast as possible around the aisles, but it wasn't all excitement, dear me no. Wayne guessed the price of a bag of peanuts and Dick said 'back bacon'; they were practically unstoppable. In the 'Scrambled Letters' round, Mandy said 'digestive biscuits', and Dale said, 'You see what happens on *Supermarket Sweep*? It can go up, it can go down, it whizzes along.' Then Dale suddenly said, 'Where am I?' I shouted back, 'Late twenties, career going nowhere, reduced to this rubbish.' But what did his question mean? Was he confirming that he really is from the Leslie Crowther school of presenters? Turned out the response he wanted was 'Lisbon' but either way the round had nothing to do with shopping. Even the commercial break that followed seemed more of a programme than the programme itself.

Only Chinese artists and Western morons habitually clap themselves in public and, since none of the contestants claimed to be members of the Bejing Opera, I leave you to draw your own conclusions. In lieu of a climax, the teams were allowed to charge around the supermarket and grab whatever they liked off the shelves. There's always something distasteful about naked greed, but the sight of six adults fighting and risking personal injury in order to stuff sacks of kitty litter and jars of pickled onions into their trolleys was somehow more pitiful than offensive. Finally Dale slipped into call-and-response mode, telling the contestants, 'You haven't won two thousand pounds, but you have had fun,' and they replied, 'Yes, it's been great just being here.' As the credits rolled, I noticed the writer's name was Susan Huntridge and wondered how she got the job. Then I saw the producer's name was Howard Huntridge. So, no great mystery there.

While some companies are paying £35,000,000 a year for their franchises, Central are paying £2,000, so why are they producing cheap trash like this for the network? If we have to have a show set in a supermarket, then frankly I'd far rather see edited highlights from Asda's closed-circuit TV. Children ramming errant trolleys into stacks of baked beans. Violent arguments in the 'Eight items or less' queue about whether twelve apples are really one item. Shoplifters being apprehended. Now that actually *would* be worth watching. As for this, throw it out down the garbage chute and for God's sake let's hope it's bio-degradable and we never see it again.

To Mention But a Few

An odd bunch, composers. Probably sitting day after day in solitary confinement, hunched over a quire of sixty-four-stave manuscript paper, doesn't do much for anyone's social skills but, if you ask me, most of them are only seven quavers to the semibreve. Sir Malcolm Arnold once instructed me (quite innocently) to accompany him to a lavatory where, as he sat on, we discussed his Seventh Symphony at length. Sir Michael Tippett invited me for a drink, then promptly sat on my Walkman and smashed it to bits. And, after two minutes' conversation, Elisabeth Lutyens suddenly showed me a picture of Muhammad Ali's head stuck on to a naked male torso and confided, 'Him and my grandson – the only men in my life.'

Elisabeth who? You may well ask. Not only was she a fine composer, but (even dead) she also provided a lone voice of reason at the outset of last night's *To Mention But a Few* (part of CH4's *Secret Chamber* season about women composers): 'I always refused to join any women's societies in England, or concerts for women only. I don't see why you should discuss being a woman composer any more than being a homosexual composer . . . it's frightfully old-fashioned.' At that point, the programme logically reached a double barline and should have concluded with some performances of her agreeably strident music. But, instead, we had to endure an hour of the most painful, incoherent cacophony I've ever heard: the sounds of the pampered, self-pitying middle classes harping on at full whinge.

The set had more than a whiff of 70s Viv Westwood about it, an appropriate backdrop to the score of middle-aged feminist contributors, whose cause also peaked in the 70s. Gathered together to give a puff to the Women in Music organization, this plummy bunch of talking heads constantly referred to 'Orff' (not composer Carl, just the opposite of 'on'), as they trotted out hard-luck stories of male indifference to their work. 'Publishers should be begging to publish this music,' wailed one, seemingly unaware that, since the advent of photocopiers, publishing new music has become an act of pure philanthropy, not business. Others lamented that there were insufficient lucrative commissions on offer, although scarcely one in a thousand wannabe composers produces anything worthwhile with the money, and the first (and last) performance is usually given in a near-empty hall. Indeed, from an aesthetic standpoint, most composers should only get Arts Council grants if they promise *not* to compose: that really would give the public value for money.

Everyone doubtless had valid points to make, but their interviews had been disastrously edited into a mosaic of disconnected, contradictory soundbites. Several times the programme derailed, and started dealing with anything from women conductors to racism and having babies. One contributor insisted that women had always been excluded from the musical establishment, the next that they had always been accepted. Wilfrid Mellers rightly highlighted the remarkable achievements of Clara Schumann and Fanny Mendelssohn but, of the numerous women who spoke, only Minna Keal came across as someone whose music you wanted to hear more of. Indeed, the hour would have been better devoted to this remarkable and unaffected composer who, from her appearance and manner of speech, is clearly related to Handel. Irene, that is.

'By the end of the day, I'd like to be able to pick up a piece of music and not think, Aha, this is by a woman composer – just that it's a jolly good piece of music,' said someone from Radio 3, a viewpoint strangely at odds with the desire for segregation which many of the women composers sought. Britain's leading female composer, Judith Weir, was nowhere to be seen, and (Keal and Nicola LeFanu excepted) this seemed to be largely a parade of second-rate scribblers, blaming lack of success on discrimination rather than on any deficiencies in the talent department. Art is frail and downtrodden enough in this country as it is, and the sight of composers attempting to tear the existing support structure to shreds was as unedifying as it was inconsistent. CH4 was clearly aware of the problems too, because it took the unusual step of substantially re-editing the programme after sending out preview copies. Take a bow producer Mary Jane Walsh, who last night created televisual *Klangfarbenmelodie* – a sad case of try to spot the theme.

Newman and Baddiel in Pieces

Michaelmas term will soon be upon us, and the new student intake is at risk of contracting a terrible disease. The symptoms are unmistakable. The victim begins to look mean and moody, experiments with an unconvincing Cockney accent, tells fellow-students that his parents were lost at sea, and buys himself a razor that leaves a three-day growth of stubble on his chin, for that authentic 'I'm too intellectually preoccupied to shave' look. But the gaffe is blown at the end of term when Daddy (a High Court judge) and Mummy (head of the WRVS) turn up in the Volvo to collect his trunk, utter the phrase 'Hello, darling' and are overheard discussing his offshore investment portfolio.

So it is with the stars of *Newman and Baddiel in Pieces*. David Baddiel and Rob Newman may sport the least convincing Cockney accents since the glorious days of Dick Van Dyke, but their loyal middle-class student audience are hardly likely to know that. The Edvard Munch titles scream out teenage angst, but sadly it is clearly some time since either of these two were students themselves. Like gentlemen in their forties cycling in Lycra shorts, you can't help feeling they're a little too old to be dressed as teenagers and touting themselves like this to a naïve campus following.

Scratch away the veneer of sneering contempt, and the little learning which they wear as heavily as army greatcoats, and what did we find last night? A structure heavily indebted to the monologues of Kelly Monteith, that 80s comedic giant who rose without trace to a position of well-deserved obscurity. In these soliloquies, they explored their innermost feelings of vulnerability, insecurity, shyness and inadequacy, feelings so profound that you wondered how on earth they were ever persuaded to step in front of the TV cameras and talk endlessly about themselves. But, despite the Freudian trappings, we were in juvenile Woody Allen territory, and it didn't take them long to get on to jokes about gherkins and marrows, and women nibbling on cucumbers. Having started with adults and adultery, we descended to infantile humour with a pie thrust into a face. Not funny, but the lads will no doubt claim that it was a deconstructionist pie.

In between these insights into human shallowness were the

sketches, and things went from Baddiel to worsiel. A pointless skit about an unsafe safety officer who caused road accidents took up a full minute, and then, blow me, exactly the same thing happened again, this time in the kitchen. Another sketch saw them dressed as The Orb, unsuccessfully trying to perform 'unplugged'. Minutes later, the same joke was repeated, this time with the Utah Saints. Their portrayal of two bickering history professors has apparently achieved cult status on campuses and, hearing them deliver such mortal lines as 'You wet your bed, your bed's like a lake,' it's easy to see why they are being hailed as worthy successors to the Two Rons. To be fair, there was one excellent sketch about sniffing aerosol cans; but to be fairer, the two of them were complete and utter aerosols to begin with.

The nadir was reached with Newman's impersonation of Jarvis, a kerb-crawling pervert so depraved and debased that he could repeat the line 'You come from Stoke on Trent do you? You know what they say, Stoke on Trent, bent' with no shame or remorse whatsoever. He continued to the audience, 'That last bit wasn't very funny, and the fact that you wanted to laugh, but couldn't, gave me pleasure.' By that point, I was beginning to resemble Munch's 'Scream' myself. The simple fact is that, while teenagers may find their mixture of arrogance, introspection and smut hilarious, adult viewers see before them a pair of fundamentally unlikeable performers with a very short shelf life. The pair often complain that the serious press ignores them, but what else can you do with an act that only the immature could find funny? There were occasional flashes of real inspiration, but not enough to justify wading through such a miasma of self-indulgence. Producer Harry Thompson is a Concorde pilot who finds himself flying a Sopwith Camel, and even he can only just about get the thing off the ground.

So how is it then that Newman and Baddiel are one of the few comedy acts able to sell out Wembley Arena? There can only be one answer. The Wembley Arena must be a pub in north London.

The Cook Report

Television people are as bad as Jehovah's Witnesses: they're always knocking unexpectedly on your door. Sometimes it's LWT's Light Entertainment Department, with Bob Carolgees saying, 'Surprise, Surprise' and barging into your hallway. Other times it's Central's Heavy Entertainment Department, which is exactly the same except that Roger Cook turns up and tells you that you've won tonight's star prize: five years in prison.

The Cook Report began its seventh series last night with a report on the Manchester triads. Not since the days of Frank Cannon has justice been pursued with such ludicrous obesity as when Roger's vast smiling bulk waddled after the man who Cook alleged was the head of the largest triad in Britain, and attempted to interview him. Of course, Mr Cook had no fear of Oriental martial arts; you would need Bovis, not Kung Fu, to throw our hero off balance.

Roger, part Esther Rantzen and part rottweiler, is a man with a mission, and that mission is to rid ITV documentaries of their dreadful ratings, by turning serious issues into entertainment. Yesterday's programme, *Meet the Triads*, had everything an LE title should have – except an exclamation mark! Even its plot would have served well as a sit-com. Jo Tan from Hong Kong 'wanted to be a good citizen', and was persuaded to open a bogus video shop in Manchester, in the heart of the triad empire, while we watched him on a secret camera. What happened next? The triads called by and Mr Tan found himself starring in a video nasty. But the inevitability of the beating, combined with Cook's enthusiasm for showing us the thuggery in full detail, made it all seem grimly funny rather than tragic, the televisual equivalent of laughing at funerals. To maximize our enjoyment, Cook solemnly intoned, 'This is not a dramatic reconstruction,' satisfying those of us who always turn up the volume whenever the newsreader says, 'Some viewers may find this disturbing.'

And it certainly was disturbing, what with the intimidation, extortion, threats and physical injury. Cook told us Jo was safe really, because Central had built a fake wall in the shop and he could run away but, when you've been beaten so badly that you can't stand up, you don't want escape routes, you want a team of paramedics. Tan's motives were simple: he wanted to help put the triads behind bars. *The Cook Report's* motives were simple too: they wanted exciting footage, and they got it thanks to Tan, continuing to film him as he crawled helplessly in the street, rather than rushing out to help him. After all, someone might have killed him, and they wouldn't want to miss footage like *that*!

This is a curious programme, and it is a mystery why its genuine violence can be shown before the watershed, when fake violence cannot. The viewers want Roger to get hit. His producer wants Roger to get hit. Roger's victims want to hit him. Worst of all, I think *Roger* wants to get hit, knowing that a physical assault gives the programme a suitable climax, unlike last night's impotent, absurd and almost genteel denouement in a police station.

The triads are a wretched cancer within the Chinese community, but self-styled vigilantes like Cook make me uneasy. I remain dubious of both his motives and his programmes, which are short on explanation and very long on sensation. Like the Guardian Angels, he often behaves more yobbishly than the yobs, and he has now assumed the role of a latter-day Witchfinder General. In an earlier series, he once stood over a pornographer and forced him to kneel down and burn his books on camera. He is so sure of the end that he feels he can justify such means. And that terrifies me more than any triad.

One thing is certain. After last night's programme I don't think we're likely to see any signs stuck to the doors of Chinese restaurants reading COOK URGENTLY REQUIRED.

Natural Neighbours

There are certain pieces of popular propaganda which I absolutely refuse to believe. Glasgow is not at all violent, so it's said, it's really a quiet, friendly, cultural place. Alcohol-free wine isn't at all vile, I've often heard, it actually tastes better than the real thing. And pigs aren't dirty, ignorant swine, they're really clean, clever and extremely affectionate. The jury's still out on the merits of Glasgow, and the stomach pumps are on standby next to the unopened Eisberg but, after watching last night's *Pigs Might Fly* (BBC1, first in the *Natural*

Neighbours series), I've become a total convert to the porcine cause.
As I'd always suspected, *Spitting Image*'s depiction of tabloid
journalists as a bunch of porkers turned out to be most unfair: pigs have
better table manners, superior personal hygiene and are manifestly
more intelligent than the average hack. As proof, I draw to your
attention Hambone and Bacon, Vietnamese pot-bellies who, every
morning, patriotically raised the Stars and Stripes up the flagpole of
their Colorado farm. Or Priscilla, the swimming pig from Texas, who
once leaped into Lake Somerville to save a drowning child, becoming
enshrined in local legend thereafter as the 'Hog Hero'. Or Lady's Maid
IV, a 'beautifully ugly' middle white from Preston, who was undoubtedly the most stunningly cute animal I've ever seen on four legs.
Certainly far cuter than the average tabloid hack, many of whom I've
also seen on all fours, late at night in Dean Street.

'The entire population of the swine world are my relatives,' said a
T-shirted American woman whose breasts sagged down to her knees
and, looking at her, I could quite see her point. A pig pushed another
pig on a skateboard and then (more novel still) we saw a pig being led
by a pig – Officer Matt Jagusak, holding a leash attached to Special
Agent Ferris. Ferris's highly trained snout could unfailingly detect a
small bag of cocaine hidden in a lorryload of baking soda and, although
a bloodhound's nostrils may be more sensitive, the police preferred
Ferris because 'Dogs have the intelligence of a rock . . . pigs are the
rocket scientists of the animal kingdom.' Sadly, battery farming has
crushed that intelligence in many of today's breeds so, in Edinburgh,
Dr Robert Young had devised Foodball (a spherical, knobbly affair
containing their dinner) to stimulate them and encourage their
foraging instincts. For a moment, we veered dangerously close to
That's Life! territory as a stadium was hired, a referee blew his whistle,
and two piggy teams duly trotted out, looking not unlike a squadron
of R101s, each balancing on matchsticks for legs. But at least we had
the rare excitement of hearing the middle eight of the *Match of the Day*
theme, a thrilling experience which (like straying into the middle bit
of the *Mastermind* sig) felt as though I had suddenly fallen clean over
the edge of the world.

Most people prefer a clear demarcation between their potential
pets and their potential dinners, but that distinction had become

blurred for many of the pig owners. When Tom Alty's middle white won first prize at the West of England show, he hugged her lovingly and said, 'She'll be back next year, one way or another . . . I do like bacon for breakfast.' And, to the backdrop of a porcine version of *Desiderata*, we visited Pigdom, a Texan swine shrine where we heard the sad tale of Jerome, a grieving pig in exile who'd committed suicide by going out in an electrical storm and getting himself struck by lightning. A tragedy, some would say. But the Mr Micawbers amongst us would see it more as a good 'n' tasty instant barbecue.

This was a sensitive but not sentimental look at pigs – dignifying them rather than Disneyfying them – and, if the series continues in this vein, it'll be a hit. The pigs had been brilliantly researched and photographed, and the programme's understatedly humorous narration (by Griff Rhys Jones) was far more persuasively inviting than the haughty cry of the Attenborough beast. Indeed, my only fear is that New Age people, tiring of whales, might be tempted to start setting the pig's limited repertoire of grunts to music. By the end, my admiration for the animal knew no bounds, but that didn't stop me immediately tucking into some pork the moment it finished. I won't tell you which part it was. Walls have ears you know. Well, I've heard that's what they put in their sausages, but it's probably just a rumour.

GMTV

The truth is out. TV-am never lost its franchise after all, the whole thing was just an elaborate ruse to get rid of Mike Morris. One night last week, everyone else simply upped sticks, moved to new premises under an alias and carried on without him: Lorraine Kelly, Dr Hilary Jones, the producers, the researchers, the sofa, they're all there on GMTV. They've even hired Morris's moustache, his suit and tie, his Christian name and his interviewing lack-of-technique, and given them to the new male presenter, Mike Wilson. Only Morris's brain was left behind at Camden Lock, unemployed. Still that's nothing new, his brain was always unemployed there.

Even the GMTV controller, Liz Howell, might be Bruce Gyngell with a frock on, because the entire set is still decked out in his favourite colour – poodle-parlour pink. With a roaring fake fire in the grate it made a cosy scene yesterday, spoiled only by a pop-out mortuary tray in the form of news footage covering murders in Ireland and the badly burned body of a young woman found in a bin liner. Then, back to cosy quizzes, diets, recipes, fashion, chats with third-division stars and human interest stories. In short, *TV Quick* magazine with moving pictures.

Jeremy Beadle told us he collects unusual facts. 'I have twenty thousand books,' he boasted, which is rather like learning that Stephen Hawking has twenty thousand pairs of trainers. 'I put everything under the day they happened and compile it under a thing called "Today's the Day",' he explained; shame there isn't a basic English grammar on his shelves. Dr Hilary Jones appeared in a denim shirt unbuttoned down to the chest hair, and was introduced as 'the world's fourth-sexiest man', just like it was a BMA conference. Linda Lusardi (that other distinguished medical authority) conducted a searing interview with Gazza, discovering that when he wants to lose weight he eats less. Then a woman went to Sri Lanka, after being inoculated against cholera, typhoid and charisma, and asked us to phone in if we knew the country's former name. I did, said, 'Ceylon,' and was cut off before I could give my name and number. Maybe that was all they wanted to know.

Simon Parkin, an ex-BBC children's presenter with a voice that really ought to be wasted on local radio, forced two 'stars' from Coronation Street to construct the Toast Office Tower out of bread and peanut butter. What did they think of the bombings in Manchester? 'It's getting stupid,' they replied. Then Fiona Armstrong, former anchorwoman at ITN, came on with a kippometer and announced the height of the toast tower as four and a half kippers. I understand that Fiona considers her transfer to GMTV a wise career move.

After a cartoon, Carla and Jemma, victims of the unfortunate but extremely stale hospital baby-swap story, were in the studio. The parents were interviewed three times, repeatedly describing how, due to an administrative bungle, the wrong label had become attached to their baby and given to someone else. I expect that is how Bruce Gyngell felt, if he were watching yesterday. They've taken his baby, switched the labels and now they won't give it back. In its franchise application, GMTV ruled out weekday cartoons and promised 'political interviews . . . authoritative family programmes and educational children's features . . . to develop a European perspective in children'. Yesterday's programme made little attempt to meet those commitments, simply thumbing its nose at the ITC. Unless it mends its ways, the ITC should revoke GMTV's licence *tout de suite*.

The worst was saved till last. 'Top of the Morning', hosted by baby-crazy Lorraine Kelly, was bottom of a very deep and much-scraped barrel. A fitting climax came when Leslie Walters, a cook, suddenly and inexplicably began performing exercises in mid-recipe. By then I had half nodded off and mistook it for an epileptic fit.

There was only one saving grace: at least Claire Rayner didn't appear. But then they announced they've booked Philip Hodson for Thursdays. I have stomached raw eggs for breakfast in Thailand. But Hodson? Sorry, that's the limit.

Pebble Mill

There's something about the name Ross that seems to guarantee mediocrity on television. Over the years we've had to endure Nick Ross, Ross McWhirter, Jonathan Ross and any number of sibling Rosses (not to mention Joe Ross, the Chinese bandleader). But for genuine, twenty-four-carat mediocrity, none of those could hold a candle to the host of *Pebble Mill* (BBC1), Ross King, a man so unremittingly disagreeable that, every time I see him, I have an out-of-body experience. Through every orifice.

The programme's opening titles depict the heads of various 'stars' (daytime-TV-speak for a roll-call of the embarrassingly available) inside tiny effervescent bubbles, an appropriate introduction for TV's biggest bubblehead. King of the first person singular (I lost count after the seventy-sixth 'I'), he's recently acquired an orange Bikini Atoll suntan, which contrasts nicely with his monochrome personality, and makes even the peripatetic lobster herself, Judith Chalmers, look as pale as a Dickensian waif in comparison. No longer content with merely presenting the programme, he's lately started performing on it as well, attempting feeble topical sight gags of the sort they do properly on *Have I Got News For You*. Call me sadistic, but there's something exquisitely satisfying in the sight of a man corpsing at his own jokes as they fall lifeless to the studio floor.

The show's young production team presumably don't care that their audience is mostly in its seventies, because they regularly book musical acts that could only appeal to teenagers. Yesterday four youths, clearly chosen for their perfect looks rather than their perfect pitch, performed an ersatz Take That routine, while five cameramen unwisely attempted a manic pop-style video, when shooting *Gardeners' World* would surely have taxed their powers to the utmost. As for the guests, I can only assume that they turned up because their agent phoned and said, 'You've got to do it.' Clive James got the best out of American humorist Dave Barry on Sunday, but Mr King got the worst, a succession of half-hearted traveller's tales with the punchlines surgically removed. Logan Murray proved to be yet another alumnus of the Craig Charles school of poetry, believing that an unfunny thought will, if you make it rhyme, suddenly become hilarious. Mr King, meanwhile, essayed the old presenter's trick of mentioning the producer (in this case Helena) at least once a show, feeding her ego and thereby guaranteeing himself another series in the presenter's chair.

Appropriately for a mill, the programme ground on and, as the camera pulled out, it was revealed (also like a mill) to be full of old bags. Silly me, I'd thought the studio set was lit blue, but it was simply the reflection from two hundred dear old blue-rinsed biddies, sitting in stony silence. Next, dressed in not so much a shirt as a test pattern for Thai TV, Vince Hill appeared and told us how he nearly didn't record 'Edelweiss'. Ah well, they nearly didn't build Auschwitz; it's just a horror we have to live with. Then he told us how he nearly became a professional opera singer, announced, 'This is *The Marriage of Figaro*,' and launched into an aria from *The Barber of Seville*. Josie Lawrence coyly asked if it was all right to mention her new ITV series, and luckily Ross said it was, because she'd already got several clips from it cued up. Finally the Take That clones reappeared and, swelp me, there were five of them now. Presumably, one of them was so excited about the booking that he'd overslept and missed the start. Still, at least they mimed their way through a fitting end to the entire programme, pretending to sing to an audience that pretended to listen.

During the show, Mr King introduced us to 'the funniest man in America', 'the best ballad singer in the land', and 'the best impressionist in the country'. So how does *Pebble Mill* consistently manage to be one of the worst shows on television? Until my campaign for the restoration of the daytime Test Card succeeds, the BBC could at least improve matters by getting rid of presenters with Lilliputian brains and Brobdingnagian egos, and running the entire programme like Jury Service instead, selecting names at random from the electoral register and demanding that we all have a turn at presenting the show. The people wouldn't want to attend, would resent taking time off work, have nothing to say, and their hearts wouldn't be in it. So (as Angus Deayton is wont to say), no change there.

The Royal Variety Performance

It's terrible, the way we British treat our Royal Family. More enlightened countries painlessly executed their monarchs when they were of no further use, a swift and dignified end. But we, sadistic nation that we are, have preferred to let our imperial family linger on so we can torture them, year after year, by making them attend *The Royal Variety Performance*.

Like most truly dreadful television, the *RVP* excuses itself at the outset by announcing 'It's all for charity' – in this case the Entertainment Artists Benevolent Fund, which looks after clapped-out performers from a bygone era. Ironically, almost every participant in Saturday night's show could equally well have qualified as a recipient, since the entire evening had apparently stepped straight out of the 1970s. After two and a half hours of frilly-shirted comedians saying, 'There was an Englishman, an Irishman and a Scotsman,' interspersed with Muppets, Mike Yarwood and excerpts from *Grease* and *Saturday Night Fever*, the Dominion seemed to be not so much a theatre as a zoo, a last refuge for species which you thought had long ago become extinct, and which clearly could no longer survive in the wild.

One after another, people introduced each other as 'a truly great star', displaying the sort of mutual blind faith normally only witnessed at group levitation sessions. Cilla – as ever, looking like a chipmunk in the throes of a static-attack – introduced Frank Carson, who told us about a Jewish cowboy called Hopalong Goldberg, waited in vain for applause, then said, 'It's the way I tell 'em,' although I think the problem was far more deep-seated than that. Cilla spoke about 'dear sweet Tommy Cooper and Frankie Howerd', but on came Brian Conley, a man with all the charisma of a Wigan bingo caller. Next was Jimmy Tarbuck, reeking of formaldehyde although, as luck would have it, 70s sideburns are currently back in fashion. He told us that he thought Nat West was a Jewish money lender, waited in vain for applause, and then went into a routine with Mike Yarwood (the first double act I've ever seen with two straight men). Tarby left the stage leaving Yarby to do a splendid impersonation of the Prime Minister. Unfortunately the Prime Minister he had chosen was Harold Wilson, but at least he had the decency to put John Major glasses on while he did it.

There was culture too. Leslie Garrett provided the bel canto, and Harry Secombe the can belto, reliving his finest hour with 'If I Ruled the World', and demonstrating his splendid knack of singing absolutely in tune while the entire orchestra played a quarter-tone flat. Forever Plaid appeared, and won the Good Taste Award with their light-hearted tale of a group of young musicians killed in a school-bus road accident. 'New talent' Bradley Walsh told us, 'I had a bit of a funny journey here this evening laygennlemen,' and waited in vain for applause. Then, unaccountably, somebody talented came on: magician Joe Pasquale who, in five minutes, displayed more comedic ability than the entire evening had warranted: he did 'something Paul Daniels couldn't do' (pulled at the roots of his hair), he sawed Snoopy in half until the kapok came out, he told us about 'the American Siamese twins who came to England so the other one could drive' and, above all, he actually entertained us. Mr Pasquale deserves better than this, and he'll undoubtedly get it.

Back to the 70s, and the Bee Gees, accompanied by lighting that was not so much rave, more a man standing in front of a dozen Bakelite switches randomly throwing them on and off. Then there was hushed talk from the electric chipmunk of 'terrible accident . . . doctors and nurses' and on came Leslie Crowther, a man whose fettle seemed to be in far finer shape than Tarby's. Finally Cilla told us that 'Michael Barrymore is next and he's liable to do anything'; sadly, although he did many things, entertaining us was not amongst the list of things he'd chosen.

It's not that they're old guard; doubtless the Baddiels and Newmans would have been even worse. But, like Miss World, this is a format that has long outrun its purpose and its public, and it should be left to moulder in peace. Watching this sycophantic pageant, I presumed that Mr and Mrs HRH must leave with an overwhelming desire to go home and have a cold shower. But, thinking about it, with their family values, they're doubtless as vulgar as the galleryites. They probably loved every minute.

A J. L. Harris wrote to tell me my review was crap, and had joined all my reviews in the Harris ash can.

Dear J. L. Harris,
Thank you for your letter about the *Royal Variety Performance*.
    I'm delighted to hear that you throw my articles into the ash can after reading them. It's where they rightly belong.
    However, for maximum benefit, may I recommend that you throw them on to the fire instead. What with the forthcoming imposition of VAT on domestic fuel but not on newspapers, my column could be viewed as a valuable additional form of low-cost heating chez Harris.
    Best wishes,

    Victor Lewis-Smith

Dear Victor,
A great pity your *Evening Standard* article is not printed nationally. A pity because fourteen and a half million viewers who enjoyed the show – rising to seventeen million for Michael Barrymore – would be able to see how totally out of touch you are as a TV critic.
    Mind you, those few poor souls who saw your BBC-2 efforts know that already.

    John K. Cooper

Facsimile for:
John Kaye Cooper
Controller of Entertainment
London Weekend Television

29. xi. 93

Dear Mr Cooper,
There follows a copy of a letter which I received by post this morning.

You will, no doubt, be as anxious as I was to realize that somebody has gained access to your personal stationery and is sending out unhinged letters, purporting to be from you.

Obviously, I realized immediately from the content and the childish handwriting that the letter could not be genuine, since no controller in his right mind would lower himself by sending, to a TV critic of all people, letters that demean both himself and his company. It would be laughable for anyone in senior management to claim that ratings were a reliable indicator of programme quality and, as for trying to rebut a carefully argued review column by making snide remarks about the ratings for my BBC2 show, that would display a playground mentality that no controller could possibly possess.

Clearly, you will be as anxious as I am to ensure that the public image of LWT does not descend to the level of a clutch of barrowboys, interested only in ratings and not quality. I have, therefore, sent a copy of this and your letter to Christopher Bland, the chairman of LWT, and suggested that he instigates an internal inquiry to discover who has been bringing the name of LWT into such disrepute.

Yours sincerely,

Victor Lewis-Smith

Behind the Headlines

My Buddhist phase, during which I became convinced that every Friday night Terry Wogan dies on air and reincarnates as Terry Christian, is over. My belief in a traditional British miracle-working God was restored yesterday when I switched on *Behind the Headlines* and found that Loyd Grossman, televisually speaking, is no more. The man whose impersonation of an American intellectual was always about as plausible as Douglas Bader captaining the British synchronized swimming team has finally gone. No one said what had happened to him, but I suspect that unsuccessful surgery is to blame. A full manual evacuation of the vowels that backfired, perhaps. One can only hope.

Loyd has been replaced by an avocado jacket containing John Diamond. Between them they introduced us to John Walsh, who appeared to have vomited over his tie; Cynthia Rose, who resembled a pipe cleaner surmounted by a blond poodle with a party-squeaker voice; and Jaci Stephen, who used to write this column and is therefore immune from all criticism. Diamond promised an analysis of the week's news: several topics of conversation, four Gucci intellectuals and a bell whose ping would end the conversation and usher in the next subject. But this simple format produced simple-minded results, half an hour of conversation that made the backs of Walkers crisp packets look like the *Encyclopedia Britannica*.

As the avocado jacket banged the bell and the topics flew by, I felt I was either watching a televised *Just a Minute* or a coachload of foreign tourists on a whistle-stop tour of abroad, determined to cram ninety-three countries into a weekend. *Ding.* It's the White House, so it must be the USA. Bill Clinton's the new President, you know. He was at Oxford, he likes the British. Does Maastricht affect the special relationship? Dunno. Quick, back on board. *Ding.* Look out the window, it's the Eiffel Tower. We're in Paris. They're banning smoking in public in France. Smoking's very bad for you. And disgusting. I'm all for it. Hurry, the driver's revving up. *Ding.* The Old Bailey, London. Family feuds. Kids divorcing their parents. It's a shame. No, it's a good thing. All aboard. *Ding.* An American campus. *The Political Correctness Handbook.* Arguments for and against, no time to hear them. Manhole covers should be femhole covers. Snigger, snigger. Bald people are follically challenged. Ho ho. Hurry up, we're late. *Ding*. Shakespeare country. Should they make cartoons of his plays? You lose the majesty of the language. Yes, but at least people learn the stories. *Ding*. Goodbye, and off to the green room. 'I was wonderful, darling, how were you?'

This was Radio 4's *Stop the Week* transferred to television, but without the perspicacity or the time to explore any topic thoroughly. Worse, all its news stories went behind last week's headlines, so the opinions sounded not only trite, but stale. This was conversation without exposition, delivered at barrowboy speed to disguise the emptiness of its content. In the end all we got was inconsequential and unsatisfying froth, verbal zabaglione, and a boxing bell would have been a more appropriate regulator, so crude were the attacks and counter-attacks.

A nice researcher phoned me in the summer and tried to book me for the show. I explained that the only way I would appear would be if I was on a plane flying over Television Centre and it happened to crash into the studio, and I was pulled from the wreckage, badly concussed, sat in front of the camera and given a powerful shot of morphine. What a news scoop for the *Behind the Headlines*. Pity they wouldn't get around to covering it until the next week.

Equinox: Beyond Love

I suppose I must be somewhat strait-laced, because the nearest I'd ever come to a *ménage a trois* would be if I had a date with a schizophrenic. I did once meet a woman who had met a man who claimed to have had sexual intercourse with the eighteenth hole at St Andrews, but such extra-curricular golfing activities seemed like an evening with Mother Theresa compared to the goings-on described in last night's *Equinox* (CH4).

It's a fundamental rule of television that, the more titillating the programme, the more clinically asexual the narrator sounds. Yesterday's edition, *Beyond Love*, had a Libby Purves factor of 10, since it was looking at paraphiliacs, people compulsively drawn towards a panoply of bizarre sexual targets, everything from safety pins and gold rings to cadavers and even Barry Manilow. Obsessed with sexual practices outside the normal spectrum of desires, their cravings vary from the merely unusual to the downright illegal, and an entire department at the Sexual Disorders Clinic in Baltimore is currently trying to classify their various illnesses, and discover the causes. Most of the sufferers are male, and the commonest groups are the autoerotic asphyxiates ('We usually only find them as fatalities') and the fetishists. Apparently, they're born with faulty sexual featural selectors in their temporal lobes, so that in infancy, instead of being aroused specifically by female breasts and genitals, they're attracted 'to other objects that are black, shiny and wet'. If I were Flipper, I wouldn't sleep soundly in my pool tonight.

But (as any curious teenager who's ever given Alfred Kinsey a good thumbing will attest) it's the case histories that contain the juicy bits, so enough of the medical preamble and cue the freak show. An Andrea Dworkin lookalike declared, 'My preferable sexual encounter would be with a young deceased man between seventeen and twenty-five,' giving a whole new meaning to the phrase 'dead good in bed'. I'd heard of cradle snatchers, but here was a coffin snatcher who used to sneak into funeral parlours, and was only interested in men for their bodies. She briefly turned from necrophilia and tried worshipping Jesus Christ (little difference, some might say), but the obsession returned, until one night she kidnapped a client and drove him away in a hearse, stopping only to consummate their love in the back: 'I always say, if the hearse is rockin', don't bother knockin'.' A perfect coupling: her boyfriend was permanently stiff, would never have answered her back and, with a girlfriend like her, he was better off dead.

'I was seventeen when I first started strangling myself in the mirror,' said Nelson who, for variety's sake, also enjoyed drowning himself in the bath. A doctor who, I thought, dribbled throughout his interview (the expression 'Physician feel thyself' passed through my mind) reminisced about a patient whose interest in stuffing plucked chickens went way beyond the Paxo stage. But the star of the evening was undoubtedly a septuagenarian who was sexually aroused only by amputees, had a video of one-legged men skipping, and (in true Victor Kyam style) liked it so much that he shot off his own leg. OK, it's bizarre, but no odder than having breast implants or a nose job and, although it probably hurt a bit at the time, I doubt if any diet book could suggest a more painless way of losing twenty pounds in a hurry. Inevitably, the programme was inconclusive because, despite the glib terminology, research into the brain's functioning is still in the Dark Ages, and all manner of biological, social and psychological factors may or may not be to blame. Temporal lobe epilepsy might explain the compulsive state that sufferers fall into, or perhaps it's society's refusal to recognize that children are sexual beings (we saw a scan of a foetus masturbating inside its mother, a scenario that even Oedipus would have drawn the line at). As for remedies, they varied from grinning and bearing it, through a variety of chemical suppressants, to castration as a last resort (the voice of ball-crushing Jenni Murray seemed to lift slightly at this point), but it was hard not to feel some sympathy for otherwise normal people, trapped by a compulsion that they didn't enjoy, didn't understand and couldn't escape. This was a well-written and coherently cut documentary, much smarter than *QED* (its BBC equivalent) but, even so, I've decided that I *do* mind about what people get up to in the privacy of their own homes, after all. It may not frighten the horses, but by God it frightens me.

This Morning

There's a fundamental law of television: the faster and zazzier a title sequence, the duller the programme that follows it. I knew I should have expected the worst when the images introducing *This Morning* rotated so rapidly that I started to feel like Linda Blair during the revolving-head scene in *The Exorcist*. Still, at least the induced sense of nausea put me in the appropriate mood for watching the programme.

This imaginatively titled magazine show is daytime TV's answer to *Hello!* magazine, except that the rich and famous show a marked reluctance to appear on it. So instead Judy Finnigan, who could be mistaken for an overgrown schoolgirl, and Richard Madeley, like a dummy straight from the window of Man at C&A, invite us into their dismal TV home in Albert Dock each day to meet a variety of guests, most of whom have only one thing in common: we've never heard of them, but they've all got a book out and are desperate to plug it.

Book number one was by Ronnie Kray's wife Kate, who was so rough she made Sharon and Tracy sound like Barbara Cartland. Asked why she had married a psychotic lifer, she retorted, 'Why did you marry Richard?' Judy loyally retorted, 'Because he wasn't behind bars in a hospital for the criminally insane.' More's the pity. Still, it's good a reason as any, I suppose. 'Didn't you marry Ronnie simply to get media attention?' they suggested, failing to spot that they themselves were the media giving attention. Book number two was by Laylan Young, a Chinese woman expert in the art of face-reading, and even more expert in the art of conning credulous TV researchers. 'The most interesting thing about Princess Diana is that she has two eyes,' she told us and, do you know, I think she's right. 'We'll move on now to Michael Parkinson,' said Richard, staring at a picture of Cecil. Look no further than Madeley for new *Question Time* presenter.

I suspect that American universities offer PhD courses on selling your book on *This Morning*, because some US pseudo-psychologist pops up on the show every other day. Book number three was by a Californian couple – grinning like glassy-eyed Scientologists – who gave advice on bringing up baby. Their own looked utterly miserable and made a noise resembling a Harrier Jump jet with faulty gaskets, so they were obviously experts. Spend every waking and sleeping moment with your baby, they said, and never smack them. All right, no smacking babies then, but how about smacking child psychologists?

In between the book promotions were the regular features – makeovers, phone-ins, transforming your urban terrace into a Tuscan farmhouse – that daytime TV uses as grouting to fill the innumerable cracks. A woman stuck a bath sponge on a cricket stump, pushed some dead flowers into it and said, 'There, they'd charge you eighty pounds for that in London.' We also had a fashion show featuring models who looked as though they'd been in a freak accident involving an Oxfam shop, a wind machine and a rubber tree. Then a Frenchman came on and taught us how to shave: 'Use foam, a brush and a razor.' No more chainsaw misery for me in future. Now I realize why I always ended up in intensive care every morning.

'What do you ask the guy who's done the lot?' said Richard,

introducing Sir Harry Secombe. He clearly hadn't got a clue, because his most inspired question was 'Do you feel any older?' Secombe has been interviewed a thousand times and if I mention the words 'Shaving act . . . Spike-tortured genius . . . heart attack . . . the Lord . . . Pickwick . . . diabetes . . . *Highway* . . .' you'll get an idea of how much new ground Mr Madeley broke. Mouth in top gear and brain in neutral, with the missus cringing whenever he makes a comment, Madeley is the show's major problem. But the entire programme resembles one of the ads for cheap carpets that appear during its commercial breaks: yes, it's tacky and plastic, but it's only 10p a yard and it covers a huge area for next to no cost.

During his interview, Secombe claimed to have interviewed the Pope. 'Your Holiness, I am from British television,' he cried. 'Good luck,' replied the Pontiff and moved on. He'd obviously seen what goes on here. Perhaps he should send a cardinal over to *This Morning* to administer the viaticum.

The Best of The Tube

No matter how insubstantial their talents may seem, most performers on television deserve to be there. The girl on the Test Card, for example. She keeps her job because she doesn't age and can sit very still all day, holding balloons and smiling, until the director shouts, 'Cut.' Then she walks off set and goes home. The extras in soap operas are highly skilled too, able to order drinks in pubs, and hold animated conversations with one other, while emitting no vocal sounds whatsoever. Ross King is there because, like banging a tray over your head, when it's over we all feel just great. But one televisual conundrum has troubled me for years, so much so that I often find myself waking bolt upright in the night screaming, '*Why* Jools Holland?'

I asked myself this question again last night while watching him introduce *The Best of The Tube*, CH4's attempt to secure legendary status for an inoffensive but long-forgotten 80s pop show. Now in his late thirties, he still feigns the blasé, laid-back, carefully studied gaucheness that surly sixteen-year-old pop bands affect on *Live and Kicking*, glancing with premeditated absent-mindedness everywhere but at the camera, casually picking flecks from his jacket, and generally evincing such contempt for his audience that I found myself transforming into an old-fashioned schoolmaster and shouting, 'Don't slouch, boy' at the screen. Helping him pour old wine into new bottles was his original co-host Paula Yates who, despite her advancing years, had unwisely chosen to bulge out of a flab-tight black PVC one-piece, surmounted by an explosion of peroxide hair, yellow roots and all. Frankly, I was reminded of the way gardeners wrap up leeks with bin liners, to keep them warm in winter.

Without so much as a script or a decent idea between them, they traversed the Newcastle studio where *The Tube* once broadcast live, smugly referring to original props as 'a bit of rock and roll history'. In an attempt to explain what the atmosphere was like, they abandoned conventional sentences and resorted to weak adjectival strings, 'fantastic, anarchic, wild, spontaneous', yet there was little sign of such frenzy when the compilation of highlights started, just a lot of homely Tyneside girls with perms like their mums, and lads with plastic jumpers bought at the Co-op. We revisited 1982, the year when Jam gave their last-ever performance (by the sound of it, not a moment too soon), while Iggy Pop had the inspired notion of appearing without a shirt. Afterwards, we heard how Mr Pop 'tried to throw himself off a train' (a very easy thing to do, yet somehow the Wild Man of Rock couldn't manage it) and how, when the inspector came into the carriage asking for tickets, Iggy would say, 'What do you mean by that?' A man that crazy could do anything; why, the anarchist probably wears the same pair of underpants three days running as well.

In between tracks, our hosts reminisced about legendary rock and roll moments, such as the time Jools was suspended for six weeks for saying a rude word – a crime which, let's face it, certainly put Auschwitz into perspective. ZZ Top mumbled through their beards, while a twenty-five-stone Divine sang 'Shake it Up' (he's since lost masses of weight on the Andy Warhol diet). George Clinton performed too ('Any relation of Bill?' quipped Jools, by now not waving but drowning), but the programme confirmed that these were, musically, some pretty lean years we were revisiting. Still, it's odd to think that there is now a whole generation of ex-punks, all fat and forty. Some, I believe, are even called Tony Parsons and write for the *Telegraph*.

The programme ended, but the question remained: *Why* is Jools Holland there? As Cosmo Landesman's dazzling article in this month's *Modern Review* points out, his celebrity exists only on television. He was peripheral to the success of Squeeze, and Jools Holland and the Millionaires never troubled the chart compilers. Have you ever heard one of his records on the radio, or met anyone who owns one? The fact is, the man is a purveyor of a watered-down, simplified style of New Orleans blues – a pale imitation of Professor Longhair (performed without the subtle polyrhythms of the original) – but he gets away with it because this is the UK. He's the musical equivalent of a second-hand car salesman from Pinner, so why is he constantly invited to front music programmes? There can only be one answer. Does he possess negatives of every British TV controller in sexually compromising positions? If so, I demand copies.

Video Diaries

There are three bits of advice that we'd all do well to pay heed to. Never play leapfrog with a unicorn. Never dine in a restaurant where the 'speciality of the house' is the Heimlich manoeuvre. And most of all, never, ever trust a tabloid photographer.

Paul Harvey – one of that fine band of professional photographers for whom the word 'glamour' is synonymous with 'Tits out for the lads' – told us considerably more about his world than we really wanted to know in last night's *Video Diary* (BBC2). Video diarrhoea would have been a more appropriate title for this hour-long stream of unformed, noxious sludge, which followed Mr Harvey and his entourage while they executed a tacky 'glamour' shoot for a northern corporate calendar. Just in case his incoherence of thought wasn't enervating enough, he'd also had the foresight not to wear a tie microphone (relying instead on the Sony compression microphone, housed only an inch away from the camera motor), so quiet rooms sounded like 747 jets, and the first syllables of sentences sounded as though Abu Nidal had just detonated one of his amusing packages on board one. Unfortunately, the sound wasn't quite bad enough to obscure the fact that, yet again, the video-diary format had encouraged a presenter to become introspective. And, as always happens when very dull people become reflective, there was a feeling that life had been turned off at the mains.

The clients had made only three stipulations regarding their calendar. There had to be nipples aplenty; one of their executives had to choose the girls, attend the shoot and generally have a good look; and, in Mr Harvey's words, the locations had to be 'laid-back, Latin and luscious', proving yet again that alliteration is the last refuge of the illiterate. Cuba was, therefore, a surprising choice for the shoot, since all public nudity is strictly forbidden there, two government moustaches were on hand to intervene the moment an errant mamilla hove into view, and the demure Cuban models who had been hired were not prepared to pose topless anyway. And so Mr Harvey (whose catchphrase was the laughably unbelievable 'Trust me') was forced to rely on the two English models he'd flown out – page-three clones with sub-Lorraine Chase accents, eagerly squeezing their nipples into erection without even being asked – and a great deal of tawdry deception to ensure that the client's breast quota was fulfilled.

In the proud tradition of British film-makers who 'go bush', there were plenty of crowd shots of Johnny Wog looking at the film crew in amazement, presumably so Mr Harvey and his cronies could feel that their work was somehow significant, when everyone could see that it was merely grubby. 'Only three days to sort everything out and already the clock was ticking,' he intoned, trying to convince us that he really might not get his twelve calendar pictures, that December might have to be cancelled, and that what we were watching was exciting rather than unutterably tedious. But at every location the models dutifully allowed their tops to slip off yet again, Mr Harvey said, 'Trust me, we won't use any of this' to the moustaches as he clicked the shutter, and the job was duly completed. Of course, the models were supposedly the ones being photographed, but it was hard to say who was *really* on display. After all, Mr Harvey did all the posing, pouting, and tantrumming; and as for the biggest breasts, if Havana organizes wet-T-shirt competitions, the company executive would surely have won first prize.

Another *Video Diary*, and another sad case of mistaken nonentity. Travelling to a foreign country, deliberately breaking its laws and customs, blocking roads, deceiving government officials and putting their jobs at risk, all for the sake of a mildly pornographic calendar, is as breathtaking as it is arrogant, and the BBC shouldn't be giving airtime to such non-stories. 'What a misunderstood land Cuba is,' said Mr Harvey, and, as a champion misunderstander who'd misunderstood pretty well everything, including himself, I suppose he'd know. In the final minute, it suddenly emerged that he'd also spent a two-week freebie travelling the country on behalf of the Cuban Tourist Board – a fascinating journey that even he wouldn't have been able to make dull – yet he'd wasted the whole of his TV hour focusing on nipples. Looking at his calendar stills, he lamented, 'My pictures are, to a great extent, missing the point.' Too right. And so are his videos.

Watchdog

We are approaching the time of year when the 'Don't have nightmares' school of TV presenters will start popping up on our screens, drooling with phoney outrage as they demonstrate how small children can choke on plastic toys in Christmas crackers, or remove the heads from Taiwanese dollies to reveal the gleaming ten-inch metal spike beneath. But on *Watchdog* it's Christmas all year round, and each week brings another stockingful of horror, with practical demonstrations of inflammable children's nighties and lacerating toasters, while the ratings shoot up even higher than the flames from an incorrectly wired deep fat fryer.

This programme is the consumer equivalent of a Stephen King novel, highlighting the hidden terror that lurks within the most prosaic and innocuous of household objects. Lynn Faulds Wood and John Stapleton are a media couple suffering from such appalling wholesomeness that they could locate pure evil in a loose-fitting ballpoint cap. Every Monday evening they tell us how a number of dense people have been robbed, conned, fiddled, burned and bruised, and become affronted on our behalf. With its pointless acres of floor space, its live transmission and its banks of receptionists ready to answer calls within seconds, *Watchdog* clearly sees itself as the kid brother of *Crimewatch*; however the cheap ghoulish simulations, trite

Cinemascope-format film reports and arch delivery reveal its true pedigree: this is the idiot son of *Nationwide*.

Last night we learned that if you heat up a single mince pie in a microwave for half an hour instead of twenty seconds then, astonishingly, it will catch fire. Lynn frowned. A man had made a lot of money out of selling leaky roofs and then scarpered with the money, which seemed like impeccably good business sense to me. John frowned. An arthritic OAP had handed over her funeral money to a splendidly callous rep, in exchange for a Cyclopad vibrator which didn't work, while another OAP from Spain was charged £13 bank costs on his £10 DSS Christmas bonus. This time, John and Lynn both frowned. Lastly, the scandal of pizza firms employing accident-prone learner motorcyclists as delivery boys was dealt with, although the crucial point – if the messenger is in intensive care, then the pizza will arrive cold – was unfortunately missed. Typical: the customer's interests are put last again.

This worthy consumer programme is very hard to consume, at times displaying symptoms of Rantzenitis by jarringly juxtaposing tragedy and low wit in an attempt to appeal to a mass audience. Why should a man (aka 'punter') who has lost several thousand pounds on faulty roofing have to dance in a puddle in galoshes while 'Raindrops Keep Falling on my Head' is played in order to seek redress? Desperate consumers are easily manipulated, and the BBC should not force them into such indignities, nor should they be making snoop tapes of perfectly legal motorcyclists. Schmaltzy interviews with the parents of fatal-accident victims are also unwarranted. And unpaid debts are a matter for the courts of law and certainly not the BBC's pay-it-back-to-our-viewer-or-we'll-run-an-exposé department.

In Lynn and John's simplistic world, the culprits who perpetrate consumer misdemeanours ideally would be paraded through the studio, head hanging down Chinese-style, before a summary execution against the wall of the *Blue Peter* garden. But in truth the victims are usually the most guilty of all: pathetic innocents, the sort who smoke in bed and then complain when their house burns down. Their stories are undeniably tragic but, if a laugh track were dubbed on, I for one would be howling and slapping my sides. There is nothing like the misfortunes of others to send us off to bed with a warm glow.

In the mean time, here is a warning of a highly inflammable George III, made by Sir William Beechey. A family who live on an estate in Windsor have had trouble with it, and both they and their house are now gutted. So, if you have one, you should return it immediately to the manufacturer. Now, have a look at this seemingly innocent pop-up toaster . . .

The South Bank Show

The presence of TV cameras is almost guaranteed to induce a severe attack of the clichés in speakers. Neighbours of a mass-murderer always say, 'He was a bit of a loner,' even if he was actually the local wag. Contestants on game shows always declare, 'I don't care if I win, I'm just thrilled to be here,' even though their eyeballs are tattooed with £ signs. And comedians always say, 'I was deeply shy at school, joking was my defence mechanism against being bullied,' when the real reason is clearly 'I was, am and always will be an egocentric prat, desperate to be the centre of attention.'

Last night's Melvyn Bragg's *South Bank Show* celebrated Norman Wisdom's heroic battle against shyness during fifty years in showbiz, and the clichés were really out in force. The dreadful, hackneyed opening parody of a 50s cinema trail (how many more times must we endure the fake film scratch and tired 50s voice?) was an appropriate start, since the entire programme turned out to be a poor, unintentional parody of a serious bio-documentary. Captain Sinex, whose hanging jowls are making him look more and more like Mr Turner from *Emmerdale*, hosted what was not so much an interview as an audience, with Wisdom discoursing on his favourite subject – himself – and his comic's cliché of a childhood: 'The terraced house where I was born . . . mother left . . . beatings from drunken dad . . . poor but happy . . . ran away from home . . . holes in my shoes . . . lived off Bovril . . . slept rough . . . all alone on Christmas Day.' Melvyn listened transfixed, or perhaps he'd had eyeballs painted on his eyelids and was already comatose, who knows? Ten minutes in and I was certainly racking up the ZZZZZs.

Having established Wisdom's comic credentials, we moved on to his mature work (if such childishness can be thus described), and a montage of archive clips served to demonstrate that his desire to entertain has never really been a blessing, more of a curse. This was not a comedy routine, but a man having a fit on stage. Every bucket of paste had to be stepped into, every staircase fallen down, every piece of fine china smashed, every hose squirted at someone pompous. Whereas great comedy continually subverts our expectation, Wisdom perennially fulfils it at wearisome length, and all in a suit three sizes too small. But this was an arts programme, so Richard Dacre, an earnest cliché of a film historian who deserves a regular spot in 'Pseud's Corner', was wheeled on to put a bogus intellectual gloss on the pratfalls: 'Wisdom's Gump fails to recognize the subtle indications of class authority . . . his recurring comic strategy is to misunderstand . . .' Hurrah for Mr Dacre. At last, a moment of true comic genius that had me laughing out loud.

As the show progressed, it was hard to escape the conclusion that Wisdom's undeniable success – a dozen Rank films, stage and screen awards, a nice house in the Isle of Man and a Rolls-Royce – has been due not so much to talent as to sheer persistence. He is an egregious little man who appears to suffer from the same affliction as Roy Castle, namely that he plays a hundred instruments, none of them very well: 'I learned to play the clarinet,' he told us, before producing a sound very much like a tom cat in the throes of evisceration. At times, the room was awash with schmaltz as Wisdom moved alarmingly easily from giggles to tears and back again in his standard don't-laugh-at-me-'cos-I'm-a-fool guise. In private, as in public, he seems to mistake tears for genuine tragedy, and laughter for genuine comedy.

Nigel Wattis' limp film glossed over the less rosy side of Wisdom's life – the two failed marriages, the abortive attempt to make it big in the USA, the sudden collapse of his film career in the late 60s – but sadly, *The South Bank Show* nowadays seems to regard itself as the *Hello!* magazine of the arts world, replacing criticism with unbridled praise, and preferring 'celebrities' to 'artists'. A few months ago, they raised George Formby shoulder-high, and they currently seem intent on bestowing wholly inappropriate intellectual cred on to music-hall acts who neither merit nor crave it. What next? The *oeuvre* of Bobby Davro? As for Wisdom, it seems appropriate that the signature tune (used throughout the programme) of someone clearly so infatuated with himself should be entitled 'Narcissus'.

Telly Addicts

More and more nowadays, television is in danger of disappearing up its own fundament. In the early years, it regarded itself as so inconsequential that it frequently did not bother to make recordings of even its most important programmes. But more recently it has acquired some worryingly narcissistic tendencies, and who today would be surprised if a Biteback report, about a *Panorama* investigation into the making of *Telly Addicts*, was reviewed on *Did You See?* and ended up being discussed on *Points of View?*

We all know the effects of prolonged in-breeding, and both *Telly Addicts* and its host Noel Edmonds display the classic symptoms. The incestuous lineage of the quiz's format is all too clear, with rounds half-inched from various shows: 'TV Times' is a mini *Rock and Roll Years*; 'On the Box' is ESN-level *Mastermind*; 'Channel-Hopping' is heavily indebted to *A Question of Sport*; with a thin grouting of TV trivia separating these three central pillars. As for Noel, anyone who laughs hysterically through eighty per cent of his own show (especially when the audience can barely manage ten per cent) must be close to certification and a rubber room with no handles on the inside.

Last night's final took place between two families – the Paynes from Hull and the Wilsons from Mansfield – an octet who looked as though they could not pass the basic neurological finger test, although they obviously manage to watch TV at least twenty-five hours a day. Had they been athletes there would certainly have been a call for an artificial stimulant test, since both teams were clearly hyperactive, applauding themselves as though they were in a US game show. Noel introduced them, putting them at their ease by talking mostly about himself; how very like the man.

The archive snippets on which they are quizzed were initially fascinating. It was delightful to see Valerie Singleton doing a Tuf shoe commercial. Russ Conway's attempts to create a more visually exciting act by undressing his piano, making ridiculously exaggerated hand

movements and flashing his choppers, were touchingly doomed. And
I never knew that the dog in *All Creatures Great and Small* was called
Tricky Woo. I shall dine out on that. Nevertheless, it soon became
clear that this was not *Telly Addicts* at all, but *LE Addicts* – sit-coms,
stand-ups, sport and adventure, topped off with a few ads and some
popular drama. Dick Emery yes, *Omnibus* no. *Thunderbirds* and *Post-
man Pat* of course, but *Civilisation* or *Monitor* no thank you.

Noel is an instantly likeable man. In fact I think that is what I don't
like about him. With his streaked hair, his nudge-nudge common
touch, his self-assured smug manner and his schoolboy puns, he is the
archetypal smooth local rep from a package holiday firm, the guy who
meets you on the bus from Rhodes Airport, assumes an instant
matiness and tells you cheerily that your hotel in Ixia is only half built.
Worse, he is a gross attention seeker, hijacking questions to talk about
himself, even walking from team to team with an absurdly affected
Max Wall gait making it impossible to avoid paying him absolute
attention. Is this Little Man Syndrome?

On and on ground a panoply of pap: Dot Cotton, Daleks, *Count-
down* and *Hogan's Heroes*, Bucks Fizz and Hilda Baker. The Paynes
won a holiday to Florida where they can (and probably shall) watch
cable day and night in their hotel, and the Wilsons received consolation mini-TVs, so they can view while at stool. But half an hour of this
was enough to make me queasy. CH4's *TV Heaven* earlier this year
worked because it juxtaposed the trivial with the consequential:
Doonican with Jung, Varney with Bronowski. But an unalleviated
diet of sweets with no meat soon becomes sickly and cloying. There are
film buffs and opera buffs, but there is no such thing as a telly buff. Nor
should there be, because only the retarded and TV critics should pay
so much attention to such an ephemeral, transitory medium.

It may be an old joke, but it's still true: TV is called a medium
because it is seldom rare and hardly ever well done.

Going for Gold

I warn you now. If daytime television gets much worse, I'm going to stop watching it altogether, pop down to the video hire shop, pick something at random and review that instead. Even *Jeremy Clarkson's Guide to the Wankel Rotary Engine* would be preferable to most of the dross currently on offer.

When choosing the presenter for a new quiz show, producers draw up a list, with the biggest names at the very top. Agents are telephoned. Offers are made and rejected. Gradually, they move further down their list. Eventually, as the cameras prepare to roll, the reluctant shout goes up: 'OK, phone Henry Kelly then.' So it must have been with the genesis of the Euroquiz *Going for Gold*, for there was the great man himself, charisma-light, hair prematurely ginger, bounding on to the cheap blue neon set and rousing the audience to fever pitch with his first exciting words: 'It's an important day, because today we'll find the third semi-finalist for the first semi-final.' The man exudes not *gravitas* but *frivitas*.

With our national cricket and football teams at their present nadir, I thoroughly approve of the BBC making three foreigners speak English when they compete against one of our boys. How else are we ever to win anything? But, although the programme claims to be pan-European, non-British contestants almost invariably hail from Scandinavia or the Low Countries, and therefore all speak better English than Henry. Yesterday's line-up was a typical Euro-bland trio in jackets and slacks, looking like a team of junior buyers from Marks & Spencer: Gert from Denmark, who resembled a hairless unconstructed photofit picture with a slashed saveloy for lips, and expressed 'a strong interest in Boy Scouts'; Stein from Oslo, who wisely talked only about his tie, since it was by far the most interesting thing about him; and our boy William from Scotland. Together with Kiki from Finland, who said almost nothing and seemed to be there principally as ballast, this was to be our afternoon's entertainment.

What followed was not a game show, but an impotent ritual in which questions and answers were meaninglessly and unenthusiastically intoned. Every expense had been spared, and there were neither picture inserts nor music. 'We have no elimination round,' said Henry, beginning a round whose sole purpose was to eliminate one contestant. His unique skill as a broadcaster – whether as TV quizmaster reading from cards, or DJ on Classic FM regurgitating sleeve notes – is that you always feel you have a better grasp of the subject-matter than he does.

Eventually it was over and, I don't mind telling you, I was intellectually stretched. Gert had a tactical win and Stein had a tactical defeat, but neither seemed remotely elated or dejected, as though this had been a job interview and they had both decided not to accept anyway. Finally, Henry told us that, if we knew which island *Bergerac* was originally set on, we could waste 48p by phoning an 0898 number 'and have the chance to win a year's free TV licence'. Such a lavish prize was offered, presumably, because they reckoned no one would bother to take up the offer, after this example of the output.

The show is certainly not gold, but the production office deserves to be knee-deep in guilt. The graphics and set are appallingly cheap and nasty, while the words of the title music plumb new depths of inanity – 'The heat is on, the time is right, it's time for you to build your game 'cos people are coming, everyone's trying, trying to be the best that they can when they're going for, going for gold' – as though they've been translated into English from Danish, via Esperanto. The whole farrago is such a dreadful warning against 'European' culture that I half expected the closing credits to reveal it as 'a Lord Rees-Mogg production'. In fact, Reg Grundy is responsible, and it can only have got on air on the strength of his name.

Years ago, Picasso used to avoid paying restaurant bills by simply signing his famous name on a napkin and presenting it to the *patron*. *Going for Gold* is Reg Grundy's free lunch.

How Do They Do That?

There's been an epidemic of punctuation in television recently. In a futile effort to inject vitality into inanimate programmes, dozens of titles now have a rejuvenating exclamation or question mark clipped on, like gentlemen of a certain age hopefully donning corsets and toupees. *That's Life!*, *Wish You Were Here . . . ?*, *See Hear!*, *Play It Safe!*,

What's Up Doc?, *Middlemarch!*. *Middlemarch!?* OK, I lied about the last one.

The makers of *How Do They Do That?* were clearly so desperate that they didn't stop with the title, but knocked up a giant polystyrene question mark for the studio set as well. The programme (made by Reg Grundy and Time Warner, who customize the global format for local consumption) had a mustachioed presenter when I first saw it in the US so, naturally, the BBC also wanted someone with a moustache to front the British version. Sadly, since Anna Raeburn wasn't available, the job went to Desmond Lynam instead. Being little more than a childish version of *How?* for grown-ups, the ideal co-presenter would have been dear old Bunty, but instead we had Jenny Hull, who began last night by revealing a cunning stunt in which Des hovered high above TV Centre before plummeting rapidly to (apparently) certain extinction. His impersonation, presumably, of the show's prospective ratings. Five minutes in, and we were still being told what was coming up later (a sure sign that a programme is going nowhere, and is merely treading water) but, when the first item was finally shown, you could understand their reticence. For no discernible reason they'd chosen to reveal the unremarkable secrets behind a US dancing baby commercial (which no one here has ever seen). Then, quite unconnectedly, a London detective sergeant called Bob Window recalled how his hand had been severed at the wrist by a yobbo with a samurai sword. 'How do they do that?' Des asked. Deprived childhood, society being to blame and knock-down sale at local samurai-sword shop were the phrases that crossed my mind, but Mr Lynam was preoccupied with the problem of sewing Mr Window's hand on to the rest of Mr Window: 'How? . . . well, a team of surgeons use micro-surgery to stitch the tendons and arteries together'. After such a detailed explanation, we could probably do it ourselves. Bob's repaired limb was working well, although admittedly you could still see the join on his forearm. Compared to the rest of the programme though, it was seamless.

'Send us a letter if you've ever wondered How Do They Do That,' begged Des, although it's most unlikely that anyone impressed with the feeble explanations we'd had so far would be able to write. 'Millions of magazines are sold every month. How do they do that?' he asked. The answer was that they have pictures of beautiful young women on them, just like third-rate TV shows. We saw acres of supermodels, and met a man whose job involved touching up Yasmin Le Bon (for the cover of *Harpers & Queen*), highlighting blemishes on her face and removing them like a join-the-dots puzzle in reverse. After a hopelessly confused attempt to explain how the Virginia State Lottery was plundered by a computer wizard, we met someone with too much time on his hands: the World Student Memory Man, who turned out to be the most unmemorable man I've seen in years. When, after he'd recited a forty-item shopping list forwards, Des asked him to do it backwards, it became very clear that the programme also had too much time on its hands.

In China, unwanted babies are not talked about, but are quietly taken upstairs to the dying room and left there. It's a cruel custom, but I fear that infanticide should have been practised at the BBC when this wretch was first conceived. The show doesn't fulfil any useful purpose, giving answers that are crassly simplistic and wholly inadequate and, while it's not the worst programme I've ever seen (though pretty close), it's certainly one of the most insulting to the intelligence. What intrigues me is that the producer, John Longley, will somehow have to defend it to his bosses when it comes up at the BBC internal review board. Now *how* will he do that?

Desmond Lynam wrote to me soon after this review was published, claiming that he enjoyed my column and that, even after reading my critique of *How Do They Do That?*, he was still able to see the funny side. What a fine gentleman, I thought.

However, a year later, when Mr Lynam was asked if he would agree to allow his letter to be included in this book, he declined, in a brusque telephone call to my agent's office, turning down my offer of a donation to charity. What a fine gentleman, I thought.

Jim'll Fix It

For some who put their heads inside the magic rectangle, the halo afforded by the studio lights is not glory enough; they want beatification too. St Esther has long believed that a good deed should never go unnoticed (preferably on prime-time television) but, when it comes to spending licence payers' money and then taking the credit for it, nobody can hold a candle to St Jim.

Jim'll Fix It is one of TV's oldest people shows, fronted, appropriately, by one of TV's oldest people. It began as the show where terminal illness merged with Light Entertainment, and where the host regularly 'fixed it' for chronically sick children; not to be cured, of course, but to be whisked off to Disneyland so that, even if they didn't feel better, the viewers did. But, in recent years, it has not just been a show for the terminally challenged. Now, the physically fit are allowed on too – just as long as they're about two coupons short of the pop-up toaster, and are able and willing to act out their sad fantasies before the cameras. We had the full set on this week's show, where the prematurely peroxide St James Savile Kt, OBE, KCSG appeared in unconvincingly self-effacing mood, as though bored with his own image. A clipboard had replaced his customary cigar but, although the danger from passive smoking may have passed, viewers were still at risk from passive condescension as he told them about the miracles he had wrought, repeating the phatic phrase 'Now then, now then' like a nervous tic. First off was Philip, a policeman from Nottingham whose life's dream was apparently 'to drive a racing car very fast around a circuit'. I thought most policemen spent their evenings doing that on council estates already. Even so, it's something he could easily have arranged for himself for fifty quid, without troubling St Jim and the BBC. In a sequence assembled by a director who is clearly wasted on this programme – he should be directing home videos – we saw (through a muddy windscreen) tedious minutes of Philip driving cautiously around Snetterton, intercut with embarrassingly staged cutaways of him biting his nails and feigning fearful expressions. In short, it was an archetypal people film, the sort where the 'punter' has been assured by the director that 'Of course you won't look stupid,' and then ends up on screen looking very stupid indeed. At least it was refreshing to see a policeman being patronized for a change.

There has always been a dubious hint of *The Minipops* about this show, and we didn't have to wait long: Cheryl, an adolescent girl gymnast, wanted to become a cheerleader. St Jim had fixed it for her, so on came a vacuity of blonde bimbos (whose careers will, I fear, probably peak doing an ad for German yoghurt) and allowed Cheryl to demonstrate that, as a cheerleader, she made a great librarian. Next were a gross of old biddies, who wanted more men for their dancing sessions; St Jim had fixed it for a dozen Lionel Blair wannabes to partner them. Lo, another young girl: 'I wannabe a fairy,' said Rebecca, and St Jim let her hold his magic wand while he fixed it for her to make him disappear, alas only temporarily. Finally, he attended a Jimmy Savile lookalike competition, and came fourth.

Jim'll Fix It is TV's answer to the collected works of Madame Blavatsky: miracles are promised at the outset, followed by a lot of tedious drivel, and then you are told that the miracles have taken place. The show's title is unequivocal, but is anything really being *fixed*? The OAPs still don't have men. Cheryl still isn't a cheerleader. Rebecca didn't really see anything disappear. Perhaps the title refers only to the show's neutered, gelded blandness (like having your cat fixed), or to the flagrant, pointless waste of licence payers' money (the show itself is a fix). Certainly, the only people who really have things fixed for them are the manufacturers; in an orgy of product placement, I counted Loctite, Castrol, Dunlop, Hitachi, Lotus and Ford, all enjoying extended plugs on the BBC at minimal cost to themselves.

Emmerdale

I've often thought someone should start a soap opera about the everyday story of country life in that peaceful rural village of Hiding. The press are always telling us that Lord Lucan is in Hiding, so why not show us exactly where he lives? Number 47, Main Street, Hiding, next door to Salman Rushdie who runs the corner shop opposite Martin Bormann's pub three doors away from Andy Warhol's cottage. What a show. What a cast list.

Unfortunately, *Emmerdale* (formerly *Emmerdale Farm*) has monopolized the rural soap slot for the past two decades. The last time I tuned in, it was little more than Emmerdale Allotment. But more recently there has been a migration away from the land and into the city, on a scale not witnessed since the early days of the Industrial Revolution, with half the action now taking place in Leeds, and Beckindale colonized by middle-class actors who prefer the wine bar to t'Woolpack.

Episode 1734 was ushered in by the old familiar theme music, but the pastoral oboes and Vaughan Williams strings have been replaced by fretless bass and ice-cream-van synthesizers, and the opening shots are of Mills & Boon bedsheets and pert botties in cycle shorts. Now, rather than foxes racing after little hares, *Emmerdale* employs foxy actresses with big hair, as the producers have finally discovered that there is more mileage to be wrung out of sex than occasional shots of an artificial inseminator sticking his arm up a herd of Friesians. Young models pout seductlessly like refugees from *Baywatch* as they talk to each other in that rare Yorkshire dialect – t'RADA. This is supposed to be the deepest rural North, where the locals drag their knuckles on the ground as they walk, slap brown paper and beef dripping on their skin and sew themselves into thick woollen underwear between the months of October and April. But in *Emmerdale*, no one is convincingly Yorkshire any more. Even the sheep seem to come from Central Casting.

The show is constructed from dozens of minuscule scenes, a mosaic structure that serves only to underline the triviality of the content. On her birthday, Lorraine rebelled and told her mother, 'I'm sixteen and I don't want jelly at my party,' the sort of facile parental conflict routinely introduced by soaps to straddle the age groups. Meanwhile, in Leeds, Rachel and her flatmate discussed how to dispose of a dead rat, the nearest we had come so far to any sign of animal life. Alan Turner, the pub landlord (and reincarnation of Katy's husband Philip from the 1950s Oxo ads), prepared a casserole and talked to Kathy, whose perpetual inane/insane smile suggested a bit of magic-mushroom cultivation had been going on in clandestine Gro-bags. When Rachel met Dave at a bus stop, we finally had our first glimpse of countryside – a garden hedge in Leeds – while they indulged in a typical Yorkshire conversation, all about being vegetarians and whether to meet at the wine bar. Frank, a freelance contractor who was now trying to contract alcohol poisoning, was berated by his daughter Zoey (good old Yorkshire name), and a student trio discussed the relative merits of 85 and 87 clarets, joined later by a blonde woman holding a Chelsea Girl bag (reet old Yorkshire shop). Meanwhile at Home Farm the phone was answered with the traditional Tyke greeting 'I'm sorry, he's in a meeting.' At the close we were finally vouchsafed a brief glimpse of the Woolpack, where old Seth, the programme's only surviving handlebar moustache, supped his ale and shook his head at such fancy goings-on, a perfect advert for the phrase 'Yorkshire-born, Yorkshire-bred, strong in t'arm and thick in t'ead'.

Farmers perennially claim that they are poor as church mice, but that excuse has now been appropriated by skint TV companies, as justification for scheduling cheap and shoddy programmes like this. *Emmerdale* was never more than a pop-up book of *The Archers* but the attempt to make it more palatable for Southerners has ruined it; in shaking off its parochial rustic themes in favour of slick urban storylines, it has lost the only charm it ever had. With good old Yorkshire names like Glen McCoy (writer) and Morag Bain (producer) high on the credits, is it any wonder?

Life With Fred

There is Fred disease rife throughout the land. Spreading faster than bovine spongiform encephalopathy through cattle, a plague of people called Fred has contaminated the media. Scientists have identified the initial source of infection as Fred Loads, an interminable bore unwisely given airtime in the early 70s, but soon outbreaks were being reported across the country, from Fred Housego in the south to Fred Truman in the north. All Freds displayed the same distressing symptoms: they became loud-mouthed and self-opinionated, they referred to themselves as 'Joe Blunt', kept calling spades spades, and they inflicted ceaseless, ill-informed, home-spun monologues on anyone unlucky enough to be within shouting distance.

Tragically, another case of media Fred has recently reappeared in the Bolton area, years after the original outbreak seemed to have been contained. Fred Dibnah, steam traction engine enthusiast and Britain's best-known steeplejack (a proud boast indeed) is back on the air, sharing a year of his tiresome existence with us on *Life With Fred* (BBC2). Combining the voice of Cyril Smith with the mustachioed appearance and intellectual muscle of E. P. Gumby, he led us last night through the relentlessly mind-numbing tedium of a Dibnah spring, continually expecting laughter or wonderment from those around him, although his words and actions rarely deserved anything other than outright contempt. In years to come, there will surely be a gold statue, the 'Dibnah', awarded to those rare broadcasters capable of equalling Fred's only recognizable talent – his ability to talk half an inch of meaning to every fifty feet of noise.

Few things in life are more depressing than the sight of amateurs feigning eccentricity for the cameras and, along with Fred disease, Mr Dibnah had clearly also contracted chronic Heinz Woolfitis. Could he just put his cap on his head? Dear me no, he had to tell us about it being a fire hazard on account of being oily, how he'd caught a disease from it and nearly gone blind, and how people in pubs would remark on its smell. And, in case the man's obsession with collapsing chimneys and steam engines wasn't already Freudian enough, Fred's anecdotes (appropriately, for a man interested in steam) were perfect examples of the syndrome known as Freud's Kettle, far too full of incident ever to be believable. Nobody minds embellishment in a hilarious story but, if it's far-fetched *and* dismally unfunny you're after, then Fred's your man.

Could he simply climb up a chimney? No, he had to stop, jump around on the scaffolding and wave to bemused children on the ground, or to his family who dutifully stood watching. Meanwhile, away from work, he pursued his favourite hobby – driving his steam engine at three mph through the town centre, blowing his whistle, causing traffic jams and making heads turn. He told us how he loved driving through the city, but got bored in the country. Hardly surprising: in the country, there was no longer anyone to look at him.

Whenever the phrase 'to my mind' is used, one infers that the speaker doesn't actually possess a mind at all and, when Fred turned to philosophy, he did not disprove my theorem. I quote the great man verbatim: 'You can't escape this feministic business, I mean half of these buggers now come home and have to get their own tea. It's a bit like the Roman Empire, they all turned queer and retracted back t'Rome from all over t'world, and had underfloor heating and went bloody bad. And now they make racing cars and washing machines.' Now that's what *I* call Fred disease. If this man is a popular after-dinner speaker, I can only assume he works the mortuary and mental-hospital circuit. The dead and the mad might just tolerate him.

This was a ridiculous documentary by Don Haworth, which appeared to be shot on 70s film stock, had a 70s-style stilted voice-over, and surely marks the final death rattle of 70s television. Like oil tankers, networks take a long time to turn round but, with two first-class controllers now at the helm of BBC1 and 2, it's hard to envisage anything like this being commissioned again. Ever. Its satanic mills, Victorian parlour music and flat-capped northerner Uncle Tom-ing for the cameras might have made a southern audience purr with delight a decade ago, but not any longer. The man may work all day with rivets but, curiously, Fred failed to be riveting once.

Lucky Numbers

Last night, I dreamed that I visited the study of Professor Mariella Frostrup, the celebrated Scandinavian thinker, columnar journalist, philosopher of renown and concupiscent star of numerous television shows, all of them broadcast in the middle of the night when nobody is watching.* Together, we pondered many of the innermost mysteries of life. Why do tourists pay to go to the top of very high buildings, then put a coin into a telescope so they can see the ground in close-up again? Why do politicians only tell the truth when they're calling each other liars? Do people in hell use the phrase 'Go to hell'? Why is there no alternative word for 'thesaurus'? But there was one conundrum even the Swedish prof could not unravel: Why on earth was Shane Ritchie ever allowed near a TV camera?

Lucky Numbers (ITV) modestly bills itself as 'Britain's biggest game show', so it's only natural that Britain's biggest ego should have been hired to present it. 'Starring Shane Ritchie' may sound like an oxymoron (with the emphasis on moron), but that's what the voice-over promised us last night; yet what we saw wasn't a presenter, it was Danny Baker after a stroke. Indeed, after watching Mr Ritchie for a few minutes, a medical condition seemed the only plausible explanation for such behaviour. His hands clearly had Tourette's syndrome, his visage was a mass of facial tics, he kept shouting insensibly into thin air and, whenever he traversed the set, he skipped, hopped, jumped or bounced, anything rather than walk normally. This look-at-me body language is, of course, familiar to paediatricians, who call it 'the terrible twos'. And Mr Ritchie was obviously also at 'a difficult age': twenty-eight, going on three.

If you find bingo too intellectually demanding, then *Lucky Numbers* is the game show for you, since only half of the conventional ninety numbers are used, and it takes thirty minutes to complete one card. Last night's contestants were Michelle, Doris and Steve, an unemployed fitter who had the bad luck to trip headlong over the set without injuring himself (if only he'd broken his leg, he could have sued and won a fortune). The trio helped to pick numbers, but that was irrelevant to Mr Ritchie who (as usual) treated the show as his own personal audition tape. Parrot-like, he attempted dozens of micro-impersonations (from Robin Williams to John Major): he could do everyone, it seemed, except himself. He pointed incessantly in all directions (I lost count after the sixtieth time) – at the contestants, the audience, the cameras, even himself – a vacuous gesture which he mistakenly believed would compensate for lack of wit. Above all, he spoke fluent drivel: 'I love you all, you know that. Big bucks bingo bonanza. What do you need? Balls. Show me your balls.' It was generous of the man to donate his brain to science, but what a pity no one told him you're supposed to wait until after death.

By the commercial break, it was clear that the only genuinely lucky numbers were 1, 2 and 4 (the only TV channel selector buttons it was safe to push). General-knowledge questions came and went, with slips aplenty from our host, even though he was reading it all from cards: 'Frascrati is a wine from where? . . . Is Siddean Sheldon an American writer?' The only question Doris got right was 'What is your name?' but Steve was overwhelmed to win £15,000 (although he was probably underwhelmed next day, when the benefit office stopped his dole money). Finally, Shane told us that 'This proves that anyone, yes anyone, can be a winner on this show.' And, after watching this fiasco, I was inclined to agree with him.

Don't get me wrong, I adore crass game shows. Watching Bruce Forsyth or Michael Barrymore toying with contestants can be a delight, but even the most lumpen members of this show's audience were more than a match for its presenter, while the only number that the producer seemed to consider lucky was the lowest common denominator. Actually, I know the producer. We worked together in radio (in fact, he was a friend until this piece appeared in print), and I always considered him passably intelligent. Maybe the show is a clever parody, some post-modernist ironic vision of the nightmare that television might one day become. But I somehow doubt it, and wonder whether he sleeps at night. *Lucky Numbers* is sponsored by the *Sun*, and programmes usually hesitate before collaborating with that newspaper, for fear of being dragged down-market. Last night, however, we witnessed a refreshing change: for once, it was the *Sun* that needed to fear for its reputation.

* Shortly after publication I received the following letter from Ms Frostrup, which made no sense to me at all.
   I understand that she subsequently left the country.

A Diverse Production for
CARLTON TV

24 January 1994

Dear Victor,

Have you been stealing my mail? It must be three years since I last received a request to do an audition and my TV work is hardly prolific. In fact if your occasional swipes are anything to go by, you probably aren't surprised.

Surely I provide enough genuine material with which to attack me without your having to resort to fiction. Or maybe not?

Best wishes,

Mariella Frostrup

Jimmy's

I'm told that the incurable and gullible in California pay fortunes to cryogenic companies, to be frozen at the moment of death and thawed out centuries hence, when a treatment for their disease has been found. Of course, if they *really* had faith in the procedure, they'd ask to be killed and frozen as soon as a terminal illness was diagnosed, because diseases are more easily cured if arrested in the early stages. But they don't because, secretly, they know the chilling truth: the cryogenic company will soon go bust, the electricity board will cut off the power and bailiffs will move in to evict a sorry cargo of melting eyeballs and brains, floating in slush. Hardly a dignified way to go.

Patients at *Jimmy's* (ITV) are treated with somewhat more dignity, but last night's edition still gave me cold feet about ever putting myself into the hands of medical science. The living (and occasionally dying) soap is now in its tenth series, and continues to chronicle, for our amusement and delectation, those cases where Germolene wasn't quite enough and, down at St James's in Leeds, the boys with the J-Cloth suits and hats had to step in and make good. Although the camera doesn't overly intrude into events, the result is nevertheless disconcertingly unreal. After all, everyone in a hospital knows the role that's expected of them, and they play it for all they're worth, with helpless patients disguising their fear by endlessly expressing ghastly gratitude, thereby feeding the vanity of egotistical consultants. As for the adults dealing with terminal child cancer victims, their irrational jollity is strangely reminiscent of medieval pomander users optimistically hoping to ward off the Black Death.

Hilary Pike had probably daydreamed about being famous, but I doubt if she ever suspected her first national appearance would be in the David Beevers Theatre, with her internal organs on public display. One of her kidneys was being removed, prior to transplantation into her son Tim, who received a horse-sized dose of anaesthetic, said, 'I have the taste of onions in my mouth' and passed out; I've been to a few restaurants like that myself. Surgeon Peter Lodge explained, 'We have to use live donors – there are fewer road crashes these days' (its self-self-self with some motorists), and continued with what was not so much keyhole as wide-open-door surgery: 'I'll just push the lung out of the way . . . this one has the lumbar vein, so it's easier to use.' The knife cut deeper and I couldn't help noticing the ceiling needed painting, before everything went black.

Angela Constantino was plundered for spare parts too, namely bone marrow for her brother Dino, who'd come in thinking 'You'll give me a pill and I'll go home' but was instead given massive chemotherapy for leukaemia. Elderly Joe Myers (who'd already had a stroke and a heart attack) arrived for a skin graft. Met by a nurse who said, 'Hello, I'm Judith,' Mr Myers replied, 'Hello, I'm Judith.' No need for a pre-med there. By now, part of Mrs Pike was lying in a dish, surrounded by admiring surgeons. 'Nice kidney,' they muttered, slicing surplus membranes from the bloody mass. Meanwhile, Bessie Prydderch was scanned for an aneurism, and the consultant gave her the results in plain English: 'This aneurism means that the aorta is dilated from the aortic valve right the way down. Inoperable.'

Illness and death are humanity's lowest common denominators, exercising a universal fascination, and *Jimmy's* panders squarely to that appeal. It offers a vicarious drip feed into a hospital, a place where life and death can be observed in safety, without the fear or the pain that usually accompany them. Demystifying the hospital is all very well, but the programme goes further than that, presenting human tragedy as entertainment, and gratifying the *schadenfreude* in us, making us feel better by showing others who are worse. Patients are captured at their most pathetic and vulnerable and, although they have doubtless agreed to be filmed, can that agreement ever be freely given in such circumstances? At times of crisis, who's going to risk making enemies by refusing to play ball with those in authority?

Anyway, I'm taking no chances. From now on, I'm carrying a medical card on my person at all times, reading IN THE EVENT OF ACCIDENT OR DEATH, I DO NOT WISH MYSELF OR MY INTERNAL ORGANS TO FEATURE IN A PRIME-TIME TELEVISION PROGRAMME.

Channel 4 Racing

There are two groups of people not to be trusted: eighty-year-olds with German names and hazy memories who live in Buenos Aires, and TV eccentrics. Luckily, the former are repaidly dying off, but the latter live for ever on our screens, and they're all as fake as a call girl's multiple orgasm. *Channel 4 Racing* has its resident eccentric too: looking like Worzel Gummidge after an incident with a letter bomb, John McCririck was originally hired for his knowledge of bookies' tick-tack, but over the years he's shown us little that was ticky and much that was tacky and, mercifully, he's now largely sidelined. Hosting yesterday's Derby Day special was Brough Scott who, despite having anchored such events for decades, still gave the impression of being an inept best man at a disastrous wedding, standing awkwardly in an ill-fitting morning suit, uncertain what to do next. The man spoke with the regal portentousness of Richard Dimbleby, but his mouth was running on low-octane vocabulary.

As he burbled, the Queen was driven slowly down the course in that Rolls-Royce (the tall one that looks like a hearse designed to carry vertical coffins). She wore a delightful primrose-yellow coat which, touchingly, precisely matched the Queen Mother's teeth, and Colmanballs dropped like bombs as the commentator strove manfully for an OBE as he uttered such rubbish as: 'The Queen Mother is using a stick, but she doesn't let it handicap her in any way.' Thousands packed the stands (not so much an audience as the basis of the statistic that we're a nation of back-pain sufferers – I'd bet half of them were blagging the day off work), and McCririck walked amongst them, conducting the first *vox unpop* I've ever seen, and telling us that he fancied Weigh Anchor. It takes one to know one, John. Meanwhile, Gary Player was unilaterally dedicating the race to President Mandela, and emotionally praising the man for his struggle against injustice. Can this have been the *same* Gary Player I heard many years ago on *Any Questions*, roundly defending apartheid? Clearly not. Strange, though: they both played golf.

A disembodied voice appeared periodically, with news of the betting – 'Three to one against, seven to two each of two, sixteen to one bar' – a stream of reassuring meaninglessness, racing's equivalent of the *Long Range Shipping Forecast*. Lester Piggott (looking taxed and sounding like Mr Senna would have if he'd survived the crash) gave another of his Keith Richards-style interviews, where even an incomprehensible half-sentence answer was a cause for celebration. Finally they were off, twenty-five suede Esther Rantzens surmounted by midgets modelling psychedelic blazers, followed by ambulances. Just as well, really, because one fell off, a delightful spectacle since it wasn't me. In fact, I won £24 in the office sweepstake, which was more delightful still. And, most delightful of all, the whole event was a catastrophe for the bookmakers. Life couldn't be better.

Sport is the saviour of daytime TV, offering endless hours of cheap schedule-fillers with thrills pretty much guaranteed. But unlike other great sporting occasions, such as Wimbledon or the Cup Final, the Derby is ninety-five per cent anticipation, with the big event itself all over inside two minutes (rather like sex, only longer), and time hangs heavy when there's nothing more substantial than relentless telephoto long shots and inane commentary to fill the aeons between races. Even so, I'd lay odds that the sport of kings will run on TV for decades to come, although hopefully without the tedious gesturing and posturing of Mr McCririck. To paraphrase Mrs Patrick Campbell, I don't care what these people do, so long as they don't do it in public and frighten the horses.

Without Walls: Heigh Ho!

1995, it seems, is the year of the luvvy. So far, we've seen luvvies having tantrums and fleeing the country, tearful luvvies on trial for rape and, every time you switch on the box, there's a luvvy telling the world that 'I'm essentially a very shy person.' Strange, because very shy people are usually too shy to mention it, or to give interviews, and certainly far too shy to strut around on stage night after night in front of hundreds of complete strangers or appear in front of millions watching TV. That paradox doubtless explains why all actors are so highly-strung. In fact, the average luvvy is so neurotically schizophrenic that he could go to group therapy all by himself.

But, as last night's *Without Walls: Heigh Ho!* (CH4) amply demonstrated, the professional problems confronting the ordinary thespian are dwarfed by those that face the diminutive performer. A theatrical midget may aspire to playing Hamlet with the RSC, but casting directors are a notoriously conservative bunch, and roles for the vertically challenged remain pitifully few. So, as each winter approaches, dwarfs reluctantly take up their picks and shovels and head towards provincial theatres in groups of seven, prepared to fall back yet again on *Snow White*, the midget world's equivalent of going on the game. Yes, it's slightly degrading and humiliating, but it's one of the few jobs where society discriminates in their favour, and at least it represents six weeks of guaranteed regular pay. Come the end of January, they know they'll all be back on the dole, and facing a far worse indignity: trying to sign on and finding that the DSS counter is too high for them to complete their P45s.

Whoever coined the apothegm 'Dover for the continent, Eastbourne for the incontinent' was surely inspired by the audience at a matinée performance of *Snow White* in Sussex's last resort where, presumably, rubber sheets are automatically supplied along with the Kia-Ora. Backstage, all seven dwarfs turned out to be grumpy, incessantly whining about overcrowding and the state of their dressing rooms, although they did have a point: they could scarcely be expected to find out who was the fairest of them all when the only mirror on the wall was six feet above floor level. Zena Camplin (Sniffly) complained that people thought 'small bodies, small brains', but said little to convince us otherwise, while Robert Gillibrand (Blusher) considered it demeaning to ask dwarfs to fall over on stage, although few actors expect to emerge from panto with their dignity fully intact. And, once we saw them on stage, marching past with profiles like the concave side of a spoon, it became obvious that they really were ridiculously short. On acting talent.

To be fair, those of normal height displayed equally stunted thought processes. Richard Cheshire (director, and Christopher Biggins soundalike) told us that 'Some of the dwarfs were very naughty last night, they stayed up drinking . . . so they had a good telling-off,' as though these were children he was dealing with, not a stroppy septet of diminutive adults. Snow White (played by Melanie, a woman who could make either of the Philadelphia-cheese girls look like Dorothy

Parker) thought that it would be nice to see short people properly represented in a soap opera, and protested, 'I have to say, "They're not very tall and some aren't that bright." Is that offensive?' Perhaps it was, but, as the weeks rolled by, the genuinely demeaning aspect of the job must surely have become clear to those of all heights: they were all having to spend six weeks in out-of-season Eastbourne.

By the end, I wasn't sure whether I'd been watching a politically correct tribute to the vertically challenged or a lily-livered freak show. The dwarfs had a hard time, but they were so over-empathized with by the programme that I almost felt they deserved it, and only their periodic outbursts of nastiness helped their cause, showing them as normal, irascible human beings. Like films made by wheelchair-bound people, who overact (archly squeezing themselves into ticket barriers, or jamming themselves in lavatory doorways) in an exaggerated attempt to convince us that public buildings are inherently un-friendly, the programme made me forget that Randy Newman's lyric about 'short people got no reason to live' was intended as irony, and only confirmed my atavistic Orwellian prejudices: six feet good, three feet bad.

Sorry, but I feel superior whenever I pass a short person in the street, and what do I care if that angers them? I'll take refuge on the top floor of the *Evening Standard* building. Dwarfs can only stretch as far as the button for the first floor. Their lift never goes right to the top.

Esther

Things to do with an old bag, part one. Small, self-sealing plastic bags are useful if you've had bad service at a restaurant. When the waiter comes to remove the dishes, utter the phrase 'That looks *particularly* nasty, I'll just take it away for analysis,' lift a small piece of food from the plate with tweezers, pop it into the bag and seal it. I guarantee the bill will be waived.

Things to do with an old bag, part two. Give her a new series, but make it only thirty minutes long, and bury it in away at five p.m. in the hope that nobody will notice it. Give her a hand-held mike and an audience to thrust it at, encourage her to address serious issues in a superficial way, then sit back and wait for her contract to expire. So it was that St Esther, our Lady of Rantzen, took to the air again yesterday, only months after her last vehicle was finally shot down in flames. The opening titles said it all, a montage of disembodied words – 'confess . . . hate . . . lie . . . fear . . . pain . . .' – that could well have been inspired by one of her production meetings. More revealing still was the show's logo, a pair of inverted commas that clung to her name like limpets: appropriate decoration for a woman who, with her unique blend of patronizing, championing and humiliating her audiences, seems to have lived her entire media existence in inverted commas.

Wife-beating was yesterday's subject, a contemptible crime deserving of a more enlightened (and less emotive) approach than we got from Esther, whose first four questions to a victim were: 1) Can you tell us about the beatings? 2) How bad were the injuries? 3) How long did this go on? 4) Was it in front of the children? It quickly became apparent that this was no serious enquiry, just a knee-jerk, tear-jerk outpouring of self-justification from abused women who, after years of being disbelieved, had finally found someone willing to believe anything they said, proven or not, with Esther treating them as though victimhood automatically conferred wisdom, rather than simply misery. 'A doctor' told us that 'Women always blame themselves,' but these women were eager to blame everyone else, with Sisters clapping delightedly as one convicted murderer (who cries in exactly the same place every time she appears on TV) recalled pouring petrol over her husband and setting him alight. The kangaroo court was in full session. Then the reformed wife beaters took over, denouncing themselves like star turns at a Stalinist show-trial. Michael explained he'd only ever been violent because he'd seen his father doing it. It was the same with me. I remember watching *Bridge Over the River Kwai* at an impressionable age, and immediately machine-gunning all the staff at my local Japanese restaurant.

Ersatz *Oprah* is one thing, but this was fake ersatz, *Kilroy* with breasts. As for the audience, they weren't your whooping *Oprah* variety either: by the look of them, whooping cough was more in their line and, although they'd doubtless got tragic tales to tell, they'd obviously taken a collective trip to Psychosis City and only bought one-way tickets. 'One of the great myths of domestic violence is that it only affects a certain type of person,' said one victim, encouraging us to disbelieve the evidence of our own eyes and, as the programme ground towards its end, you couldn't help wondering who it was intended for. Not the law makers, who wouldn't bother to watch it. Not the victims, who certainly didn't need to hear lurid details of mindless abuse. No, it's really intended for mindless couch potatoes with no interest in the subject, who'll switch over unless they're regularly fed salacious titbits.

There was a number you could ring, but we all know that a helpline is simply the fig-leaf of propriety with which a nakedly sensationalist programme attempts to clothe itself. By the end, I'd had quite enough of the Lady Thatcher concerned expressions, and the Oprah trot across the studio (can't we bring back the boom mike, that acoustical fishing rod that used to work a treat before hand-held mikes became *de rigueur* for presenters?). This show was a curious paradox – *Oprah* without the teeth, yet simultaneously *with* the teeth – and, although Esther may run and run around the studio, the show most definitely *won't* run, because the woman has no idea how to talk to people (witness the débâcle when she recently hosted R4's *Midweek*) and is clearly uneasy when too far away from a carrot that looks like a penis. How long will it be, I wonder, before somebody sets up an Esther Line? For women who have run out of causes.

Witness: Consider the End

However much we may try to forget it, we all know that we are born into a condemned cell. The best we can hope for is that the executioner is detained elsewhere for as long as possible, or has a pretty bad limp and, when he does finally arrive to dispatch us, that he isn't sadistic or incompetent.

Those unlucky enough to suffer a slow and agonizing end to life are scarcely in a position to argue the case for voluntary euthanasia, so for many years Ludovic Kennedy has publicly championed their cause. *Consider the End* was his latest plea for more enlightened and compassionate treatment of the terminally ill, in an age when our ability to prevent the human body dying has far outstripped our ability to cure it. Where once the old and the sick were allowed to die with dignity, now they die with indignity, buried under a scrapyard of chrome and rubber resuscitators and pumped full of drugs, with plastic tubes thrust into every available entrance or exit. They are no longer even allowed the hope that pneumonia – for centuries the old man's friend – will come to alleviate their suffering.

This was not an overview of the subject, but a petition for a change in the law and, like the shrewd criminologist he is, Kennedy bolstered his case with a plethora of the good and the eminent, all speaking in euthanasia's defence. He had assembled a furniture shopful of professorial chairs, many of them stating frankly that they themselves had performed mercy killings, legal or not, when they were GPs. Indeed, most of those who spoke for the defence had witnessed a painful, hideous death at close quarters. Sir Dirk Bogarde told how he was converted to the cause during the war when, after a bombing, he found himself in a trench next to a 'thing' – a head attached to an arm – that kept screaming, 'Kill me.' And Tony Cocker recalled how, after helping his suffering wife to die, he was given a life sentence for murder, a sequence of events so grotesquely ridiculous that even Monsieur Feydeau would have been taken aback.

Moving on to the attack, Kennedy laid into the Roman Catholic Church – 'medieval in its thinking, barbaric in its lack of compassion' – which condemns euthanasia as a mortal sin and (on the quiet) pours millions of dollars into American PR companies to fight against legislative reforms. In the Vatican, an insufferably smug Archbishop Foley proclaimed, 'Suffering in the last minutes of life helps us to share in Christ's pain and helps us to imitate Christ more closely . . . When I go to the dentist, I often think of Christ's Passion.' I hope I'm there to remind the archbishop of that hideously trite point, if he should end his days terminally ill, doubly incontinent, vomiting, nauseous, racked with pain and covered in bed sores: I fear that the closing stage of a terminal disease is not as simple as Take a rinse and see you again in six months.

The pusillanimous BMA has also set its face against euthanasia although Dr Fisher, its tongue-tied equivocating spokesman, had apparently volunteered to die in front of the camera. Practising what he preaches, Ludovic dispatched her quickly and painlessly; I doubt if she felt a thing. Lastly he moved to the Netherlands, where euthanasia has been decriminalized. Holland is so terminally dull that I fully expected to see the entire population eagerly queuing up to be put out of their misery, but no. In a series of moving testimonies, we heard how hard it was for patients to obtain permission, and how much harder for the doctors to bring themselves to administer the lethal injection. But, when all hope is gone and only suffering remains, what greater act of human kindness could any of us wish for?

Ironically, this sober, unhurried enquiry into death was far more vital and alive than most of the fast-moving but empty programmes that nightly jostle for space in the schedules. Brian Wenham and Tim Cooper at Hed Productions have produced an intelligent and uncluttered documentary and together with Kennedy – a first-class writer-presenter of the old school – have demonstrated that television is at its best when tackling issues from a clear, committed standpoint. Few people appear inside the magic rectangle for any reason other than to further their own careers, but it seems that Kennedy has always been motivated by compassion rather than ego, by an angry kindness and a belief that dying well is part of living well. May he long continue.

Index of Reviews